D1559518

Making *The Best Years of Our Lives*

THE WILLIAM & BETTYE NOWLIN SERIES
in Art, History, and Culture of the Western Hemisphere

Making *The Best Years of Our Lives*

The Hollywood Classic That Inspired a Nation

ALISON MACOR

University of Texas Press ◆ *Austin*

This book has been made possible in part by the National Endowment for the
Humanities: Democracy demands wisdom.

Requests for permission to reproduce material from this work should be sent to:
    Permissions
    University of Texas Press
    P.O. Box 7819
    Austin, TX 78713-7819
    utpress.utexas.edu/rp-form

♾ The paper used in this book meets the minimum requirements of
ANSI/NISO Z39.48-1992 (R1997) (Permanence of Paper).

Library of Congress Cataloging-in-Publication Data

Names: Macor, Alison, 1966– author.
Title: Making The best years of our lives : the Hollywood classic that inspired a nation /
    Alison Macor.
Description: First edition. | Austin : University of Texas Press, 2022. | Includes
    bibliographical references and index.
Identifiers:
    LCCN 2021041568
    ISBN 978-1-4773-1891-1 (cloth)
    ISBN 978-1-4773-2505-6 (PDF)
    ISBN 978-1-4773-2506-3 (ePub)
Subjects: LCSH: Best years of our lives (Motion picture) | Best years of our lives (Motion
    picture)—Influence. | Best years of our lives (Motion picture)—Public opinion. |
    Post-traumatic stress disorder in motion pictures. | Veterans in motion pictures.
Classification: LCC PN1997.B2765 M33 2022 | DDC 791.43/72—dc23/eng/20211027
LC record available at https://lccn.loc.gov/2021041568

doi:10.7560/318911

In honor of Michelle E. Melland (Captain, USA) and Harvey R. Mitchell (Sergeant, USMC), in memory of George S. Macor (Staff Sergeant, USAF), and for all who have served

Contents

Making *The Best Years of Our Lives*

Introduction

I wondered why so few films and so few plays honestly reflect the conflicts of our times. Every age, every generation, every decade, every year, has some battle of mind, of emotion—some social cause that favors the time. Why does the screen seldom find these conflicts?

WILLIAM WYLER, "Escape to Reality"

Homer Parrish busies himself in the dimly lit kitchen, the glow from the open refrigerator glinting off the steel hooks that have replaced his missing hands. A shadow appears across the filmy curtain obscuring the window of the kitchen's back door. Hearing a knock, Homer looks up from the counter where he is assembling a late-night snack. His girlfriend and next-door neighbor, Wilma, stands on the porch.

Inviting her in, Homer offers her a piece of cold fried chicken and a glass of milk. He is nonchalant, even distant, while Wilma appears nervous, her soft brunette waves framing a pretty but anxious young face. "Homer, my family want me to go away," she begins as he stares down into his glass of milk. "Tomorrow," she says, adding, "up to Silver Lake at my Aunt Vera's place."

Homer shifts his body away from her, as if to shield himself, and shoves his hooks into the pockets of his worn bathrobe. He retreats to a corner of the kitchen and then turns to face her. "I want you to be free, Wilma. To live your own life. I don't want you tied down forever just because you've got a kind heart."

"Oh, Homer!" Wilma cries out in frustration as she rises from a chair and moves toward him.

"Cut."

Director William Wyler's quiet, authoritative voice stopped the scene. Harold Russell and Cathy O'Donnell, playing Homer and Wilma, walked slowly toward the foreground of the kitchen set. Russell, an army veteran, was costarring in his first picture. O'Donnell, a young actress from Alabama, was one of the latest discoveries by the independent producer Samuel Goldwyn. They were shooting on one of the soundstages at Goldwyn's West Hollywood studio, at the corner of Formosa Avenue and Santa Monica Boulevard. The studio had been the home of Charlie Chaplin silents, Douglas Fairbanks swashbucklers, and Mary Pickford melodramas. Wyler and his cinematographer, Gregg Toland, heads bowed toward each other, stood conferring about the take.

In the late spring of 1946, when production was beginning on *The Best Years of Our Lives*, Wyler had something of a reputation in Hollywood. Nicknamed "40 Take Wyler" or even "50 Take Wyler" (depending, as several biographers have noted, on who was telling the story), the filmmaker was a stickler for striking just the right note with a scene.[1] Six years earlier, while directing Bette Davis in *The Letter* for Warner Bros., Wyler had received a confidential memo from the studio's head, Jack Warner, who was "astounded" to learn that Wyler had shot fourteen takes of a particular scene. "You must not realize that there is a war going on," Warner chided the director. "You are a very good director and no one can tell me you can't make a scene in at least 2 to 4 takes tops." Wyler responded, "If I found it necessary to make 14 takes of one scene there must have been a very good reason—as I also should much rather make just 3 or 4 as you suggest."[2]

On *Best Years*, although Wyler moved quickly and decisively through many of the scenes without dialogue, he took his time when shooting others, particularly those with Harold Russell. Russell was a bilateral hand amputee with no acting experience except for his "role" in *Diary of a Sergeant*. He appeared in this military training film to instruct other World War II amputees in how they too could adapt to life without their limbs. Russell's can-do attitude and easygoing personality made him a natural poster boy for the War Department's rehabilitation campaign. Wyler, however, needed Russell to be able to mine Homer's anger and grief over his missing hands in order to play up the tension in *Best Years*, a drama about three veterans readjusting to life after World War II. At one point during filming, the forty-four-year-old Wyler threatened to send Russell to an army hospital for several weeks to get him "unadjusted" and, Russell later joked, to "rehabilitate my rehabilitation."[3]

The dramatic scene between Homer and Wilma was part of a longer, pivotal sequence toward the end of the film in which Homer, worn down by anger and anxiety after returning home, asks Wilma to follow him up to his childhood bedroom so that she can witness firsthand what it would be like to be married to him. Standing together in Homer's starkly lit room, Wilma watches as he takes off his robe, undoes the leather harness securing his hooks to his upper arms, and struggles into his pajama top. Even today, the bedroom sequence has the ability to evoke a powerful and compelling mix of emotions in an audience: fear, anxiety, hope, dread. Will Homer, who has lashed out violently before, hurt Wilma because of his own frustration over his disability? Will Wilma be repulsed by his stumps and reject Homer? How far will the filmmakers go in showing an unmarried man and woman together in a bedroom?

As Wyler later said of shooting the scene, "There were delicate problems in bringing a boy and a girl to a bedroom at night . . . without presenting Homer's hooks in a shocking or horrifying manner. As a matter of fact, we felt we could do quite the opposite and make it a moving and tender love scene."[4]

Including such an intimate scene in a 1940s Hollywood film was a daring move, but not as risky as making the movie itself. As with all films released by major distributors during this time, *Best Years* had to adhere to the strict moral guidelines in the Production Code, an antiquated list of rules that governed what could be said and shown onscreen, especially depictions of sexuality and alcohol consumption. There were other problems, too. Wyler had been back from the war for less than a year, and like Russell, he had sustained a debilitating injury: he lost hearing in his right ear while photographing aerial shots for the documentary *Thunderbolt* (released in 1947). Privately, Wyler worried that he wouldn't be able to direct again. And the screenwriter and playwright Robert E. Sherwood, who had led the Office of War Information and written speeches for President Franklin Delano Roosevelt during the war, had to be coaxed onto the project by Goldwyn because, as Sherwood initially told the producer, "by [1946], this subject will be terribly out of date."[5]

But none of this seemed as risky as casting a bilateral hand amputee in one of *Best Years'* lead roles. Russell was one of only sixty-three similarly disabled vets in the country, and at the time, even the American media had an informal policy against publishing images of severely wounded servicemen.[6] Except for *Diary of a Sergeant*, the army training film in which Wyler and Sherwood "discovered" Russell, the thirty-two-year-old veteran had no acting experience. In late 1945, when Russell received the call from Goldwyn's office about the part, he was running children's sports programs at the local YMCA in Cambridge, Massachusetts, and he thought the offer was a hoax.

In short, making *The Best Years of Our Lives* was a bold move for all involved, even the inveterate gambler Goldwyn.

The motion picture that resulted from Goldwyn's gamble ultimately burnished his reputation and set a precedent in Hollywood. Winner of seven Academy Awards, plus an honorary award for Russell (who also won for best supporting actor) and the Irving G. Thalberg Memorial Award for Goldwyn, *The Best Years of Our Lives* broke new ground with its documentary-inspired visuals and socially relevant story about three servicemen struggling to rebuild their civilian lives. The veterans meet when they catch the same transport plane back to their hometown in the Midwest. Fred Derry (Dana Andrews) is an air force captain heading home to Marie (Virginia Mayo), the fun-loving blond he married shortly before heading overseas. Homer Parrish (Harold Russell) is a sailor who lost both hands when the aircraft carrier he was on was torpedoed. He is worried about how his girlfriend, Wilma (Cathy O'Donnell), will react to his disability. Sergeant Al Stephenson (Fredric March) is eager to return to his wife, Milly (Myrna Loy), but conflicted about resuming his prewar job as a banker. As Fred searches for a decent job and tries to cope with lingering war trauma, Homer struggles to find purpose, and Al develops a drinking problem as a way to deal with his disillusionment at the bank. A blossoming relationship between Fred and Al's adult daughter, Peggy (Teresa Wright), threatens Fred's rocky marriage and his friendship with Al. The film ends with Homer and Wilma's wedding, which reunites the three veterans and offers a hopeful but realistic path forward for each of the characters.

While *Best Years* wasn't the first film to depict characters experiencing postwar trauma, it was the first prestige motion picture to feature top box-office stars struggling with such symptoms. And while *Best Years'* finale superficially promises a conventional happy ending, a reunion between Fred and Peggy in the background of the same scene offers a more sobering postwar outlook. The film's realistic, even downbeat tone and documentary-style cinematography—shades of both the film noir cycle and the relatively short-lived social problem genre, which were already taking hold—were also somewhat new for Hollywood in 1946. Ultimately, the film's record-setting grosses proved that a star-studded, big-budget drama could tackle adult themes in a believable but still box-office-friendly fashion.

In the late summer of 1944, two months after Britain, the United States, and other Western allies had invaded the coastal region of Normandy, Frances Goldwyn, married to Sam, read "The Way Home," a two-page *Time* magazine article about US servicemen from the First Marine Division returning home after serving overseas.[7] Frances was always on the lookout for potential movie properties for her husband, who had relied on her taste and judgment since the early years of their marriage. She even had her own office at the studio, just down the hall from her husband's corner suite. But Frances also had a personal stake in reading the *Time* article: the Goldwyns' son, Sammy, had recently enlisted in the army.

Though brief, the *Time* article captured the mixed emotions of its subjects, 370 furloughed marines. Traveling across the country from San Diego on a troop train that they nicknamed the "Home Again Special," the servicemen struggled to imagine their homecomings in big cities such as Chicago and Rochester and in small towns such as Moberly, Missouri, and Chicapee Falls, Massachusetts. "I'm a little worried about how I'll look to them, about how much I've changed," said one marine. The reporter who accompanied the men took note of the tense atmosphere inside the Pullman cars: "The silence came back. Suddenly two marines began to wrestle, to break the monotony, to relieve the strange embarrassment of coming home."[8]

Frances Goldwyn shared the story with her husband, encouraging him to consider it as the basis for a picture about postwar reintegration. Sam put her off, at least initially. He doubted that audiences would be interested in such somber themes once the war was over.

By the time the United States had entered World War II, Samuel Goldwyn was known for prestige pictures such as *Wuthering Heights* (Wyler, 1939) and *The Little Foxes* (Wyler, 1941), big-budget films with top box-office stars, including Laurence Olivier and Bette Davis. The self-made independent producer, whose bulbous nose and large upper body gave him the physical appearance of a prizefighter, had an unflattering reputation for toughness. Despite Goldwyn's renown for infusing films with the "Goldwyn touch"—an indefinable mark of taste, quality, and class—he had had more success during the war years with "escapist comedies" such as *They Got Me Covered* (Butler, 1943) and *Up in Arms* (Nugent, 1944), which had made him significant amounts of money. Anxious that these lighter movies would overshadow his reputation for making quality films, the sixty-five-year-old producer began to reconsider his wife's suggestion.

The article in *Time* was one of the first pieces in a national magazine to hint at what experts around the country had been referring to as the "veterans problem."[9] Nearly three years earlier, not long after the US entry into World War II, social workers, military personnel, and other qualified professionals had begun preparing a campaign to ready the American public for "the likelihood of a major social crisis" resulting from the "sudden demobilization of millions" of military men, "able-bodied and disabled alike."[10] This campaign led to articles like the one Frances read as well as to advertisements in women's magazines and similarly themed home-front propaganda, much of it specifically targeting women and families, subtly and not so subtly urging them to take responsibility for this massive reintegration. (Margaret Tallichet "Talli" Wyler, married to the director, became acutely aware of such "advice" as she struggled to help her husband readjust after the war.) Compounding the readjustment transition, according to these experts, was the fact that nearly one-third of these veterans had most likely spent time in a hospital for "neuropsychiatric causes" in the final year of World War II. As the historian David Gerber observed of the time, "Every veteran was a potential 'mental case,' even if he showed no symptoms."[11]

The term "post-traumatic stress disorder" (PTSD) was coined after the Vietnam War, but the roots of the condition date back at least to ancient times, when any kind of violent stressor, from an attack by a predatory animal to armed conflict, could produce similar kinds of psychological and physiological responses. Panic attacks, sleep problems, and depression or sadness over missed loved ones were just a few of the symptoms soldiers reported to the Austrian physician Josef Leopold Auenbrugger in 1761. Auenbrugger wrote about this "nostalgia" among soldiers who had experienced "military trauma," and his description was used as a model for similar types of psychological "injuries" up to and through the American Civil War.[12]

During World War I, the English psychologist Charles S. Myers had observed firsthand the long-term psychological effects of wartime trauma on soldiers while serving as a captain in the Royal Army Medical Corps.[13] Myers's ongoing research, along with similar observations by psychiatrists and psychologists during World War I, did much to draw attention to "nervous disorders of war" such as shell shock, which were deemed a "major drain on manpower," particularly during the first year of the war, when rough estimates suggested that thousands of British soldiers were taken off the battlefield in France and sent back to England.[14]

By the start of World War II, the term "shell shock" had been replaced by the more clinical-sounding "combat stress reaction" (CSR). This phrase was meant to reflect the military's attempts to address the fallout from war as a result of advances in weaponry and changes to military strategy since World War I. Differences in the ways that soldiers fought—enduring longer stretches of fighting, for example—led to use of the phrase "battle fatigue" to describe the kind of combat exhaustion they experienced. Efforts to rehabilitate servicemen diagnosed with CSR were implemented, and research revealed the benefits of relationships within military units for preventing stress and encouraging recovery. Such relationships, in fact, created the spine of Robert Sherwood's script for *Best Years*, establishing connections among the three main characters, servicemen of varying ranks from different divisions of the armed forces.

Perhaps the "veterans problem" was on Sam Goldwyn's mind in September 1944. It was then, a month after reading the *Time* article, that Goldwyn decided to pursue a project about returning soldiers. He reached out to MacKinlay Kantor, a writer whose novel *Long Remember* was set during the American Civil War and who had recently reported on World War II from overseas. Goldwyn shared the *Time* article with Kantor and commissioned him to write a treatment and a story for $20,000. Goldwyn instructed him to use the article only as inspiration, telling Kantor, "The story you have to tell from your own knowledge"—using the slightly muddled syntax that was one of the hallmarks of Goldwyn's communication.[15]

Having served as a London-based war correspondent for a Los Angeles newspaper, Kantor had extensive knowledge of soldiers and battles. He had flown combat runs with the Royal Air Force and the US Eighth Air Force (based in England), and he had done in-depth interviews with many wounded servicemen. Kantor captured their experiences, coupled with his own harsh observations, in a novel he called *Glory for Me*. He made the somewhat un-orthodox decision to write the novel in blank verse, and he gave a completed draft to Goldwyn in March 1945. The novel's form was the least of Goldwyn's concerns. *Glory for Me*, its title inspired by a Protestant hymn, was marked by a dark, brittle tone. Its three main characters were for the most part unsympathetic, but perhaps the most disturbing was the "spastic" Homer Wermels, a gunner's mate whose ship had been struck by a torpedo: "Alive on its right side, and dying, jerking on its left / It walked with pain and twisted muscles." Kantor added that Homer's body wasn't the only thing affected: "In his brain a little telephone was doing things / And all so wrong, so very wrong indeed."[16] Years later, Harold Russell described Kantor's version of the character as "a gargoyle in human form."[17] Goldwyn had trouble imagining what this character would even look like onscreen, let alone which of the leading men under contract to him (David Niven? Danny Kaye?) could be convinced to play the part. For the time being, Goldwyn shelved the project.

But he still needed a film from William Wyler. The director had worked with the independent producer since the mid-1930s, when Goldwyn had hired Wyler to direct *These Three* (1936), based on Lillian Hellman's controversial play *The Children's Hour*. Like Goldwyn, Wyler had emigrated from Europe to the United States as a teenager, but his path to Hollywood was made easier by his relationship with his distant cousin Carl Laemmle, the founder and head of Universal Studios. "Uncle Carl" gave Wyler a start, but the émigré with the intense eyes had to prove himself as an office boy and in other low-level positions at Universal. His break came in directing two- and five-reel westerns, which led to Wyler's briefly becoming an assistant director and then a director on feature films and, eventually, to meeting Goldwyn and making *These Three*. Wyler had renegotiated his contract with Goldwyn before the war, and now he owed him one more project. Goldwyn wanted him to direct a film about Eisenhower, which he had hired Robert Sherwood to write. But Wyler, leafing through books in Goldwyn's personal library, became intrigued by Kantor's *Glory for Me*.

The Best Years of Our Lives tackles infidelity, alcoholism, and sexual anxiety. It also tiptoes through a political minefield: the screenplay's mention of communism during the ideologically charged postwar months sparked more than one FBI investigation during production. Later, *Best Years* was targeted as the House Un-American Activities Committee waged its battle against suspected communists living and working in Hollywood.

Most of *Best Years'* stars, supporting cast, and crew had served during the war. Some, like the handless Russell and the partially deaf Wyler, were haunted by their injuries. Their experiences infused the film with an authenticity unlike anything on the screen at that time. Audiences went to *Best Years* in droves, making it the highest-grossing film since *Gone with the Wind*, released seven years earlier. It was, wrote one historian, a "cultural event, deeply rooted in its time and the conventions of the Hollywood system."[18]

Best Years also mainstreamed the conversation about the "veterans problem." While *Till the End of Time* (Dmytryk, 1946) and other contemporaneous films likewise dramatized postwar trauma, *Best Years'* bold depiction of what today we call PTSD brought the issue front and center. As one critic wrote at the time, *Best Years* was "the first big, good movie of the postwar era" to do so.[19] The film and its cast humanized even the most troubled and disturbing veterans and showed audiences how to have compassion for those struggling to leave the war behind.

From the average moviegoer and lowest-ranking veteran to the most celebrated officer, viewers were deeply affected by the film. An anonymous pilot who flew for the Royal Air Force wrote to Goldwyn after *Best Years* had played in London: "Things are just about as tough over here as they are in the States for an ex-serviceman. . . . Apart from our families, we receive little sympathy. That's why when I went to see 'The Best Years of Our Lives' I felt overwhelmingly grateful."[20] The *Stars and Stripes* correspondent and Pulitzer Prize winner Bill Mauldin, known for his satirical cartoons skewering the army brass and celebrating the average GI, wrote to Goldwyn after watching the film at his neighborhood movie theater. In an uncharacteristically emotional letter, the cartoonist called *Best Years* "the first honest-to-God sincere thing I've seen about the war and its aftermath."[21]

But the impression the film made at the highest levels of the military carried the most potential to change how war trauma was regarded and treated at the time. "Sometimes we forget that when men are veterans they are also men, carrying with them the imprints that war leaves on the lives of men. Here is a movie that takes those men with their wounds, their pride, their hopes, their setbacks and tells what happened to the lives of three of them—what happened to the lives of their girls, their wives, their families," wrote General Omar Bradley to Goldwyn after viewing the film.[22]

Yet this esteemed motion picture—beloved by fans of classic Hollywood movies and film scholars alike, included on the Library of Congress's National Film Registry—seems little known among the general public today.[23] It is ironic, in fact, that Frank Capra's 1946 feature *It's a Wonderful Life* is more widely recognized and has become a generation-spanning holiday staple. Capra's film was the first production released by the newly formed independent company Liberty Films, in which Wyler was a partner. Yet at the time of *It's a Wonderful Life*'s opening, a week after *Best Years'*, Wyler and Goldwyn's final collaboration trounced Capra's film at the box office, effectively bankrupting Liberty Films. As the film critic Jonathan Rosenbaum has observed, "It says something about the American public of 1946 that they preferred the realistic, astringent honesty and quiet resolution of *Best Years* to the fantasy feel-good solution that papered over the panic-stricken despair of *It's a Wonderful Life*."[24]

By telling the powerful story of *The Best Years of Our Lives*' journey from script to screen, this book offers insights into the film's key players as well as its era. In particular, this story follows three men—the producer, Samuel Goldwyn; the director, William Wyler; and the film's breakout "star," Harold Russell—and examines the making of this multiple-award winner through their experiences. Wyler's and Russell's profound wartime injuries shaped the film's screenplay, and Goldwyn worked exhaustively to make a prestige picture about World War II that might finally earn him a Best Picture Academy Award. This story also traces the evolution of treatments for war trauma, offering context both for Wyler's and Russell's postwar rehabilitation and for the subsequent handling of the characters' trauma in *Best Years*. It is this focus that helped the film become—for a time, at least—a unifying force in a nation grappling with its walking wounded, thanks in part to Russell's touring alongside the film in the year following its release. *Best Years*' success gave Russell a second act as a veterans' advocate and champion for the rights of the disabled, a platform that endured through eight presidential administrations and culminated in the Americans with Disabilities Act of 1990.

Produced more than three-quarters of a century ago, *The Best Years of Our Lives* and its characters' struggles continue to resonate. Writing about the film after it screened at Manhattan's Film Forum during the first anniversary of the September 11 terrorist attacks, Frances Davis observed that directors of contemporary war films like *Pearl Harbor* (Bay, 2001) seem to lack the skill possessed by Wyler and his *Best Years* associates to "portray the emotional toll that war exacts even on the winners." The film's stark portrait of a disabled veteran and its willingness to tackle tough questions about veterans' mental health made it a forerunner of contemporary films dealing with similar issues, including Hal Ashby's *Coming Home* (1978), Oliver Stone's *Born on the Fourth of July* (1989), and Kathryn Bigelow's *The Hurt Locker* (2009).

Bigelow's film in particular includes moments reminiscent of those in *Best Years*. The scene in which Staff Sergeant William James (Jeremy Renner) wanders a grocery store's frozen food and cereal aisles in a kind of consumer daze at the end of *The Hurt Locker* owes a debt to *Best Years*' skeptical drugstore clerk, Fred Derry (Dana Andrews). Derry's sales pitch in reverse to Peggy Stephenson (Teresa Wright), when he talks her out of purchasing any number of new beauty products, reveals a war-scarred veteran unwilling to embrace the country's postwar optimism and consumerism. As with Derry, James's disorientation in the grocery store is only a symptom of his inability to readjust to life stateside. And James's domestic scenes in *The Hurt Locker* mirror the kind of malaise that *Best Years*' characters feel as strangers in their own homes.

The Best Years of Our Lives has also had a profound influence on a generation of filmmakers who followed in William Wyler's footsteps. Francis Ford Coppola acknowledges *Best Years* as one of the ten greatest movies of all time, and Steven Spielberg screens the film annually "to bring people to see it for the first time, so I can relive it through their eyes."[25] It is one of a select group of postwar films, Martin Scorsese believes, whose authenticity has the rare ability to speak to audiences then and now. "The greatest filmmakers were moved to create meditations on existence, on the miracle of life itself," writes Scorsese. "They didn't look away from harshness and violence—quite the contrary. Rather, they dealt with them directly and then looked beyond, from a greater and more benign distance."[26]

Speaking with a journalist on the eve of *Best Years'* release, William Wyler described his unsettled mind-set immediately after his discharge from the service: "I wish that I could go back [to Hollywood] quietly and make a small picture just to get the feel of things."[27] *The Best Years of Our Lives* would not be that small picture for Wyler—nor for anyone else connected with it, for that matter. Instead, it would become much more.

CHAPTER 1

Warstruck

Pearl Harbor came to my rescue.
WILLIAM WYLER

It wasn't the first time Helmut Dantine had been a Nazi.

By the late fall of 1941, the chiseled blond from Austria had played a series of German officers in such films as *International Squadron* (Mendes and Seiler, 1941), *Desperate Journey* (Walsh, 1942), and *Edge of Darkness* (Milestone, 1943). But it was on the twenty-three-year-old's current production that he would have the chance to make his Nazi shine. Dantine had been cast in *Mrs. Miniver*, a drama about a middle-class English family's experience during the early days of the Battle of Britain. In the film, Dantine's German officer sneaks into the family's garden and threatens the mother after his plane is shot down near their house.

Dantine was working under the direction of thirty-nine-year-old William Wyler, also a German-speaking émigré. Dantine and Wyler both owed their careers to relatives who had offered safe passage to the United States. Dantine suffered at the hands of the Germans before emigrating. After the Nazis annexed Austria and took over the country, Dantine was sent to a concentration camp outside Vienna. For three months, he and forty-nine other men were confined to a small room with nothing to do but imagine their fate. Dantine got lucky: an uncle who was a vice president at Consolidated Aircraft in San Diego managed to get his nephew on a ship bound for the United States.[1]

Of Dantine's performance in *Miniver*, one journalist wrote, "Out of the calm of *Mrs. Miniver*'s garden rose a new kind of masculine menace.... Hard, merciless, bitter as a dose of arsenic, who was the man who played the Nazi officer?"[2] It was a small but attention-grabbing role, and Dantine's scene opposite the picture's British star, Greer Garson, was one of the film's most memorable. Holding Garson at gunpoint in her kitchen, he shoves hunks of fresh bread into his mouth and guzzles milk from the bottle as she looks on in horror and disgust, a captive in her own perfectly appointed English home.

Without *Mrs. Miniver*, perhaps, there would have been no *Best Years*. Before Pearl Harbor could "rescue" Wyler from sitting out a war that he desperately wanted to witness, *Miniver* gave him the opportunity to be involved from afar. And when he finally went overseas, Wyler made documentaries for the war effort, experiences that later helped shape the screenplay and direction of *Best Years*, giving him an understanding not only of how the film's characters might think and feel about being in the war, but also of what they felt on returning home. And although Wyler told *Miniver*'s wartime story to the best of his ability, he realized months later, after arriving in bombed-out London, that the film had failed to achieve his desired level of authenticity. He would not make the same mistake again.

Production on *Miniver* began in mid-November 1941. Wyler was energized to make the film because of its potential as propaganda. "The most satisfaction I get out of a film aside from its critical and financial success, is its contribution to the thinking of people, socially or politically," Wyler told a biographer years later. "In this sense every film is propaganda. But of course, propaganda must not *look* like propaganda."[3] At the time, making *Miniver* was the closest Wyler could get to the war, which had deep personal meaning for him. His parents, Melanie and Leopold, and his older brother Robert had emigrated from Mulhouse, France, near the Swiss and German borders, to Los Angeles years earlier, but many of his Jewish mother's relatives remained in the town, which in 1941 was under German occupation. Once Wyler established himself in Hollywood, he wrote letters, petitioned the US State Department for visas, and committed to sponsoring financially at least two dozen relatives in the way that his mother's cousin Carl Laemmle had sponsored him. But by the time Wyler had begun working on *Miniver*, the State Department was no longer granting refugees of German-Jewish descent entry into the United States.[4]

When Sidney Franklin, a producer at MGM, approached Wyler with the script for *Miniver*, Wyler knew immediately that he wanted to make the movie. He also knew he *had* to: under a new contract to the producer Samuel Goldwyn, Wyler had been loaned out to MGM while Goldwyn was engaged in a lengthy lawsuit with his distributor, United Artists. The loan-out was a key Goldwyn move, and one he often used to fund his own productions: it enabled him to make money from the directors and actors under contract to him even when they refused to work on a particular Goldwyn project or when Goldwyn was unable to make another picture, as was the case during his legal battle with UA. Written and rewritten in a matter of weeks, the script for *Miniver* was based on the novelist Jan Struthers's series of essays about a suburban London family living through the Blitz and participating in the daring rescue of Allied soldiers from the harbor surrounding Dunkirk.

By Thanksgiving, production on *Mrs. Miniver* was in full swing on the MGM soundstages in Culver City. May Whitty, who played the imperious gardener Lady Beldon, was a Liverpool native who had begun her career on the London stage. She, Garson, and many other members of the cast and crew discussed the latest war news from overseas between takes on the set. Teresa Wright, a Goldwyn find who had made her screen debut in Wyler's previous film, *The Little Foxes*, was cast in a pivotal role as Garson's daughter-in-law, newly married to the Minivers' son, who was away in the Royal Air Force. Goldwyn had been so impressed by Wright's performance in *Foxes*, in fact, that he had allowed his rising star to add a codicil to her contract before *Miniver* started production. The modest—and savvy—ingenue insisted that her image remain as true to her idea of professionalism as possible. Subsequent contracts stated, in part, "I will not pose in shorts, playing with a cute cocker spaniel. I will not be shown happily whipping up a meal for a huge family."[5]

Production on the *Miniver* set shut down every six days. Wyler left the MGM soundstage as twilight fell on Saturday, December 6, and made the twenty-five-minute drive to his home in Bel Air. The house, which Willy and Talli had purchased less than two years earlier from the director Frank Lloyd, was located across the street from the University of California campus on Copa de Oro Road. The two-story house was the perfect size for a growing family: in 1939, Talli had given birth to a daughter, Cathy, named for the heroine in *Wuthering Heights*, the picture Wyler was making when she was born. Now, in December 1941, Talli was pregnant again.

The next morning, December 7, dawned clear and sunny, and Wyler had a tennis game planned with John Huston. The two directors had been friends since Wyler's days at Universal, when he was just starting out behind the camera and Huston was still writing uncredited dialogue on projects like *A House Divided*, in which Wyler directed Huston's father, Walter. The morning edition of the *Los Angeles Times* was full of news about President Roosevelt's sending a note to Emperor Hirohito in an attempt to broker peace with the Japanese. Closer to home, the city was grappling with a massive sewage problem that had been polluting beaches and discoloring the ocean waters off Malibu.[6]

Inside the house, Talli had the radio on. It was popular at the time to listen to the weekly broadcast of the New York Philharmonic. On that particular Sunday, the pianist Arthur Rubinstein was playing Brahms's Concerto in B-flat Major when the broadcast was interrupted by a live news bulletin. Four months pregnant, Talli ran out of the house and down to the tennis court to tell Willy and Huston the news: Pearl Harbor had been attacked.[7]

The Japanese bombardment of the US Pacific Fleet changed everything, of course. When Wyler received a note from Mary Pickford thanking him for a recent gift, she mentioned that her husband had just left for a three-month training course with the Naval Air Corps. "It certainly is a new life for us all, isn't it?" she mused.[8] But some in Hollywood had been involved in the war effort before Pearl Harbor. The screenwriter Robert Sherwood, a playwright and member of the Algonquin Round Table, had begun writing speeches for President Roosevelt in the late 1930s, around the same time he was working on scripts for *Abe Lincoln in Illinois* and *Rebecca*. When the news broke that Adolf Hitler had invaded Poland in the spring of 1939, Sherwood was at the Trocadero on Sunset Boulevard. "And so it has come," he wrote later in his diary. "The dance floor was packed with Joe Schenks and L. B. Mayers and agents dancing La Conga with blonde, fake-breasted cuties. At one ringside table a group were huddled over a little portable radio, listening to a maniac who had just condemned millions of decent, helpless people to death."[9]

Like many men at the time, Wyler was eager to participate in the war, and Pearl Harbor suddenly made it possible. In December 1941, however, he was an out-of-shape thirty-nine-year-old husband and father with a second child on the way. His personal circumstances alone would have allowed him to stay home. "He couldn't stand the thought of sitting on the sidelines," Talli said years later. "He just didn't want to miss the war."[10] On December 18, Wyler submitted an application to join the Signal Corps, a division of the Army Pictorial Service.

First created as a communications entity before the Civil War, the Signal Corp expanded its role over time to keep pace with such technological advances as telegraph and radio. In the years before Pearl Harbor, the actors Melvyn Douglas and Burgess Meredith had met with the poet Archibald MacLeish, then serving as the librarian of Congress, to discuss the formation of a temporary government agency that could use Hollywood talent to disseminate and circulate propaganda during wartime. Darryl Zanuck, the head of Twentieth Century–Fox, had a similar idea, and as a lieutenant colonel in the Army Reserve, he had access to the army chief of staff, George C. Marshall, who signed off on a plan to use Hollywood's filmmakers and technical experts to make training films.[11] Frank Capra, who was between film projects and received his commission before Wyler did, headed to Washington, DC, in January 1942 to begin overseeing the production of training films.

Tensions ran high in Los Angeles in the days following the disaster at Pearl Harbor. The city was home to four major aircraft factories, and its location on the Pacific coast made some feel as if it were a natural next target for the Japanese. "Enemy Planes Sighted over California Coast" warned a local headline on December 9.[12] Wyler reluctantly turned his focus back to *Mrs. Miniver*. The British actor Henry Wilcoxon, cast as the vicar in the film, informed Wyler that he had enlisted in the US Coast Guard, and left almost immediately to begin his service. Wyler tried to wrap up as many scenes as possible before Greer Garson departed to join other stars involved in a war bond drive in Canada.

By early March, Wyler had yet to shoot the film's final scene, which featured Wilcoxon giving a sermon in the village's bombed-out church. In *Miniver's* original script, the vicar's speech concluded with lines from the Ninety-First Psalm, emphasizing trust in God above all else. In light of all that had happened since December 7, Wyler knew the movie's final words had to do more. Wilcoxon received a two-day leave from the coast guard to return to the MGM set, and on the eve of shooting, he and Wyler rewrote the vicar's speech. While Wilcoxon's monologue still included words from the psalm, the sermon quickly turned personal, referring to the hardships and tragedies sustained by individual characters throughout the course of the film. "Why?" asks the vicar as he addresses the congregation. "Surely you must have asked yourselves this question. Why in all conscience should these be the ones to suffer?" Because, he continues, the war is not just about the battlefield and those who fight there. "This is the people's war! It is our war. We are the fighters. Fight it, then! Fight it with all that is in us. And may God defend the right."[13]

Even without the finished film's dramatic accompaniment—Herbert Stothart's orchestration of "Onward, Christian Soldiers" and Joseph Ruttenberg's final, upward tilt of the camera to the hole in the church's roof as six groups of planes fly past in formation—Wilcoxon's speech made an impression on set. An emotional Greer Garson teared up during the actor's first take. When Wyler caught sight of this, he gave her more specific direction than he usually offered his actors. "The tears in the eyes," he said. "That was very good. But you let them spill over just a second too soon. Now, if you can get the tears again, I want you to hold them there. And *then* I want you to let that tear run down your cheek." Garson, on the verge of "hysterical laughter" in response to Wyler's pointed request, managed again to summon her character's emotional reaction. As the camera tracked in on her upturned face, a single tear formed on her lower eyelid, then slid down her glowing cheek. Wyler extended the shot in the final cut of the film, intercutting between Garson and the vicar before ending the scene—and the movie.[14]

Although Wyler still needed to complete postproduction on *Mrs. Miniver*, Wilcoxon's rewritten scene, one of the last to be shot, seemed like a fitting end to a project that Wyler had chosen as his contribution to the war effort. "We all felt and sought to convey the profound determination that dramatized those days," said Teresa Wright years later. "It was a picture produced in the shadow of headlines, and those of us who appeared in it would never forget it."[15]

The opening of *Mrs. Miniver* was scheduled for early June, but for two months after finishing the project, Wyler worried about its relevance. Combat films had quickly become a popular genre in the aftermath of Pearl Harbor. Movies such as Universal's *Eagle Squadron* (Lubin, 1942) not only included battle sequences (and actual combat footage) but also showcased the combat unit as a group of characters worth caring about. Wyler knew about projects such as Paramount's *Wake Island* (Farrow, 1942), which would open two months after *Miniver* and quickly go on to become a box-office and critical success, thanks to its gritty portrayal of a group of American marines struggling to defend their isolated location in the Pacific.

Wyler was somewhat unprepared, then, for the overwhelmingly positive response that greeted *Miniver* after it premiered. "Perhaps it is too soon to call this one of the greatest motion pictures ever made," wrote the *New York Times* critic Bosley Crowther, "but certainly it is the finest film yet made about the present war." Despite Wyler's fears that the film would seem irrelevant or out of date, Crowther cited *Miniver*'s home-front setting as a strength: "This is a film about the people in a small, unpretentious English town on whom the war creeps up slowly disturbing their tranquil ways of life, then suddenly bursts in devastating fury as the bombs rain down and the Battle of Britain is on."[16] *Variety*'s Herb Golden called the film "quiet yet actionful," describing it as "one of the strongest pieces of propaganda to come out of the war."[17]

Not everyone was a fan. Wyler's good friend Lillian Hellman, who had seen *Miniver* at an early preview, exited the theater crying. "You ought to be ashamed of yourself," she scolded him through her tears. Hellman, whose integrity and dedication to her craft had inspired him to take himself and his work seriously, labeled *Miniver* a "piece of junk," telling Wyler, "It's so below you." On the ride home from the screening, Hellman's partner, Dashiell Hammett, told her she shouldn't have been that blunt. "Why shouldn't I do that?" demanded Hellman. "This man is a great director, and he ought not to be touching stuff like this."[18]

The critical and box-office success of *Miniver* seemed to propel Wyler out of the purgatory of waiting for a commission. Cooling his heels in Washington, DC, where he had arrived shortly after the birth of his and Talli's second daughter, Judy, Wyler ran into the screenwriter Sy Bartlett, the friend who had recruited him the previous December to apply to join the Army Pictorial Service. No longer with the Signal Corps, Bartlett was serving as an aide to General Carl Spaatz of the Army Air Force. Bartlett invited Wyler to be his guest at a private party to be held on the eve of Spaatz's departure for Europe. Although it wasn't yet common knowledge, Bartlett told Wyler that Spaatz was heading to England to establish a base of operations for the combat-oriented Eighth Air Force. By the time Wyler arrived at Spaatz's DC row house, Bartlett had prepared Wyler to meet the guest of honor, a World War I fighter pilot who had worked his way up the chain of command. Bartlett introduced Wyler as the director of *Mrs. Miniver*, and Wyler wasted little time on party chitchat. "General, I don't know where you're going or what you're going to do, but somebody ought to make a picture about it," Wyler said, pretending he knew nothing about Spaatz's mission in Europe.[19]

Within days, William Wyler, filmmaker, had become Major William Wyler, assigned to produce documentary films for the Eighth Air Force. His military physical noted he had an "insufficient number of teeth," and at five feet, seven inches tall and 165 pounds, he was deemed "obese." "No training, nothing. I was simply sent someplace to buy a uniform," Wyler said years later.[20]

More than six months passed, however, before Wyler began making an actual documentary. One of his first assignments had him flying back to Los Angeles in August to use his Hollywood contacts in order to secure equipment and a crew. The job proved more difficult than he had anticipated, and he was particularly disgusted with the lack of cooperation regarding a donation of equipment from MGM, the studio that had released *Mrs. Miniver* to such acclaim just two months earlier. He eventually assembled a small crew that included a writer, two cameramen, and a sound recordist. Lieutenant Jerome Chodorov had worked as a reporter before turning to writing for the stage and screen. William Clothier, who had shot aerial footage for *Wings* in the 1920s, was commissioned into the unit as a captain, as was William Skall, a longtime Hollywood cinematographer known for his Technicolor expertise. Wyler also recruited Harold Tannenbaum, an RKO soundman who was also a World War I navy veteran.

Wyler and his small crew had arrived in England by the fall of 1942. The Eighth Air Force had taken over a former Royal Air Force station in Bassingbourn, a village in the countryside a few hours north of London. General Spaatz had established his headquarters in London, and Wyler was given an office nearby. While waiting for his orders to come through, Wyler drew up a list of projects that he and his crew could make about the Eighth Air Force. He was also waiting for film equipment to arrive from the United States. His group had secured more than a half-dozen 35 mm cameras, including several fixed and handheld Eyemos, which were known for their precision and indestructability. The cameras, along with portable sound-recording gear, were being sent by boat from Ohio. When the shipment failed to arrive, Wyler was forced to use 16 mm handheld cameras that he borrowed in London.

By November, Wyler had been in the army air force and away from Talli and their girls for a few months. "Things are progressing slowly," he wrote in a letter home. "He didn't know anything about chains of command and people or organizations, requisitions and that sort of stuff," recalled Talli. "He felt stymied. Getting a typewriter was a major project."[21] Wyler appealed to Major General Ira C. Eaker, a Texan who had flown raids during World War I and who had recently been named commander of the Eighth Air Force in England. Eaker understood from his own wartime experiences what kinds of images and information were necessary to educate the public about the military's activities. "These films are conceived as documentary motion picture stories exploiting the human element, as contrasted to factual and newsreel material," Eaker wrote in his directive.[22] Besides laying out exactly what kind of equipment Wyler should receive, Eaker's order assigned Beirne Lay, a career military man who had studied at Yale, to help Wyler navigate the army's bureaucracy.

By February 1943, Wyler, Clothier, Skall, and Tannenbaum were taking a four-day course that would prepare them to recognize different types of aircraft and to operate relatively new radar technology so that they could identify enemy planes. Chodorov was by then no longer part of the crew. One night over dinner the previous fall, Lay had witnessed a heated disagreement between Chodorov and Wyler, with the writer challenging Wyler over his quest for authenticity. Not long after, Lay arranged a transfer and Chodorov was sent back to the States.[23]

Later in February, Wyler traveled to Bassingbourn to participate in his first combat mission, aboard a B-17 bomber dubbed the *Jersey Bounce*. The mission had two German targets: the northwestern harbor city of Bremen and the coastal town of Wilhelmshaven on the North Sea. Wyler had been on training flights before. He and his crew had already shot footage of and from B-17s, trying to capture basic elements of each mission such as the unique "choreography" of getting planes off the airstrip and into the air, and the massing of bombers from several air bases to create one protective formation.[24] But this mission on the *Jersey Bounce* was a potentially dangerous air raid.

Wyler had had plenty of time to observe the bombers the previous fall when he toured bases in England and Ireland. And he had spent hours studying the planes as they took off and returned from missions, so he was somewhat familiar with the hulking aircraft known as the Flying Fortress. In production for only a decade, the Boeing B-17 quickly became known for its durability and engine power. The Japanese dubbed them "four-engine fighters," and the pair of supercharged engines on either side of the cockpit produced a drone so loud that crew members had to communicate via radio inside the plane. Each B-17 was equipped with a dozen .50-caliber machine guns and could carry eight thousand pounds of bombs. One of the plane's most distinctive features was its clear, Plexiglas nose, which housed a gunner who sat on a swivel chair and operated a mounted machine gun. Three years later, Wyler and Robert Sherwood paid tribute to the B-17 and this particular feature in one of *Best Years'* most memorable scenes.

Wyler accompanied the men of the Ninety-First Bomber Group, a crew that included Robert K. Morgan (pilot, twenty-four years old), Clarence "Bill" Winchell (waist gunner, twenty-six), and Vincent Evans (bombardier, twenty-two). Morgan and the nine other crew members typically flew the *Memphis*

Belle, but that bomber had sustained heavy damage during a previous mission and was undergoing repairs. Wyler was more than twice the age of the crew's youngest member, a nineteen-year-old washing machine repairman named Tony Nastale, who was one of the bomber's two waist gunners.

Initially, the crew was dubious about the "over-age major" in their midst. Once up in the air, the young men got a glimpse of Wyler's fearlessness as the filmmaker paced the open catwalk around the bomb bay, desperate to capture the action taking place all around the *Jersey Bounce*. Wyler carried a 16 mm camera in one hand and, in the other, a stainless steel walk-around oxygen bottle to which he was tethered. An awkward electric flight suit, worn to insulate him from the frigid in-flight temperatures, further restricted Wyler's movement. Dogged by German fighters, the B-17 flew through dense flak bursts and thick cloud cover. Unaccustomed to shooting in such challenging conditions, Wyler struggled to get usable footage. "We could hear him cuss over the intercom. By the time he'd swing his camera over to a flak burst, it was lost," Evans, the bombardier, remembered.[25]

Morgan brought the *Jersey Bounce* up to 28,000 feet as it closed in on Wilhelmshaven. Forced to stay put at such a high altitude, Wyler positioned himself in the plane's nose and tried to record frontal attacks. The oil in his cameras froze at the low temperature. Wyler returned from the mission without any usable footage, but the experience stoked his daredevil spirit. He understood the technical challenges that he was up against. In total, seven planes were lost during the raid, and within the Ninety-First Bomber Group, forty-one men suffered injuries, including frostbite. Despite the mission's heavy human toll, Wyler felt rejuvenated. He described the hazards of air combat in a letter to a Hollywood friend, writing about being pushed to one's limits in an environment "where human resistance and wit are taxed to the maximum, where things happen faster than any man can think." Citing the vast divide between "the comforts of Stage 18 in Burbank or Culver City" and his wartime situation, Wyler concluded, "This is life at its fullest."[26]

Less than two weeks later, Talli attended the Academy Awards on his behalf. *Mrs. Miniver* had been nominated in twelve categories, including a best director nod for Wyler. This was his fifth nomination in the category, and in years past he had made a joke of not winning by carrying a small black satchel to the ceremony, telling friends it would come in handy on the off chance that he would have an Oscar to bring home.[27] On March 4, 1943, nominees, presenters, and guests crowded into the Cocoanut Grove at the Ambassador Hotel in Los Angeles. In a nod toward wartime sacrifices, women were encouraged to forgo wearing evening gowns.

Colonel Frank Capra, on temporary leave and smartly dressed in his army uniform, announced the nominees for best director. When he called out Wyler's name as the winner, Talli rushed to the stage. "I wish he could be here," she said as she clutched the statuette, made of plaster because of metal shortages. "He's wanted an Oscar for a long time and I know it would thrill him an awful lot to be here. Probably as much as that flight over Wilhelmshaven did. Thank you so much."[28]

Wyler received the news in Bassingbourn when a reporter arrived to interview him about the award. He dashed off a telegram to Talli: "Darling, terribly thrilled family enlarged by Oscar, must make postwar plans to build trophy room . . . All my love darling and don't let Cathy play with my new doll."[29] Since beginning his wartime service in England, Wyler had been feeling somewhat embarrassed by the film. For a director who strove for authenticity, he realized as soon as he got close enough to the war that he had made "small errors of emphasis, little details unimportant in themselves but just enough to make it seem less than real."[30] Wyler even tried to duck a command screening of *Miniver* for London's top military men, but General Eaker insisted he attend.

Delighted as he was with his first Academy Award, Wyler quickly returned to the business at hand. The *Memphis Belle* was back in service, and Wyler accompanied its crew on three missions between April and mid-May 1943. Wyler had been forbidden to fly on the last of these by General Eaker, who feared that Wyler's recent acclaim for *Miniver*, a film purportedly disliked by the Germans, coupled with his Jewish ethnicity, would put a bull's-eye on his back if the plane went down and Wyler was captured. He went on the final mission anyway. During the flight, the tube connecting Wyler's mask to his walk-around oxygen tank came loose, and he passed out. Beirne Lay gave Wyler a sharp rebuke for his recklessness but did not report the incident to Eaker.

King George VI and Queen Elizabeth were scheduled to visit the base at Bassingbourn in late May. Wyler pulled some strings to have the royal couple inspect the *Memphis Belle* as both a surprise for the crew and as a photo opportunity for his documentary, which by then was being called *25 Missions*, after the number of raids an American crew had to fly before qualifying for a visit home. The *Belle* was among the first to reach this milestone, and the film re-created the final mission by using footage from multiple raids and flights.[31] On May 26, the king and queen arrived at Bassingbourn in a fleet of Rolls-Royces. Morgan and the other crew members stood at attention next to the *Belle* as the royal couple made their way down the line. Wyler was introduced to Queen Elizabeth as the director who had made *Mrs. Miniver*, and she gave him a smile. "It was very nice," said the queen.[32]

Three days later, Wyler went on his fifth mission. He and his cameramen had already shot enough footage for the documentary, but for Wyler this mission was personal. In Europe, upon completion of a fifth sortie, every bomber crew member was eligible for the distinctive bronze Air Medal embossed with an eagle carrying two lightning bolts in its talons. Wyler wanted the Air Medal maybe as much as, if not more than, he had wanted to win an Oscar. The mission took Wyler over three heavily defended targets in western France, including "Flak City," the name bomber crews had given to the submarine base at Saint-Nazaire. It was a difficult, dangerous raid; thirteen B-17s didn't return. Wyler's bomber—not the *Belle* this time—easily could have been one of them, and he admitted years later that going on the mission had been a dumb decision.[33] Months later, when the crew of the *Memphis Belle* visited the Wylers' home in Bel Air, its pilot, Robert Morgan, noticed that Wyler's Air Medal was prominently displayed in his office, alongside his Oscar for *Miniver*.[34]

In June, just as the ten-man crew of the *Memphis Belle* was being sent home to the United States to begin a cross-country war bond tour, Wyler received a sixty-day leave to edit the 16 mm footage into a feature documentary. As he had explained to General Eaker, the footage had to be blown up to 35 mm for the theatrical distribution that the army air force envisioned for the film, and that level of technical work had to be done in the States. "Suggest brushing up Cathy on the use of word Daddy and prepare Judy for an early introduction," Wyler cabled Talli on June 4. Catching rides on military planes, Wyler flew from the United Kingdom to Iceland, Greenland, and Nova Scotia before arriving in Washington in mid-June. "Please attend meeting at Carlton Hotel Washington . . . don't bring children," teased Wyler in another telegram to his wife.

It had been nearly a year since they had last seen each other, and after another delay or two, the couple finally reunited in New York at the Hampshire House, a hotel overlooking Central Park South. Aspects of their first wartime reunion later found their way into *Best Years*. Willy had written to Talli many times over the previous months, joking that he wanted her to remain just as she was when he left, with her brunette waves gracefully framing a lineless face. But things had changed. They had endured wildly different experiences in their year apart. "You're not supposed to be strangers, but you are strangers for a moment," Talli recalled years later. She waited for Willy in the doorway of their room, located at the end of one of the hotel's long hallways. Willy, room number in hand, stepped off the elevator. They rushed toward each other.[35]

By the time the Wylers met in New York, the clock had already begun ticking on Willy's two-month leave. After settling back home in Los Angeles, Wyler established himself at Hal Roach's studios in Culver City, which the army air force had been leasing since September 1942. There, top Hollywood stars like Ronald Reagan, a captain and adjutant for the AAF's First Motion Picture Unit, oversaw the creation of military training films.[36] Located about thirty minutes from Wyler's Bel Air home, Fort Roach offered the necessary facilities and equipment for Wyler and a small crew to complete the documentary's postproduction, which included editing the footage, finalizing a script for the film's narration, and recording a voice-over track, a score, and atmospheric sound effects. Wyler's first order of business, however, was to send the 16 mm footage to the Technicolor Corporation. The company would handle the process of making a 35 mm projection print of the raw color footage, which could then be edited and finished for theatrical release. But Wyler soon discovered that *25 Missions* was a lower priority than the military's training films, many of which were ahead of it in Technicolor's queue. The work print wouldn't be ready until late August.

Meanwhile, the "stars" of *25 Missions* were a month into a whirlwind trip across the United States. Originally billed as a war bond tour, the *Memphis Belle*'s home-front mission focused more on boosting the morale of workers at aircraft factories and allowing the crew to put on something of an air show, buzzing the tops of downtown buildings and doing flyovers. Starting in Memphis, the tour crisscrossed the country, making stops at factories and plants in places such as Oklahoma City, San Antonio, and Las Vegas. Crowds turned out to greet the returning fliers, swarming around the bomber and the men.[37]

Wyler realized midway through the *Belle*'s summer tour that the documentary needed to capitalize on the bomber crew's tremendous reception around the country. He began to think of the film as a five-reel feature rather than a short, and he decided to incorporate footage from the *Belle*'s Los Angeles stop as part of the documentary's final sequence. He arranged to film the crew's visits to the Douglas Aircraft plant in nearby Long Beach and Lockheed's plant in Burbank, and he made plans for the men to rehearse and record "wild" lines to simulate the intercom dialogue they had exchanged during bombing missions over France and Germany.[38]

In the middle of his leave, Wyler had appealed to Beirne Lay about lengthening the film beyond the planned two reels, which would necessitate Wyler spending more time in Los Angeles. Wyler and Lay had grown close during the ten months they had worked together, and Lay had even stopped by Copa de Oro during one of his stateside leaves earlier in the year to check on Talli and the girls. After hearing through the grapevine that Wyler planned to remain in the United States an additional month, however, Lay reminded Wyler that he had a job to do. "Two months was the target for the whole trip. Remember?!" wrote Lay. He painted a grim picture if General Eaker were to hear about Wyler's plan to extend his leave. "90 days in USA = 10 years in Folsom," Lay scrawled at the bottom of his letter.[39] But by the time the 35 mm Technicolor work prints arrived in late August, only two weeks remained on Wyler's leave of absence, and the documentary was far from finished. The music had to be written and recorded, the intercom chatter re-created by the *Belle* crew had to be edited, and sound effects and dubbing needed to be added. Even on a tight schedule, the remaining work wouldn't be done before late September.

Wyler cabled General Eaker, asking for an additional two months. "You come back or I get a replacement," was Eaker's reply. In late October, Wyler returned to England to make his case in person. He requested more time (an extension of orders "until completion") and the authority to make creative decisions such as hiring a new writer and extending the documentary's length beyond the prescribed two reels. By the end of his stay, Wyler had received permission to make a longer film and for a two-month extension.[40]

One of Wyler's first decisions upon his return was to go back to an earlier, longer cut of the film. He knew that for the film to do well in theaters, it needed to play as dramatically as a Hollywood feature film. New narration would be scripted by Lester Koenig, a writer who worked for the First Motion Picture Unit. A clean-cut twenty-four-year-old, Koenig had worked at Paramount before the war, but he had a greater affinity for—and later, greater success with—producing music, thanks to an early introduction to the legendary producer John H. Hammond. Koenig's ear for rhythm and tone shaped the narration of *25 Missions*. Lines spoken by the narrator such as, "'Keep your voices down over the intercom,' he's likely to say" became "Don't get excited and yell when you're talking on the intercom," creating a tighter, less expositional voice-over that better communicated a bomber mission's sense of urgency and danger.[41] Satisfied with the new direction of the narration, Wyler huddled with Koenig and the cutters to put together a final version as quickly as possible. Working many late nights, the team shipped off a completed work print to Technicolor in early January.

A small item appeared in *Variety* in mid-February 1944 under the headline "Col. Wyler's 'Missions' Ready for Release." That same month, Wyler headed to Washington with Talli, where the top military men were eager to attend an advance screening of *25 Missions*. Wyler accompanied the film to the White House, and when President Roosevelt was introduced to the filmmaker, he requested that Wyler sit next to him during the screening. As the lights went down and they settled into their seats, a title appeared on the screen informing viewers that "all aerial combat film was exposed during air battles over enemy territory." The president leaned toward Wyler and inquired about the weight of the bombs flown on the *Belle*. He asked a couple of other questions and then grew quiet as the pastoral scenes of Bassingbourn dissolved into a series of shots of bombers lined up on the edge of a field. "This is a battlefront," intoned the narrator, "a battlefront like no other in the long history of mankind's wars. This is an airfront."[42]

The Technicolor footage shot by Wyler, Tannenbaum, and Clothier produced compelling images: an eight-hundred-year-old church overlooking a makeshift airstrip, bomb payloads being lifted onto the *Memphis Belle*, B-17s in formation against a brilliant blue sky clouded by inky black puffs of flak. Lester Koenig's scripted narration, delivered in a no-nonsense voice-over, introduced viewers to the ten-man crew of the *Belle* and led the audience step-by-step through the bomber's final mission, over Wilhelmshaven. The documentary concluded with shots of the king and queen visiting Bassingbourn and saluting the crew of the *Memphis Belle* for a job well done. After forty-one minutes, the documentary ended and the lights went on in the White House screening room. The president remained in his seat, his eyes glassy behind oval wire-rimmed lenses. "My! That's a great picture, one of the best I've ever seen," he told Wyler.

After a world premiere in Memphis on April 6, 1944, the documentary was released by Paramount to theaters around the country. By then the film had been retitled *The Memphis Belle: A Story of a Flying Fortress*, and the *New York Times* film critic Bosley Crowther praised it as "a thorough and vivid comprehension of what a daylight bombing is actually like." Crowther's review ran on the front page, the first time in the newspaper's history that an American film had received such coverage.[43] By the end of May, the documentary had been shown in approximately fourteen thousand theaters around the country. Samuel Goldwyn, who saw the film in Hollywood, sent a congratulatory telegram to his top director: "It is by far the best thing that has been done for the Air Forces to date and you should be very proud of your accomplishment."[44]

Interviewed for a radio program while he was working on the documentary, Wyler shared his impressions of flying air raids with the crews of the B-17s. "When you get into the plane you are full of confidence, in the ship, in the crew, in yourself. But then, there are minutes—which seem like hours—and hours, which seem like days—before you reach the target—and after you've left, on the way home," he told his interviewer. "Fear. . . . It's deep down in the pit of your stomach. But there's another feeling that is also strong—and it helps a lot. As you look around and see a sky full of Fortresses—as you look down and see the enemy coast—you'd rather be where you are than down there, with them coming at you."[45]

Thanks to Wyler's dogged perfectionism, the feelings and experiences he described in his interview all found their way into *The Memphis Belle*.

CHAPTER 2

Every Veteran a Potential Mental Case

I was constantly troubled by doubts and fears. No matter how firmly I made up my mind about something by the light of day, when the shadows lengthened and darkness came, I began to waver and wonder, and to question myself. That was the worst part of being crippled.

HAROLD RUSSELL, *Victory in My Hands*

Harold Russell glanced at his wristwatch. The baby-faced army staff sergeant was doing a routine final inspection of the explosives that he planned to use during a demolition training exercise that afternoon at Camp Mackall, in North Carolina, the primary training site for the US Army's airborne troops during the war. Raised in the quintessential college town of Cambridge, Massachusetts, with its town squares, campus quadrangles, and seasonal foliage, Russell considered the sandy, swampy camp a vast wasteland. And like many of the men at Mackall, he was desperate to see combat in Europe.[1]

Like William Wyler, Russell had seen the war as an opportunity. He enlisted to escape small-town living and the nagging suspicion that his own life was headed nowhere. Russell was transferred to Camp Mackall and the 513th Airborne Division in the spring of 1944 after training for more than a year. He had spent a month at parachute school, making his way through the four stages of the specialized program. Afterward, Russell had volunteered to be an instructor in the army's newly established parachute demolition school, hoping it would eventually get him closer to combat. Instead, he spent eighteen months as an instructor at Fort Benning until finally, with the help of the school's commandant, he secured a transfer to Camp Mackall, the last stop before being sent overseas.[2]

As the late-spring sun blazed overhead, Russell turned his attention to gathering nitro-starch packages and blasting caps for the outdoor demolition exercise. Looking around for a place to sit, he lowered his stocky body onto a nearby fifty-pound box of TNT. Russell picked up a quarter-pound package of nitro-starch, explosive orange powder neatly wrapped in brown paper bundles the size and shape of a stick of butter. He crimped the explosive's fuse to a blasting cap. As he inserted the cap and fuse into the explosive, he checked his watch again. It was 2:25 pm on Tuesday, June 6. At lunch that day, the camp chaplain had shared the news that Allied forces had landed on the northern coast of France. D-Day had begun.

The afternoon was already broiling, and the supplies for Russell's course had been sitting on the grass during lunch. Russell noticed that the blasting cap felt warm as he inserted it into the nitro-starch bundle. In an instant, a searing red light blinded him. Russell felt himself being jerked violently backward, and his helmet flew off his head. Seconds later, he opened his eyes. He was lying on the ground, and when he lifted his head and looked down at his muscular arms, he saw that his hands were no longer there. Instead, Russell saw a bloody tangle of skin, muscle, and bone, shredded and exposed. He began screaming, less from pain than from the immediate shock of seeing his mutilated arms. The camp's medics came running. They swaddled his exposed stumps and carried Russell on the run to a nearby jeep. Camp Mackall's hospital was fifteen miles away from the training site. "I was afraid of dying," Russell recalled later. "That was the last, the final coherent contemplation that crossed my mind before I slipped into unconsciousness."[3]

The paratrooper wasn't even scheduled to teach the demolition training class that June day. He was filling in for a fellow instructor who wanted the afternoon off after his girlfriend had arrived unexpectedly from out of state. Badly hurt as Russell was, none of the troops around him at the time of the explosion were injured. By some miracle, the fifty-pound box of TNT on which Russell sat hadn't blown up in a chain reaction. And when his wristwatch was found after the accident, it was still ticking.[4]

The thirty-year-old spent ten days at the base hospital, where he drifted in and out of consciousness. The doctors bandaged his arms and suspended them from a wooden frame above his head. Wrapped in thick strips of white gauze, the stumps reminded him of his life before the war, when he worked full-time in a neighborhood meat market. He thought his arms looked like "two sides of beef hanging on hooks." But it was the searing pain he felt in his chest and stomach, where the explosive had torn through his body, that surprised him the most. It felt as if his organs were on fire, and the churning pain was relentless. The wounds in his torso would have been worse, in fact, if not for the protection provided by the pistol belt he wore the day of the accident. Sometime in the first week after he lost his arms, Russell had a dream about his late father. Mr. Russell had managed a Western Union office when Harold was young and the family still lived in North Sydney, Nova Scotia, where Harold was born.

In the dream, he was sitting on his father's lap and typing a message that read, "What hath God wrought?"[5]

Russell stayed less than two weeks in the hospital at Camp Mackall, where the doctors and nurses tended to his wounds and kept him sedated most of the time to help manage his pain and shock. Still, he had periods of awareness, when he cried uncontrollably over the loss of his hands. He also struggled with phantom pains that made it feel as if his fingers were tied in knots, as he later recalled: "I tried to pry them apart, but I couldn't. . . . Yet the more I tried to separate my imaginary fingers, the more it hurt. And I couldn't stop doing it. Just like you can't stop touching an aching tooth."[6]

In mid-June the army transferred Russell to its Washington, DC, medical center. Walter Reed General Hospital, founded in 1909, was named for an army major who led the team that discovered the link between mosquitoes and the transmission of yellow fever. Constructed in the Georgian Revival style popular at the turn of the century, the hospital's redbrick main building sat on more than eighty acres of mostly undeveloped land in the middle of the nation's capital.[7]

Russell was admitted to ward 32, a wing devoted to the care and rehabilitation of amputees. He quickly learned the ward's lingo. Men with only one leg were known as "Limpy," and double amputees answered to "Shorty." One-armed men were "Paperhangers," and Russell and a guy named Tony, the only other bilateral amputee at Walter Reed, were known as "Hooks." Russell took some comfort in being surrounded by similarly injured servicemen, but he was especially self-conscious that he had been wounded during training and not in combat. Life in ward 32 revolved around physical therapy, camaraderie, and, to Russell's surprise, alcohol. Walter Reed's nurses and administrative staff tended to look the other way when the men began their daily happy hour, reaching under bunks and even inside their prosthetic limbs for hidden bottles of beer or liquor. This ritual sometimes began as early as eleven in the morning and extended into the evening, interrupted by the hospital staff only if one of the ward's occupants got out of control.[8]

Within a few weeks, Russell underwent surgery to shorten his right arm so that it matched what remained of his left one. This was one of the first steps toward fitting him with prosthetics. Around this time, Russell received a visit from a gentleman who had lost his hands as a child. In their place were steel claws. The man spoke to Russell about his experience in adapting to and using his hooks. No matter how convincingly the gentleman operated his steel claws, however, Russell wasn't buying it. The hooks terrified him: "That would mean I'd be openly advertising the fact that I was a cripple and a freak," he wrote later. The visit convinced Russell that he needed to replace his own hands with "cosmetics," prosthetics that resembled real arms and hands.[9]

Russell's prosthetics were specially made for him in the hospital's orthopedic workshop. Once they were ready, he struggled to learn to operate them effectively. He was disappointed to discover that he had to exert a constant pressure with his upper arms if he wanted to grasp anything with his "fingers." And not every finger of his prosthetic hands moved, which seemed pointless to him and detracted from the illusion of having actual hands. By the next morning, Russell had changed his mind. He traded in his "cosmetics" for a pair of steel hooks. But he became disheartened all over again when he realized that getting the hooks was just the beginning. Not only would he have to relearn basic tasks such as brushing his teeth, tying his shoes, opening doors, and dialing a telephone, but he also began to realize how much effort it took to do these everyday things. Russell felt like a five-year-old going to kindergarten for the first time.[10]

Russell had been at Walter Reed for about two months when he watched an army training film that gave him some hope. *Meet McGonegal* (1944) introduced him to a bilateral amputee named Charles McGonegal. A veteran of World War I, McGonegal was a confident and gregarious middle-aged man who had married and become a successful real estate agent. During his retirement, McGonegal moved to a California ranch, where he began raising horses in what would become another profitable venture.

The training film was less than twelve minutes long, but it captivated Russell. Produced by the War Department's Signal Corps, which included many Hollywood filmmakers like Frank Capra, *Meet McGonegal* begins with a waist-level shot of its subject looking at his reflection in a bathroom mirror as he prepares to shave. "This is my neighbor Charles McGonegal. I'd like you to meet him. I think he's an interesting fellow," says the narrator. After half a minute or so, McGonegal lifts his razor to his lathered cheek, and viewers see for the first time that he has hooks for hands. The short film follows McGonegal as he completes his morning routine, eats breakfast, and leaves his house to get into his automobile, parked at the curb. At the end of the film, McGonegal speaks to the viewer, sharing that it took him about three months to relearn how to do ordinary tasks. He spent those months at Walter Reed, and while not completely independent, he was able to return home and eventually find a job and get married. Over a final shot of McGonegal playing billiards and successfully making a corner shot, the narrator assures viewers, "He had faith in himself, and he knew it could be done. It took a little while, but he got there."[11]

A few days later, McGonegal visited Walter Reed on behalf of the American Legion. He took the men of ward 32 into town, where he treated them to sodas and cigarettes. The outing was about more than the free drinks and smokes, of course. McGonegal wanted to show the amputees that it was possible to exist in the outside world again, to move among able-bodied civilians and live one's life, and even to find joy in doing so. He also wanted to demonstrate how to deal with strangers' stares and interest. After he passed around cigarettes to all the men, McGonegal made a big show of removing one from a pack and lighting it. "Everyone in the store watched him as if it were some kind of theatrical performance," recalled Russell, who was mesmerized by McGonegal's charisma and ease. "As it turned out, it was."[12]

Inspired by McGonegal's visit, Russell continued to work on his physical rehabilitation so that he could master things like putting on his clothes and grooming himself without help. The thought that had scared Russell most in the early days and weeks following his accident was that he would always need help. He had worked since the age of ten, and the idea of not being able to hold a job terrified him. He was also worried that his girlfriend, Rita, who had been writing to him almost daily since the accident, would never be able to comprehend his situation. The sister of his high school friend Charly Russell (no relation), Rita was back in Cambridge, where his mother, a nurse, also lived. "How could [Rita] know what it meant to be a helpless cripple, to be fed, kept clean and dressed, to have someone else perform all those intimate services that you could no longer do for yourself?" Russell wondered.[13]

Eventually, it was time for Rita to find out. The army gave Russell a thirty-day furlough, and in mid-fall he headed home to Massachusetts. He spent time with his mother and with Rita, going out in Cambridge to the movies and to favorite eateries and bars, but he felt on edge no matter how Rita, his mother, and others responded to him. Russell later described the visit as his "own private D-Day," and he didn't fully relax until he took his seat on the plane heading back to Walter Reed. "I'm going home now," he soothed himself, even though he didn't want to admit that he had come to feel more comfortable in ward 32 than anywhere else.[14]

Russell was grateful to be back at the hospital, and he threw himself into his routine of daily rehabilitation. When a friend asked him how his visit with Rita and his family had gone, Russell described it as a month of hell. He blamed others for the awkwardness he had felt, rationalizing that it was difficult for Rita and old friends to grasp the reality of his situation. "It's tough for them to understand. It's tough trying to get them to adjust themselves," he told his friend.[15] Robert Sherwood later mined Russell's first visit home for details included in the homecoming scene in *Best Years* when Homer's parents invite his girlfriend, Wilma, and her family to an uncomfortable gathering on Homer's first night back from the war.

In reality, Russell's comment about Rita and his friends could have applied to himself. Despite the hours of rehabilitation, the camaraderie of his fellow amputees, and the encouragement from successfully rehabbed veterans like Charlie McGonegal, Russell found himself ill prepared to deal with the "inquisitive questions of well-meaning strangers, the naked stares of barflies and the self-conscious embarrassment of everyone I met."[16] Only later did he realize that a few sessions with a mental health professional might have given him the psychological tools to adapt to life after losing his hands. "The Army spent millions of dollars and many months training men to make amphibious landings, parachute drops, ski assaults, saturation bombings and tank attacks," Russell observed, "yet it did little or nothing to train us to make a beach-head on the civilian world."[17]

Russell faulted the army for its inability to prepare him and his fellow amputees in ward 32 for life beyond the redbrick walls of Walter Reed. By the mid-1940s, however, the military was doing more for its injured veterans than it had during World War I, when public concern about the effects of warfare on soldiers was at an all-time high. Still, the "simple mental hygiene course" that might have helped Russell adjust more easily in 1944 was a year away from being widely available within the military. By 1945, military treatment for wartime neuroses was almost "unlimited," but before then, and mostly because of personal biases among generals and other high-ranking officials, treatment options to address the mental health of injured veterans were few and far between.[18]

Before there was post–traumatic stress disorder and shell shock, there was nostalgia. Josef Leopold Auenbrugger, a physician of Austrian descent, recorded European soldiers' psychological responses to wartime stressors in the late eighteenth century. It was not uncommon for these soldiers to experience heightened anxiety, feelings of sadness, and even panic attacks as a result of witnessing or engaging in warfare.[19] Auenbrugger used the term "nostalgia" to refer generally to such symptoms, and by the start of the American Civil War a century later, the diagnosis had made its way stateside.[20] During that war, Dr. Jacob Mendez Da Costa reported treating soldiers for an increased pulse rate, trouble breathing, and anxiety. He identified these symptoms as "soldier's heart," proposing a link between physical wartime injury and the onset and persistence of psychological symptoms.[21]

By the time of World War I, the conduct of battle had been marked by "monstrous innovations," and the jargon used to describe the fallout caused by such advances likewise evolved.[22] The automatic weapons first used in the American Civil War gave way to a new type of industrial firepower. In the early 1900s, artillery shells contained materials such as lyddite (primarily picric acid) and cordite, which were highly explosive, instantaneously combustible, and "cleaner" in the barrel. Compared to gunpowder, these compounds allowed shells to have a wider and longer reach, leaving behind no smoke to identify the location of the weapon and little or no deposit in the barrel, which allowed combatants to fire shots quickly. World War I soldiers also engaged in trench warfare, crouching or lying for hours at a time in deep ditches that often went on for miles. These trenches offered protection but also obscured the enemy, and in the words of one young lieutenant, "It gets on one's nerves waiting always for the next bang."[23] The word "nostalgia," then, gave way to "shell shock" as a means of describing soldiers' psychological and physical responses to such high-powered artillery.

The term first appeared in 1915 in the medical journal *Lancet*, less than a year into the war. Charles Myers, a British psychologist, was one of the first medical professionals to write about what he had seen while treating soldiers in France. He used the cases of three men with very similar symptoms to explore the effects of shelling and trench warfare. In all three instances, the patients experienced a loss of taste and smell after being close to exploding shells, and they admitted to feeling "nervy" in the aftermath, symptoms that Myers noted as closely resembling those of "hysteria."[24] But despite Myers's best efforts to draw attention to what he saw as the disastrous side effects of modern warfare, the work that he and his colleagues were doing in hospitals close to the front was often met with resistance by military men at the highest levels.

By the end of 1915, particularly in Britain, public support and published findings by medical professionals like Myers had made a small impact. Military policy for the first time acknowledged the existence of shell shock as a condition, although the army persisted in making a distinction in a soldier's record between mental anguish "earned" in battle and a preexisting condition that might be "hereditary and untreatable."[25]

Another two years passed before real change was made in the British military regarding the treatment of and reaction to cases of shell shock. After the United States declared war on Germany in April 1917, a no-nonsense fifty-six-year-old helped turn the tide. John J. Pershing, a career military man, was chosen to lead the American Expeditionary Force in France. By 1918, Pershing believed that he finally had enough men to help the Allies in France, but even then he bemoaned the state of his troops. The general, who once declared that "only the hardest souls can win against the army we are fighting," complained to a friend about the "prevalence of mental disorders" among American troops.[26] Pershing's acknowledgment of this problem may have made a difference among his peers. In the months afterward, psychiatrists like Charles Myers met with less resistance from the military when assessing soldiers' mental conditions and recommending treatment.[27]

During the final year of World War I, the British military started to recruit doctors to treat psychologically wounded servicemen. These doctors in turn made connections between the types of warfare that soldiers had experienced and their corresponding psychological reactions. "The problem for the psychiatrists, though, was that they could not simply respond to their patients' suffering and tease out the intellectual puzzles they posed," writes the historian Ben Shephard. "They were also supposed to send them back into battle."[28]

By the end of the war, those familiar with the psychiatric fallout of battle began using the more general term "war neuroses" in place of "shell shock," especially in published accounts. But the army and the public were not easily dissuaded from using a term that had become familiar. "It was shell-shock's very vagueness which made it so useful," notes Shephard, "offering a neutral, physical label for a psychological condition."[29] For Charles Myers, the widespread acceptance of the term "shell shock" grew troubling. An academic scientist by training, Myers appreciated the nuances of the condition, which in many cases was about more than a soldier's single psychological response to one type of stimulus. Over two decades later, at the start of World War II, Myers was more convinced than ever that the term "shell shock" should be replaced, because of its implication that a soldier's nervous condition could be caused only by the shock of an exploding shell.[30]

In 1940, when Myers published a collection of his World War I diary entries, the stage seemed set for the United States, at least, to be in a strong position to address a new generation of soldiers' war neuroses if the nation joined the European conflict. Beginning with the Civil War and Mendez Da Costa's identification of "soldier's heart," the US medical community had established a rich body of literature about the stresses of modern warfare on the human nervous system.[31] Psychiatry as a field of study was gaining acceptability in the United States. By 1940, approximately 2,500 psychiatrists were practicing throughout the country, although most were located in major cities.[32]

In Topeka, Kansas, the psychiatrist William Menninger operated the Menninger Clinic with his brother, Karl, also a psychiatrist, and their father, C. F., a family physician. While Karl was the more intellectually ambitious of the Menninger brothers, William had the managerial and personal skills to make sure that the clinic became a success, introducing modern psychiatry to Middle America. William later published a history of psychiatry, noting, among other things, that in the decades separating the two world wars, the US government had spent nearly a billion dollars on veterans' psychiatric problems.[33] In 1940 alone, treating the war neuroses of veterans cost the government an estimated $42 million, suggesting that the money might have been better spent on addressing the problems preemptively.

Despite advances in psychiatry, enormous institutions like the military and the government were slow to change their views about how best to treat war neuroses. A few people, however, were able to make a difference. Thomas W. Salmon was a former bacteriologist from upstate New York who was put in charge of psychiatric care at Ellis Island in the early 1900s. By 1917, he was the director of the National Committee for Mental Hygiene, an organization dedicated to improving the country's system of care for mental health, and the precursor of the National Mental Health Association (today Mental Health America). Shortly after America's entry into World War I, Salmon was sent overseas to learn about the psychological effects of warfare, in anticipation of him developing a new mental "hygiene" program at the request of the US surgeon general.[34] By the end of the war, Salmon had established a three-tiered system of identification and treatment that was adopted by the military.

At Salmon's insistence, psychiatric care was made available to combat soldiers within several miles of the front lines at the division level, at a treatment center a few miles beyond, or at the base hospital. But as Ben Shephard notes, Salmon's most important contribution to the military was to create a role for a division psychiatrist: "His job was to sort . . . to make sure that lightly affected cases of fatigue, concussion or very mild neurosis were not sent miles back but kept near the lines until they had recovered. He was there to prove that shell-shock, far from being complex and dangerous, was 'relatively simple and recoverable.'"[35] In effect, Salmon wanted to remove the stigma attached to a shell-shock diagnosis as well as to eliminate the chaos and uncertainty within the military regarding soldiers who needed treatment.

Salmon's organizational and treatment innovations remained in effect at the start of World War II. But further progress required a professional who not only understood the nuances of war neuroses but was also expert at communicating with the military's top commanders. Frederick R. Hanson, a young American neurologist, was working in Montreal at the start of the war. He accompanied the Canadian Army to England, and by 1943, Hanson had witnessed enough combat in France—the failed Allied assault at Dieppe, for example—to pique his interest in war neuroses, specifically, soldiers' emotional responses to their experiences in battle. Hanson concluded that "sheer physical exhaustion" was to blame for even the most debilitating cases of shell shock. But Hanson knew he needed to do more than simply state his case to someone like General Omar N. Bradley, who, after several wartime promotions, had become deputy commander in Europe under General George S. Patton. "You have to have a graph when you go to see a general," Hanson explained to one battalion surgeon. At the end of April 1943, Bradley sent around a memo stating that for all psychiatric cases in the US Army, "exhaustion" would be the initial diagnosis.[36]

But setbacks still occurred. When visiting a hospital in Palermo, Italy, a few months after the memo had been circulated, one of Bradley's commanders, General George S. Patton, slapped Private Charles Kuhl across the face with one of his gloves. An eighteen-year-old being treated for exhaustion, Kuhl had explained that his nerves got the best of him when he heard shells exploding. Patton responded by calling him "a goddamned coward." Months later, General Dwight D. Eisenhower forced Patton to apologize publicly to the men in his division and then relieved Patton of his command.[37] Later that same year, General George C. Marshall, another of Bradley's superiors, circulated a report that railed against "the spread of psychoneurotics" in the US Army, blaming the country's educational system and "environmental background since 1920." Marshall clamped down on medical discharges and implemented stiffer rules about handling psychological cases.[38]

Heading into 1944, the year that Harold Russell was injured at Camp Mackall, advances in military psychiatry appeared to be at a standstill. But change slowly continued. Between 1943 and 1945, for example, psychiatrists on the front lines began to lose faith in chemical treatments such as using barbiturates, insulin-induced comas, and even ether to help soldiers recall traumatic episodes. They favored a return to the kinds of "simpler methods" used during World War I, such as basic talk therapy, and allowing affected soldiers to get some rest without being discharged or even removed far from the field of battle.[39]

The reason for this last method of treatment was the recognition by American psychologists that a soldier's top loyalty during wartime was to his group. Championed in 1940s popular culture by the war correspondent Ernie Pyle and the cartoonist Bill Mauldin, the idea that men did better when they were surrounded by fellow soldiers intrigued medical professionals, who wanted to discover how to use this as a tool to reinforce a soldier's psyche and avoid a mental breakdown. Many military commanders were anxious about the effect of "wastage" due to psychiatric casualties on the size and strength of troops, and some American doctors wondered whether the concept of group loyalty might help stem the tide.[40]

William Wyler had experienced firsthand this group support while making *The Memphis Belle*. "You're inclined to worship the skipper, adore the ship, and look on all the other men on board as brothers," Wyler said while being interviewed during postproduction on *Belle*. "I heard a waist-gunner say: 'I've got a whole new family. There's ten of us, and I know 'em better than I know my *own* brothers and sisters, and it's just as tough to lose one.'"[41] In fact, the men of the Ninety-First Bomber Group, with whom Wyler grew close, and others like them typified a unique breed to wartime psychiatrists. The "bomber boys" were unusual among servicemen: they had days when they could rest, eat well, and even enjoy the company of women when the weather wouldn't allow them to fly missions. According to Ben Shephard, US Army Air Force psychiatrists in particular believed that "the strains of operational flying gradually wore everyone down, but that the psychodynamic forces such as leadership or group loyalty might create defences against breakdown."[42]

While Harold Russell was facing down his demons at Walter Reed in the summer of 1944, Wyler was back in Europe after the successful theatrical release of *The Memphis Belle: A Story of a Flying Fortress*. Wyler's next assignment was to make a documentary about the Fifty-Seventh Fighter Group and Operation Strangle, a strategic plan to use P-47 Thunderbolt fighter planes to attack key supply routes behind German lines. Nicknamed the Juggernaut, or "Jug" for short, the P-47 weighed seven tons and was built to fly large payloads of five-inch rockets at high altitudes. Their size and strength made them nearly indestructible in battle, and despite their ungainly appearance, P-47s were surprisingly fast.

Once Wyler arrived in Caserta, Italy, in May 1944, he became convinced that this next documentary needed to have a different structure from that of *Belle*. In part this had to do with the fact that he wouldn't be able to shoot aerial footage himself: the P-47's cockpit could not accommodate both a pilot and a cameraman, so Wyler would need to rely on mounted cameras. Thunderbolts came equipped with cameras to record images of downed enemy planes, and Wyler supplemented these cameras with ones that filmed the pilot and his instrument panel and simulated his point of view, front and back. He positioned additional cameras under the wing, in the wheel well, and next to the interior side-mounted machine guns, the cameras timed to film as the weapons fired. Besides the technical limitations, Wyler didn't want to repeat himself with this documentary. An early screenplay treatment, which he worked on that summer, moved away from concentrating on a single mission, the structure that organized *Belle*'s narrative.[43]

That same summer, Wyler shot ground footage north of Rome, capturing the ragged remains of churches and houses and a bombed-out landscape, all destroyed in the fighting. But in the wake of Italy's liberation by the Allies in late April, Wyler worried that his documentary would be out of date by the time it was released. The project seemed to lack the urgency that had fueled the making of *Belle* in 1942 and 1943.

In November, Wyler received a terse telegram from William Keighley, a fellow director who was now head of the Signal Corps' motion picture unit, demanding an update on the status of the project. Wyler had been working in Paris with John Sturges, an American film editor who later moved into directing. Neither man was satisfied with the footage they had shot up to that point, and Wyler communicated this to Keighley. "First, the subject matter is very difficult. It's not a simple story of one mission, from start to finish, like *The Memphis Belle*. . . . Second, I didn't have a crew of my own," wrote Wyler, adding that the difficulty of getting quality color footage at high altitudes was another problem. Rain and unusually cool temperatures in the early fall had grounded the filmmakers and kept them from shooting additional film.[44]

Sturges and Lester Koenig, both assigned to the documentary, now titled *Thunderbolt*, had drafted a script for the documentary's voice-over. Sturges had shot preliminary ground footage with Wyler, and he and Koening had written the narration based on that and on the aerial footage recorded by the cameras mounted on the P-47s. Koening had worked with Wyler on *Belle*'s narration, most notably rewriting the documentary's final lines. Despite Wyler's earlier insistence that *Thunderbolt*'s focus needed to be different from *Memphis Belle*'s and not tied to a single mission, he had a change of heart once he read Sturges and Koenig's script. Now he wanted the narration to build to a climactic moment with the appropriate level of drama. "For my money," wrote Wyler, "give everything to the destruction of the enemy . . . and then finish quick."[45]

Wyler headed back to Italy to film additional aerial footage that might pull together the material they already had. Sturges asked Wyler specifically to get images of the damage left behind by the bombing in Rome and on the island of Corsica, where the P-47s were stationed, at Alto Air Base. This footage would provide "atmosphere shots," images that weren't essential to the action but would fill out the documentary and add flavor. Late on the afternoon of March 28, Wyler climbed into a B-25 headed to the Allied Italian headquarters in Grosseto, about one hundred miles northwest of Rome. Although Wyler was accompanied by two cameramen, he wasn't happy with their sloppy footage, which had captured the tips of the bomber's wing and glimpses of the engine cowling. As the daredevil filmmaker had done many times while filming *Belle*, Wyler made his way into the waist of the bomber, lay down on his stomach, and positioned an Eyemo camera above the lower turret, recording the devastation in Corsica and along the coastline toward Grosseto.[46]

Wyler stayed in this position for the remainder of the flight, with the loud engine noise and high-pitched screeching of the wind echoing in his ears. By the time the bomber landed at Allied headquarters in Grosseto, Wyler had lost hearing in both ears. This wasn't the first time, so he disembarked and waited for the air pressure to equalize and for his ears to pop. But the familiar rush of sounds didn't come. The flight surgeon examined Wyler and ordered him to be sent to the larger navy hospital in Naples. Doctors there instructed a nurse to write their verdict on a piece of paper for Wyler, who could no longer hear: he was deaf, and he was being sent home.

Wyler would be taking no more flights to film footage for *Thunderbolt*. In fact, he would no longer be flying, period. Grounded because of the damage to his ears, Wyler made his way back to the United States by sea. On April 10, he boarded a troopship in Naples bound for Boston. His fellow passengers were other wounded veterans, some of them catastrophically so. Unable to hear, Wyler took refuge in reading, making his way through the longest books he could find in the ship's small library during the nine-day crossing. Like nearly every other injured veteran, Wyler worried about the future. Would he be able to direct again? How would his injury affect his marriage to Talli? In essence, what would become of him?

Wyler arrived in Boston in mid-April, where he caught a train to New York. From there he traveled out to Long Island and the hospital located at Mitchel Air Force Base. He was examined by several surgeons, and all made the same diagnosis. Wyler had suffered irreparable nerve damage, and his deafness was incurable. Although the hearing in his left ear was coming back a bit—enough that if people shouted, he could make out some words—hearing in his right ear had been permanently affected. Air force doctors recommended that Wyler undergo an adenoidectomy, removal of the lymphatic tissue between the back of the nose and the throat, to improve and preserve the hearing that remained.

One day that April, the phone rang at the Wyler residence in Bel Air. Talli was in the kitchen with Cathy and Judy when she picked up the receiver. "Instead of a happy voice, I heard an absolutely dead voice, toneless, without any timbre, without emotions," she said of hearing Willy on the line. It had been nearly a year since their last phone call, and the expressionless voice on the other end was not how she remembered her animated husband. Instead, she heard desperation and despondence. "He talked as if his life was over, not only his career. I was shocked," Talli recalled. Willy told her what had happened and what the doctors had concluded. He mentioned his upcoming adenoidectomy but told her not to come east, that he would let her know when he was headed back to Los Angeles.[47]

Wyler remained for a time at Mitchel Field after the surgery. His friend and former collaborator Lillian Hellman visited him there. Like Talli, she was unprepared for the somber change in Wyler. What had happened to the madcap adventurer who used to ride her around Los Angeles on the back of his motorcycle, weaving in and out of traffic? "I've never seen anybody in such a real state of horror in my life, that he never would direct again," Hellman recalled years later.[48]

Wyler stayed on the East Coast for a few weeks, traveling by train to Washington, where he touched base with colleagues at the War Department. He also met with Lester Koenig about *Thunderbolt*. Koenig had revised the earlier draft of the narration script, and Wyler was somewhat cheered by its improvement. Still, his deafness, although not complete, colored everything. He wasn't eating, and he had tremendous anxiety about reuniting with Talli and the girls.[49]

Finally, Wyler boarded a train for Los Angeles. Talli and his mother, Melanie, were at Union Station to greet him. When her fifty-two-year-old husband disembarked, Talli almost didn't recognize him. Wyler's clothes hung on his much thinner frame, and his face, indeed his whole spirit, seemed sapped of vitality. Wyler's wife and his mother were immediately confronted with his injury, having to get used to taking turns as they spoke to him, enunciating each word carefully and speaking directly into his left ear.[50]

Wyler was desperate to find a cure for his deafness. He visited many doctors and specialists, but they all told him the same thing: a nerve in his right ear had been destroyed, and there was no fix or treatment that would restore hearing in that ear. Some said that his hearing loss could have been avoided if he had protected his ears with plugs or even cotton before the flight. Wyler remained anxious about what his injury might do to his career and how it could change his relationship with Talli, so much so that even talking about the experience three decades later still made him emotional. "It was tough getting adjusted, particularly with an injury," he said in 1981, tears in his eyes. "It took me a long time to get settled and to make the best of it." Less than a year after his accident, Wyler drew on those feelings as he worked with Robert Sherwood on the screenplay for *Best Years*.[51]

Wyler's final attempt to restore his hearing took him and Talli up the coast to Santa Barbara, where the air force had a rehabilitation center. Despite the military's move away from chemical treatments for war trauma by 1945, the specialists whom Wyler saw gave him sodium pentothal, popularly known as "truth serum," to determine whether his injury had been brought on by psychological trauma sustained during the flight to Grosseto. At the end of the appointment, Talli found Willy in a padded cell. "He could barely stand up," she recalled of having to help him walk off the effects of the drug. "It was all I could do to get him out to the car." The psychiatrists who treated Wyler explained to him that under the drug's influence, he had been able to overhear conversations in nearby treatment rooms, and they told Talli the same thing. It took several years for her to realize these lies were part of her husband's treatment, an attempt to give her and Willy hope.[52]

Talli Wyler's experience was supported by the advice literature of the time. By the spring of 1945, when Wyler returned home, efforts to educate the public about veterans' difficulties with readjustment were in full swing. Ernest R. Groves, a sociologist, described veterans' reunions with their loved ones as "one of the greatest of all the ills that accompany warfare." Approximately 16 million US veterans were expected to return from the war, and beginning around 1944, a virtual army of medical professionals, writers, and speakers began dispensing advice about how best to help them readjust to the home front.[53] Most of this advice was aimed at women: the mothers, wives, girlfriends, and siblings who had remained behind. And just as women had been critical to the war effort by taking factory jobs and doing other work they had previously been unaccustomed to, they were now called on, by women's magazines, newspaper columns, and other forms of popular media between 1944 and 1946, to act as social workers and therapists: it was up to them to help the men readjust to life during peacetime. Women, writes Susan M. Hartmann, were portrayed in the advice literature as "responders and adapters." And in the words of Alexander G. Dumas, a psychiatrist who worked with veterans, these women, wives in particular, should show tremendous "understanding and patience."[54]

Films of the time sent a similar message, especially movies that included characters suffering from war trauma. Although *Random Harvest* (LeRoy, 1942) is set in World War I, its release a year after the bombing of Pearl Harbor reminded viewers, particularly women, what could happen to their loved ones fighting overseas. Produced by Sidney Franklin for MGM, the same team behind Wyler's *Mrs. Miniver, Random Harvest* is an adaptation of James Hilton's best-selling 1941 novel. Ronald Colman's John Smith, a British soldier who has no memory of his prewar life, stutters and stammers his way through social situations, blaming his tics on "nerves" when he first meets Greer Garson's Paula, a showgirl who takes pity on the veteran when he escapes from the Melbridge County Asylum and wanders into the nearby town to buy cigarettes. An accident undoes Smith's amnesia, returning him to his prewar identity as the wealthy Charles Rainier. The character's war trauma functions mostly as a plot device, and its effect on Smith/Rainier's life is fairly superficial. His character arc focuses less on how he struggles with the trauma than on his reunion with Paula.

Random Harvest was one of the first films released during World War II to explore shell shock, but a few older films also touched on the subject. In *I Am a Fugitive from a Chain Gang* (LeRoy, 1932), for instance, Paul Muni plays James Allen, a veteran wrongfully convicted of a crime. In *Fugitive*, based on the World War I veteran Robert Burns's autobiography, Allen's PTSD-like symptoms complicate his postwar life and ultimately lead to him spending time in prison. In one scene with his employer, the sound of a nearby explosion triggers a defensive response from Allen, who instinctively ducks for cover. Despite Allen's decorated military career, the film suggests, his inability to cope with shell shock eventually leads to his unwitting involvement in a robbery and, ultimately, a life on the run.[55]

Just before the Christmas holiday in 1944, producers Dore Schary and David O. Selznick released *I'll Be Seeing You*, a wartime drama starring Joseph Cotten and Ginger Rogers. Based on a radio play and originally titled *Double Furlough*, the film was renamed to capitalize on the success of Sammy Fain and Irving Kahal's sentimental ballad. Cotten's shell-shocked soldier meets Rogers's prison inmate when the two end up on the same train heading home for a holiday furlough. An early scene between Zachary Morgan (Cotten) and Mary Marshall (Rogers) hints at Morgan's traumatic war experience. Exiting a movie theater on their first date, Mary asks, "Is the war really like that?" referring to the combat film they've just seen. "I guess so," Zach responds. When Mary presses him about his experience, he elaborates slowly: "Sometimes it's all full of noise and sometimes it's quiet. . . . It all depends on what you're thinking about . . . how scared you are," he continues. After he admits that soldiers usually don't like to talk about their experience and Mary apologizes, he quickly reassures her, saying, "No, I feel kind of good." The film's generally thoughtful representation of Morgan's war trauma has much to do with the low-key performances by Cotten and Rogers, which give the sense that their characters' developing romance transcends the script's pairing them simply because they're both potential social misfits.

I'll Be Seeing You was one of the few wartime films to feature a lead character suffering from war neurosis, but *A Walk in the Sun* (Milestone, 1945) offered an equally nuanced examination of combat fatigue. The ensemble piece about a Texas platoon was released into theaters in December 1945 just as Hollywood's cycle of combat films was coming to an end. Thanks to Dana Andrews's success a year earlier as Detective Mark McPherson in *Laura*, he received top billing in *Walk in the Sun* despite the movie's group focus. Then in his midthirties, Andrews had been working fairly steadily in Hollywood since 1940. One of his earliest film roles, in fact, was a small part in Wyler's *The Westerner* from that year. A widower with a young son when he moved to Hollywood from Texas, Andrews did not enlist after Pearl Harbor, nor was he drafted. Instead, he appeared in several combat films while under a contract split between Twentieth Century–Fox and Samuel Goldwyn's independent company.

Early in *A Walk in the Sun*, as the platoon prepares to take a farmhouse in Italy located near the bridge they have been assigned to destroy, a young sergeant (Herbert Rudley) breaks down under the pressure. As he lies sobbing on the ground, Private Craven (John Ireland) speaks to him in soothing tones: "You're crying because you're wounded. You don't have to be bleeding to be wounded. You just had one battle too many." Telling the sergeant that he has imprisoned himself in a foxhole in his mind, Craven continues, "Go ahead, Porter. Keep crying. We understand." Andrews's Sergeant Tyne then takes over the mission, replacing his fellow sergeant after Porter is sent away for treatment. Perhaps it was *A Walk in the Sun*'s minimal inclusion of battle scenes that helped this combat film appeal to audiences even after the war had ended. The film's clipped dialogue interspersed with extended moments of silence and seemingly random bursts of violence certainly enhances the realism of the picture, which was named to the National Board of Review's Top Ten for 1945.

That same year, another equally authentic film was making its way onto movie screens around the country. *Diary of a Sergeant* was an army-issued short, a training film for amputees in the style of *Meet McGonegal*. The lead "actor" was none other than Harold Russell. In the fall of 1944, the bilateral amputee had eagerly returned to Walter Reed's ward 32 after his disastrous monthlong furlough in Cambridge. But even some of the experiences he endured during outings away from the hospital left him feeling dejected. When an overzealous patron repeatedly pestered Russell and his fellow amputees while they were relaxing at a local bar, Russell threatened the gentleman with his hooks, shaking them in the man's face to make him leave their group alone (much as he would do in a scene in *Best Years* two years later). Another time, Russell found himself sitting next to a flirty young woman at a movie theater. When the theater lights went down and she reached for Russell's hand in the darkness, she recoiled in horror, screaming, "He's got an iron hand!"[56]

By the end of 1944, Russell's physical rehabilitation was nearly complete. He was adjusting to life without his hands physically, but he was still struggling mentally. "The first, and greatest, obstacle I had to overcome was Harold Russell," he later wrote.[57] His encounter with Charlie McGonegal had certainly helped him. But it was a lunch with Major General Norman T. Kirk just before the end of the year that gave Russell the hope that he could feel purposeful again. Appointed surgeon general during World War II, Kirk was responsible for the health of approximately 10.4 million soldiers and airmen during wartime. A trained orthopedic surgeon, Kirk had performed more than seven hundred amputations on veterans after World War I, and he had perfected techniques that enabled amputees to recover more quickly than before and with fewer infections. For this reason, he took a special interest in seriously wounded veterans like Russell.[58]

"Sergeant, I want to make an actor of you," Kirk said to Russell after they sat down to lunch. The surgeon general proceeded to tell his guest about the difficulties the army was having in reaching out to disabled GIs. Though Russell had been inspired by *Meet McGonegal*, the average disabled GI wasn't buying it. Here was a guy, they said, who, as a veteran of World War I, had had nearly two decades to relearn the skills he displayed in the movie. To these newly disabled veterans, McGonegal's claim that they too could learn to dress themselves, take care of their personal hygiene, and drive themselves to whatever jobs they were able to secure all seemed like so much bunk.

But, Kirk said, if they were to see someone like Russell—a veteran of the same war, disabled like them—demonstrating how he had learned to use his steel hooks, that might provide the inspiration they needed. At the time, Russell was the only double-hand amputee at Walter Reed, and Kirk emphasized that his involvement would be crucial if a new film were to be made. The assignment was exactly what Russell needed. "It did wonderful things for my ego," Russell wrote later. "What was more important, though, was the knowledge that I was doing something useful again."[59]

Not long after that lunch, Russell met Julian Blaustein, who was directing films for the Army Signal Corps. Before becoming a reader in the story development department at Universal in the late 1930s, Blaustein had briefly trained as a fighter pilot. He had the instincts of a producer (he would helm his first picture, *Broken Arrow*, a few years after the war ended), and he sketched for Russell the general outline of the training film they wanted him to make. It would follow Russell's own story closely, from his first surgery and the ups and downs of his rehabilitation to his first visit home. The film would even re-create the turning point in Russell's rehabilitation, when he first watched *Meet McGonegal*. *Diary* would end with Russell's furlough, but unlike his own difficult experience, the film's version would be more positive.[60]

Diary of a Sergeant was shot over several weeks in October and November 1944 at Walter Reed, using the hospital's facilities to reenact Russell's first surgery and subsequent rehabilitation. The army's medical department came up with a script, which was polished by a young Australian sergeant named Irving Goff. Unlike *Meet McGonegal*, which followed Charlie McGonegal through an average day, the short film envisioned by Blaustein and the Signal Corps' Captain Joseph Newman was a narrative with a beginning, a middle, and an end. "We want the submerged seven-eighths of your story," Blaustein told Russell of their desire to tell the tale not just of his physical rehabilitation, but of his mental journey as well. As Russell later recalled, "Instead of being a dry, dead, training film demonstrating how I operated my hooks, the picture was going to be a narrative drama with me as its hero."[61]

With a budget of around $25,000, *Diary of a Sergeant* was meant to be completed quickly, by the end of 1944. But the production soon went over schedule as Blaustein and his crew moved from Walter Reed to the old Paramount Studios in Astoria, Queens, where the Army Pictorial Center was based during the war. Scenes of Russell being discharged from the hospital after completing his rehabilitation and taking a train "home" were staged at the studios, as were sequences that showed him trying to acclimate to life with his new hooks. The film was shot silent and in black and white; narration by the Broadway star Alfred Drake and an orchestral soundtrack were added in postproduction in early 1945.

Russell began the new year as a civilian: on January 3, 1945, he received an honorable discharge from the army. He was proactive about his new life, registering to begin college classes back home in Cambridge. Starting that spring, the thirty-year-old Russell was enrolled as a freshman at Boston University, where he planned to take courses in the business school. Like many veterans of World War II, Russell took advantage of the benefits afforded by the relatively new Serviceman's Readjustment Act, more commonly known as the GI Bill. Aside from a few retakes that Russell did on the BU campus, *Diary of a Sergeant* had wrapped shortly after the Christmas holidays. Russell began to acclimate to life as a college student, continuing his relationship with his girlfriend, Rita, and picking up a part-time job at the local YMCA, where he ran evening athletic programs for neighborhood boys.[62]

A few months into the spring semester, Russell received a call from Major General Kirk inviting him to a preview of *Diary of a Sergeant* in Washington, DC. Russell arrived in the nation's capital on April 12, the same day that President Roosevelt died. General Kirk and Captain Blaustein hosted Russell at the Pentagon, where the screening was attended by some of the army's highest-ranking officers. When the Treasury Department approached Russell about appearing with the film at war bond rallies, he agreed to do so even though it meant giving up his job at the YMCA, which added a much-needed $25 a week to the $200 monthly disability check he received from the government.[63]

"In 1945 all that concerned me was getting started on my new life," Russell said later. But he also understood that he could do for others what Charlie McGonegal had done for him. He was still struggling with everyday tasks like bathing and dressing himself, so he worked overtime on what he would later call his "private" rehabilitation. In addition to mastering basic self-care, Russell's plan involved getting out and in front of as many people as possible. He dined in restaurants, joined friends for drinks and billiards at local bars, went to the movies, and attended parties and baseball games whenever he could. Like his mentor McGonegal, he also worked on several icebreakers to cut through any awkwardness people might feel about his hooks. Russell dreamed up gags and stunts, including an homage to McGonegal's showy performance of opening a pack of cigarettes and "ostentatiously" lighting one for himself. "I was going to try to make people forget about my hooks and treat me as an equal," Russell said later, "not as a cripple or a freak."[64]

CHAPTER 3

The Way Home

With all respect to Sam Goldwyn, what did he know about returning veterans?
What did he know about how they felt? Wyler had been through it himself.
HAROLD RUSSELL

On his first day back at Twentieth Century–Fox after serving as a commander
in the Army Signal Corps, Darryl Zanuck, the studio head, called a meeting of
his top producers and directors. Returning servicemen, he told them, will come
back changed because of what they had seen and where they had been. Zanuck
himself had been stationed in London during the Blitz and then sent to North
Africa, where he commanded a film unit that photographed the Allied invasion
for the Signal Corps. Returning veterans would have "new thoughts, new ideas,
new hungers," said Zanuck. "We've got to start making movies that entertain
but at the same time match the new climate of the times. Vital, thinking men's
blockbusters. Big-theme films."[1]

One need not have been stationed overseas to comprehend the changes that
World War II had wrought. Samuel Goldwyn's wife, Frances, understood this
when she read "The Way Home," a *Time* article about returning marines, and
convinced her producer husband to consider the subject for a possible postwar
project. Although Goldwyn was more interested in making a biopic about General
Dwight D. Eisenhower and adapting Robert Nathan's 1928 best-selling
"angel" story *The Bishop's Wife*, he had had the foresight—with a nudge from
Frances—to have Kay Brown, a story editor, register "The Way Home" as a possible
motion picture title.[2]

Perhaps more than most Hollywood wives, Talli Wyler also realized that
life would be different after the war. "You think it's just euphoria," she said of
Wyler's return and eventual discharge in the summer of 1945, "but it's not that
simple." And it went beyond what Talli called the intimate "inter husband-wife
readjustment" that most couples faced after being separated for long periods of

time. For the better part of three years, Talli had been raising two children—an infant and a toddler—and keeping a household going while doing her best to maintain a long-distance relationship with her husband. Despite the impulsive beginning of their union, Willy and Talli had one of the stronger marriages in postwar Hollywood. Willy's confidante Lillian Hellman described it as "one of the wisest marriages I've ever seen."[3] The Dallas-born Talli was just twenty-four when she first met the thirty-six-year-old Willy in September 1938. Still, she was drawn to him. During their first week of dating, he played a tune for her on his harmonica from the opera *Hansel and Gretel*. "I was so enchanted he would know this that it was just very special," she recalled years later. She also sensed a solid person beneath the Harley Davidson–riding daredevil with a twinkle in his eye, and much later she realized that they both were ready to settle down.[4]

After Willy returned home from the war and they made the rounds of all the specialists up and down the West Coast, they returned to Los Angeles and began to deal with the reality of his hearing loss. Their two-story colonial, which before the war had been filled with music, was now much quieter. They no longer listened to records spinning on the stereo, and Willy avoided picking up the violin that he had liked to play. Because he could no longer hear melody without distortion, he and Talli stopped attending concerts, an activity they had enjoyed. Wyler's accident, said Talli, "changed our lives distinctively." More troubling, perhaps, was the deep depression that seemed to overtake her husband. "I don't know what kind of life we're going to have," Willy said to Talli at one point. "We might as well move out and go someplace and try not to do anything again."[5]

A small item in *Variety* in late August announced Wyler's honorable discharge from the Army Air Force. Wyler may have officially been done with the military, but there was still the matter of releasing the documentary *Thunderbolt*. John Sturges and Lester Koenig, who had returned to Los Angeles that summer, had been overseeing the film's postproduction at Fort Roach in Culver City. Koenig had finalized the documentary's narration by the end of July, and Wyler had approached Jimmy Stewart, who had flown twenty missions with the Army Air Corps, about recording a prologue for the film. When Wyler traveled to New York in mid-September to consult with more hearing specialists, Koenig kept him updated on *Thunderbolt*'s progress. Wyler's friends and colleagues had begun to relay messages to him via phone calls to Talli or in writing. "The picture is definitely a box office attraction," Koenig assured Wyler in a letter.[6] In turn, Wyler sent a four-page missive to the Army Air Force's public relations department, making a case for the documentary's release: "It films a story of air power in a way that people have never had a chance to understand it."[7] In addition, Wyler began to reach out to his Hollywood contacts about the film's distribution. "I consider it as good or better than 'Memphis Belle,'" Wyler boasted to a Paramount executive who had been involved with *Belle*'s release.[8]

Privately, however, Wyler was anxious. V-J Day (August 15, 1945) signaled the official end of the war. Would American moviegoers be eager to see a documentary about a mission to weaken the German front several months after the Nazis had unconditionally surrendered to the Allies? Wyler sent a letter to General Eaker, updating him on efforts to find a distributor. He pitched his former commanding officer on a series of screenings to raise interest in the film, suggesting that the army show it at the White House before hosting another event in Hollywood. But efforts to finish the film were held up by military red tape. The army air force needed to sign off on the final cut, so Wyler appealed to General Henry H. "Hap" Arnold at the War Department: "May I respectfully urge you to give this approval and let nothing delay further the release of the picture to the press and public as it loses daily in value."[9]

Finally, in mid-October, *Thunderbolt* was previewed for the West Coast press and a select audience of industry insiders. Wyler, who was still under contract to Sam Goldwyn, arranged to screen the documentary at Goldwyn Studios. Shortly before five thirty, representatives from the *Hollywood Reporter*, *Box Office*, *Variety*, and other trade publications took their seats. Wyler was there with the film's editor, John Sturges, and writer, Lester Koenig, and he said a few words before the start of the film. Days later, *Variety* ran a short piece about the screening. Since the documentary still needed approval from the War Department, the brief article was in lieu of a traditional review, but *Variety* still gave the film high marks. "AAF's 'Thunderbolt' Crashing Epic of Italy Air War," the headline declared, and the article mentioned its "spectacular fast action" and the fact that the footage had been photographed mostly by automatic cameras overseen by the pilots flying the P-47s. "It is thus an accurate, first-hand record of air action," *Variety* concluded.[10]

The positive press didn't sway distributors, however. RKO's Ned Depinet turned down the opportunity to release *Thunderbolt*, telling Wyler that the studio's schedule was already overburdened with "top picture releases." Wyler received similar responses from other studios, including Paramount, which had distributed *The Memphis Belle* a year earlier. Frances Harmon, who had overseen the newly disbanded War Activities Committee, told Wyler what everyone else was probably thinking: "It is too bad that this wonderful film could not have been made available closer to the date in which the events portrayed took place."[11]

For the time being, Wyler turned his attention to other projects. The same *Variety* article announcing Wyler's discharge mentioned his involvement in a new production company that had many in Hollywood buzzing. Liberty Films was the brainchild of Frank Capra, who spoke publicly about wanting to head his own company as an alternative to working for a studio. He and Sam Briskin, the production chief at Columbia, who would handle the behind-the-scenes details for each picture, approached Wyler not long after he returned to Los Angeles. In exchange for putting up seed money, each partner would receive a weekly salary of $3,000 and own a percentage of stock in the company. Wyler and George Stevens, who would join later, both had 25 percent, while Capra owned 32 percent.[12] Most importantly, the company's founders would have total control over their films. "No more arguments with producers about what picture to make" is how Wyler summed up Liberty's appeal years later.[13] In addition to the creative freedom the company promised, Liberty represented financial stability for Wyler. Although his latest contract with Goldwyn earned him a higher salary and a greater share of each picture than his prewar deal, it did not protect him from suspensions and "vacations" without pay if he decided not to do a movie that Goldwyn wanted him to direct. Each of the four partners was required to invest $150,000 up front, so Wyler borrowed against his life insurance policy, and by the fall of 1945, he had officially become an independent filmmaker.[14]

Except that Wyler still owed a film to Goldwyn. By 1945, Willy and Sam had made seven movies together. Their relationship had had its ups and downs, but after nearly a decade, they had reached a level of grudging respect. During their first few years together, Wyler would become so stressed while working on a Goldwyn picture that he would sometimes grind his teeth in his sleep.[15] But by the early 1940s, Wyler was able to compartmentalize his problems with the producer. When Teresa Wright, who had worked with Wyler on *The Little Foxes* and *Mrs. Miniver*, confided that she was having issues with Goldwyn, Wyler offered some advice. Goldwyn might scream at every person on the set, Wyler told her, but it was important to understand that while they all might go home upset, Goldwyn did not. "He goes back to his office and he walks home and he has a great time," Wyler said, referring to Goldwyn's daily habit of walking to and from the studio. Wyler and Goldwyn both liked to gamble and sometimes would meet in the evenings during a production. "We'd play poker and so on and he's a marvelous host in his home and (the anger) is gone," Wyler told Wright. "With Sam it's sort of a rite of passage. 'I'm the producer. I get to yell at everybody, and I scream and yell and it's done.'"[16]

Now that Wyler was out of the service, Goldwyn was eager to put his top director to work. The producer had already interested Robert Sherwood in the Eisenhower biopic and had gone to great lengths to arrange a meeting in July 1945 with the highly decorated general, whom Goldwyn revered. Plans were made for Wyler to join Goldwyn and Sherwood in Washington, but at the last minute Wyler told Goldwyn to go on without him. While Wyler also had great respect for Eisenhower, he was not interested in a project that would focus on someone whose rank and accomplishments placed him on a level well beyond that of the average moviegoer.[17] Goldwyn was also eager to make an "angel" picture, a postwar trend that included *It's a Wonderful Life*, Frank Capra's first project for Liberty Films. But if Wyler had little enthusiasm for an Eisenhower biopic, he had even less for *The Bishop's Wife*, a comedic fantasy that Goldwyn hoped to develop for his top star, David Niven. Wyler had called the war "an escape into reality," and now he wanted to make movies that spoke to the people with whom he had lived and worked during the previous three years. "I've learned so much dealing with real people in very real roles of life that I dread the day when I have to get back to telling actors how to get into a plane or put on a hat," he said.[18]

One Goldwyn property did appeal to Wyler. Browsing a shelf of potential titles in Goldwyn's library, Wyler came upon *Glory for Me*, the novel that the producer had hired MacKinlay Kantor to write the previous year. Goldwyn had a history of hiring authors and playwrights to develop his scripts, considering it part of the prestige associated with his brand. But after receiving a disappointing screen treatment of the novel from Kantor, Goldwyn had worked hard to interest Robert Sherwood in adapting the book.[19] Goldwyn had first approached Sherwood about the project in the spring of 1945, sending him the galleys of Kantor's book and asking for his thoughts. Sherwood's wartime work as a White House speechwriter was winding down, and he had begun to write a new play. But the president's unexpected death on April 12 leveled the forty-nine-year-old playwright, who described the period as "an inexpressibly sad moment in my life as a worker."[20] This grief may have been partly responsible for his dismissal of Goldwyn's offer. Taken to lunch by one of Goldwyn's story editors, Patrick Duggan, Sherwood explained that he was only interested in writing "escapist" material. Pressed further, he told Duggan that he disagreed with *Glory for Me*'s premise that all returning soldiers were "maladjusted." Goldwyn persisted, even bringing Sherwood to Hollywood to meet with him and Wyler once the filmmaker had indicated that he was interested in the material.

In late August, Sherwood wrote to Goldwyn again, expressing his doubts about the project and suggesting that Goldwyn "drop it," adding, "This is entirely due to the conviction that, by next Spring or Fall, this subject will be terribly out of date." By late 1946, Sherwood reasoned, the majority of veterans would have been demobilized and most likely settled into their postwar lives. "I do not believe that more than a small minority of these men will still be afflicted with the war neuroses which are essential parts of all of the three characters," he wrote of Kantor's novel. It was less about Sherwood's "reneging" on the project, he wrote, than about his concern that Goldwyn would be wasting his money on a movie that, "in my opinion, will be doomed to miss the bus."[21]

A week later, and just two days after the official end of the war, Goldwyn telegrammed his reply to Sherwood. "I have more faith in it now than I had six months ago," he stated, arguing that he believed the subject matter would be increasingly relevant in the months to follow. Goldwyn also included a brief analysis of the three main characters in Kantor's novel, assuring Sherwood that he would be able to make changes. "Homer need not be a spastic and be painted as the Kantor book paints him," wrote Goldwyn, addressing the book's most problematic characterization.[22] The character of Homer did indeed worry Sherwood, he said later, "because there has been so much about psychopathic veterans and it is so difficult to tell honestly how their disabilities may be overcome."[23]

Perhaps it was Goldwyn's confidence in the project or his assurances to Sherwood that he would have carte blanche in shaping the screen version of Kantor's story. It may have been Wyler's persuasiveness, too. When the three men met to discuss the project in Los Angeles that July, something Wyler said made a strong impression on Sherwood. He told the writer that the film had the potential to "prevent a lot of heartaches and even tragedies among servicemen who were confronting demobilization and return to civilian life."[24] Who better to make a case for the picture's potential healing power than Wyler, himself a wounded vet?

Whatever the reason, a week after Goldwyn cabled Sherwood, *Variety* announced the project, reporting on Wyler's return from the East Coast with a "finished" adaptation of *Glory for Me* written by Sherwood. "Wyler will direct the pic which winds up his contract with Goldwyn," stated the article, which also announced that principal photography would begin on December 1.[25] Goldwyn and his publicity chief, William Hebert, had been working hard to pitch an overly optimistic update on the project, whose screenplay Sherwood had barely begun. Still, the momentum behind the project helped pull Wyler out of his funk. He was still uncertain how his hearing loss would affect his ability to direct, and he continued to seek out specialists. Writing to him during another of his visits to the East Coast, Talli reminded her husband to make an appointment with a doctor recommended by a family friend. She alluded to the fact that tensions between the couple were easing somewhat. "I am feeling better than when you left and hope that by the time you get back all this first discomfort will be over," she wrote.[26] As time went on, Talli came to understand the profound impact of Wyler's war injury: "What a hearing loss does to people is, it just puts them under a strain, it makes everything more difficult because what everybody else is doing, totally relaxed, they are having to work at."[27]

Wyler reported to work at Goldwyn Studios on October 1, and a few days later Goldwyn hosted a luncheon to welcome his top director back to the lot and officially announce Wyler's involvement in *Glory for Me*. At one point in the film's development, however, it had seemed as if Goldwyn had someone else in mind to direct. John Ford, sidelined with a broken leg, received an advance copy of Kantor's novel, along with a note from Goldwyn asking him for his "reaction" to the material.[28] Ford, who had risen to the rank of captain while overseeing the Field Photographic Division for the Office of Strategic Services (precursor of the CIA) during the war, had fallen off a platform while setting up a shot on *They Were Expendable*, his first feature film since the war. Goldwyn asked him to read *Glory for Me* while he was recuperating in the summer of 1945. Ford wasn't interested in the project, and it is unclear whether Goldwyn truly wanted him to direct it. Sarah Kozloff, for one, believes Goldwyn reached out to Ford as a way to convince Wyler to commit to the picture.[29]

The forty-four-year-old Wyler would be making $6,250 per week on the picture, which was budgeted through July 1946. He would also be earning 20 percent of the film's net profits on its release, tentatively scheduled for 1947.[30] While Wyler began preproduction in Los Angeles, Sherwood remained in New York, struggling to finish a draft of the script. In November, he sent the first forty pages to Goldwyn, who shared them with Wyler and Duggan. In a memorandum asking them to read and respond to Sherwood's pages, Goldwyn mentioned in an aside, "It looks as though we will be able to get the boy who lost his hands."[31]

The casting of *Glory for Me* was in flux during the fall of 1945, and the character of Homer had proved especially problematic. During the war, the rising film star Farley Granger had signed with Goldwyn before enlisting in the navy. He had small parts in the wartime dramas *The North Star* (Milestone, 1943) and *The Purple Heart* (Milestone, 1944), both of which starred Dana Andrews. When Granger reported to Goldwyn shortly after V-J Day, the mogul told him about *Glory for Me* and hinted the part of Homer was being scripted for him. Granger's discharge wouldn't become official until the following year, however, and Goldwyn insisted they couldn't hold up production on the film.[32] Goldwyn had given Sherwood his blessing to reimagine the character as someone other than Kantor's armless "spastic," if only because he and Wyler couldn't conceive of how an actor would portray the character effectively onscreen without the use of prosthetics and other special effects.

The story of the "discovery" of Harold Russell in *Diary of a Sergeant*, the training film that Russell had made for the army a year earlier, has several versions and as many authors. Both Wyler and Goldwyn claimed credit, although Russell tended to believe Wyler's account, in which the filmmaker viewed the documentary at a war bond rally (possibly accompanied by Sherwood) and then alerted Goldwyn.[33]

As Wyler watched the twenty-two-minute documentary, he was impressed by Russell's naturalness in front of the camera. He later told a reporter, "He had a wonderful face which expressed strength, courage and great faith in the future."[34] Although Russell doesn't speak in *Diary*, he does a fine job of communicating his easygoing and appealing personality. With the slight smile that flickers across his open face and the good-natured determination that characterizes his onscreen rehabilitation, as when he practices putting coins in pay slots and opening drawers with knobs, Russell comes across as an approachable person. Speaking about him years later, Wyler said, "You know instinctively what he is feeling just by the expression on his face or the way he tilts his head or covers his hooks."[35]

Sometime in the fall of 1945, Wyler and Sherwood toured a number of West Coast military hospitals in an attempt to understand Homer's disability while they worked on the script. At one facility in Los Angeles, three bilateral amputees seemed especially bitter, not unlike the novel's Homer. They were suspicious of the filmmaker's motives and spoke grudgingly about Harold Russell. "We know him," one of the vets offered. "He's a lucky guy. He's got his elbows. When you've got your elbows, they can put claws on."[36]

Diary of a Sergeant ends with Russell successfully approaching a girl on a commuter train for a date. In real life, Russell was still seeing Rita, his girlfriend from before the war. By the fall of 1945, Harold Russell had satisfied his commitment to the Treasury Department to make appearances with the documentary at bond rallies. He was in his second semester of business courses at Boston University, and he had resumed his part-time job running athletic programs at the local YMCA.

That November, Russell received a call from Miriam Howell, a Goldwyn story editor based in New York. She told him that Samuel Goldwyn had seen him in *Diary of a Sergeant* and was interested in casting him in his next film, *Glory for Me*, based on the forthcoming MacKinlay Kantor novel about returning veterans. She also said that William Wyler, himself a newly discharged veteran of the army air force, would be directing the film, and that Robert Sherwood was at that moment finishing the screenplay. When Russell expressed interest, Howell suggested that they meet a few weeks later at the Ritz-Carlton hotel in downtown Boston. "I had pictured Miss Howell as a soft, fluttery blonde," admitted Russell years later. "Instead I found she was a crisp, brisk brunette, dressed in a tailored tweed suit."[37] This wouldn't be the last time that Russell's expectations of Hollywood didn't match its reality.

Russell won over Howell immediately. "He has a round, apple-cheeked, Irish pan and a wonderful smile," she later told Pat Duggan. "He is one of the most winning and likable people you could possibly meet, and it is my hunch that you and everybody at the studio will be eager to do everything to make him comfortable and happy."[38] During her meeting with Russell, she told him that Goldwyn was willing to pay him $5,000 to play the part of Homer. His salary would cover ten weeks of work beginning in early 1946, and he would receive an additional $500 a week if his services were needed beyond the initial period. She produced a letter of agreement and made it clear that Russell would need to decide on the spot if he was interested, which he was. He had already discussed the matter with Rita, viewing it as an opportunity for them to become engaged. He would take a leave of absence from Boston University, and the pair could travel to Los Angeles and get married there so that Rita could remain in California while Russell worked on the film. Soon after Howell returned to New York, Russell received a telegram from her telling him to keep the arrangement confidential until further notice. Although his experience with Hollywood was limited, Russell was beginning to see similarities between the movie industry and the army: both entities, he said, liked "to cloak even the simplest operation in an atmosphere of hush-hush and mystery."[39]

During her December meeting with Russell, Howell had revealed a few details about the film's casting. Fredric March and Myrna Loy hadn't been signed, she told him, but it was almost certain that they would say yes to the roles of Al and Milly Stephenson, the long-married couple who live in a downtown high-rise. Goldwyn originally had offered the role of Al to Fred MacMurray, who, after years of appearing in light comedies and melodramas, had surprised audiences the previous year as a deceitful insurance salesman in Billy Wilder's *Double Indemnity*. Having become Hollywood's highest-paid actor by 1943, MacMurray turned down Goldwyn's offer because the part, he later said, was too much like being a "third banana."[40] Goldwyn had considered Olivia de Havilland for Milly, but again was told the part was too small.

Wyler liked the forty-eight-year-old March, who had built an impressive career on both the silver screen and the Broadway stage, where he often appeared opposite his wife, Florence Eldridge. Wyler was equally enthusiastic about Loy, whose reputation as the perfect screen wife came mostly from her sparkling pairing with William Powell in the *Thin Man* films. But convincing Loy to take the part was proving difficult. The actress had all but left Hollywood during the war, going to New York to work for the Red Cross and returning only to make *The Thin Man Goes Home*. Howell also told Russell that Dana Andrews, under contract to Goldwyn and enjoying recent success since appearing as the lovelorn detective in Otto Preminger's *Laura*, was being considered for the part of Fred in *Glory for Me*.[41]

Around the time that Goldwyn began courting Russell for the project, the publisher Coward-McCann finally released MacKinlay Kantor's novel. *Glory for Me* was his fourteenth work of fiction, and it received significant attention, which may have been boosted by Goldwyn's PR machine. "I shall be surprised if *Glory for Me* is not one of the best loved and most widely read stories that has been begotten of the homecoming," raved the *Los Angeles Times* in a review that more accurately foreshadowed reaction to the novel's screen adaptation.[42] Kantor's book received a mixed reception on the opposite coast. Paul Griffith's review for the *New York Times* took issue with the novel's lack of realism and stereotypical characters and dialogue. And while the critic for the *New York Herald Tribune* labeled it an "angry, disturbing novel in free verse," he acknowledged that "the graphic detail which has long characterized Mr. Kantor's work gives effectiveness to these pages."[43] The book's happy ending disappointed more than a few critics, something that Wyler and Goldwyn would struggle with while editing *Best Years*. And while some of the reviews were mixed, nearly every critic who wrote about *Glory for Me* acknowledged the timeliness of its story about three veterans struggling to adjust to postwar life.

By December, when Kantor's novel was beginning to appear on some critics' year-end lists, the film's preproduction process was moving forward.[44] Sherwood had sent additional pages of the screenplay to Goldwyn around Thanksgiving, but health problems hampered his progress in writing dialogue for the film's final few scenes.[45] Goldwyn, who had paid Sherwood $100,000 for the project, invited the writer and his wife, Madeline, to be his and Frances's guests at their Georgian-style estate. Located on a cul-de-sac behind the Beverly Hills Hotel, the Goldwyn mansion had a guest suite on the main floor, where visitors could come and go through a private entrance. Like the rest of the home, the guest quarters were inviting and thoughtfully appointed by Frances, but "did not encourage long visits."[46] Although the producer liked to keep a careful watch over his productions, he gave Sherwood space to work and respected his writing routine. When the Sherwoods and the Goldwyns sat down to dinner in the rose-colored dining room, which happened often during the Sherwoods' stay, Sam kept the conversation off work. But he always made himself available if Bob wanted to discuss anything in the script, and it was during this December visit that the writer finally was able to break through and finish the screenplay. While he had retained much about Kantor's characterizations of Al, Fred, and Homer and the obstacles they faced on their return from the service, Sherwood intertwined the trio's stories more closely by complicating Fred's rocky marriage to Marie instead of ending it outright, and by amplifying the attraction between Fred and Al's daughter, Peggy.

Harold Russell began 1946 en route to Los Angeles. The immediate postwar housing shortage meant that Goldwyn was having trouble finding a Hollywood bungalow where Harold and Rita could begin their married life. A new plan was hatched: Russell would initially be accompanied by his younger brother, Leslie, recently discharged and eager to return to California, where he had been stationed in the 211th Coast Artillery before the army sent him overseas. The Russell brothers made a preliminary stop in New York so that Harold could sign a newly revised contract. He would still be making just $5,000 for the role, but Goldwyn extended the contract from ten to twenty weeks to accommodate the production's new start date in mid-April. Russell's contract now included an additional $100 a week for living expenses. An entourage of Goldwyn employees accompanied the Russell brothers on their cross-country trip. On the afternoon of January 26, the group boarded a C-47 bound for Los Angeles. The no-frills military transport aircraft bothered a few of the executives, but Russell didn't mind. "There was something beautifully symbolic about jumping into a new life from the same kind of ship I had jumped from so many times as a paratrooper," he recalled.[47]

Just as Russell had had stereotypical expectations about how Miriam Howell would look, he thought Samuel Goldwyn would be a more dramatic, even theatrical version of himself. The quiet, dignified gentleman with whom he met on his arrival in Hollywood bore little resemblance to the fast-talking, excitable mogul that Russell had imagined since first learning about the project. And while the former meat cutter had expected a steady stream of Goldwynisms—inadvertently humorous turns of phrase like "include me out"—he wasn't quite prepared for the producer's rather high-pitched voice. One of the first things Goldwyn said to Russell concerned his weight, which was twenty-five to thirty pounds over what Goldwyn deemed acceptable for the screen. When Russell protested politely, saying, "I like to eat, Mr. Goldwyn," the producer's button-like eyes flashed as he replied, "I didn't bring you here to eat. I brought you here to act."[48]

William Wyler's first meeting with the handless veteran took place at the Brown Derby restaurant over lunch. Russell had heard the rumors about Wyler's penchant for multiple takes, and he was a little wary of the director. His initial impression was that Wyler was quiet, even bland. But as they talked, Russell watched Wyler's eyes become "electrifyingly alive" throughout their conversation, especially when he was talking about their upcoming film. At the end of the meal, the two men headed out of the restaurant to Wyler's new Rolls-Royce. He had had the car shipped over from England after spending what Talli described as several "miserable" months riding together without talking unless she shouted at him. He finally realized that by sitting on the right-hand side of the car, as drivers did in Britain, he could both drive and converse with his passenger, whom he could hear with his undamaged left ear.[49] As Wyler and Russell approached the Rolls, an acquaintance stopped Wyler to say hello. "Gee, that guy does a pretty good job with his hooks," he said, thinking Russell was out of earshot. "He does a fantastic job," Wyler agreed. "He ate his steak, did the shrimp cocktail and the salad, but the one thing he can't do is pick up the check."[50]

Russell met Robert Sherwood soon after that lunch. He was struck by the playwright's resemblance to one of his former subjects, Abraham Lincoln.[51] Once the two men began meeting to talk about the character of Homer, Russell gained an appreciation for Sherwood's warmth and sense of humor. "Sherwood had a curious trick of pausing before he said anything," Russell recalled, "as if combing the precise words out of his mind."[52] Russell shared intimate details of his rehabilitation at Walter Reed with the writer, who was still fine-tuning the screenplay. Russell told Sherwood about the despair and fear he felt initially, and then the hope and even optimism he cultivated after meeting Charlie McGonegal.

Some of Russell's initial time in Los Angeles was spent working with Wyler on the script, and the pair toured a nearby veterans' hospital together. The men often met at the Wylers' new home, on Summit Drive, where the family had moved after the first of the year. By late 1945, Talli was pregnant again. Fred Astaire, who owned the Summit Drive house, had decided to build a more contemporary house on a bigger lot up the street. The Wylers purchased Astaire's two-story gray Georgian for $95,000. It sat on nearly an acre and included a pool and a cantilevered tennis court, one of the first such designs in the country. Charlie and Oona Chaplin and their children lived on an estate next door, and the storied Pickfair, originally purchased by Douglas Fairbanks for his new bride, Mary Pickford, in 1919, was farther up the street. Surrounded by olive trees, the Wylers' house had twelve rooms and enough space for the soon-to-be family of five. Writing to Lillian Hellman in early February, Wyler described "living a little like gypsies" as Talli, "heavy with child at this moment," did her best to unpack while he continued to tinker with the script. "We are having plenty of trouble with the Goldwyn picture," Willy told Hellman, "and it doesn't look like we'll get started shooting until sometime in March, if then."[53]

One of the holdups on the picture was the signing of Myrna Loy, whom Wyler very much wanted for the part of Milly. While the actress had never worked with Wyler, the politically active Loy was friendly with Bob Sherwood and his wife. The "Queen of Hollywood," as Loy was known during the late 1930s, hailed from a small town in Montana and had intended to make a career as a dancer. In Los Angeles, she worked as a "prologue dancer" between movie screenings at Grauman's Egyptian Theatre. Her Welsh, Scottish, and Swedish roots gave her a face initially too exotic for Hollywood, and her early silent-film roles as vamps and "Orientals" reflected this. Loy's casting opposite William Powell in *The Thin Man* (Van Dyke, 1934), a low-budget "quickie" made in less than twenty days for MGM, gave her an unexpected break when the film became a hit. Loy also credited the *Thin Man* series for its modern approach to onscreen marriage. "There was this wonderful relationship between these two people; they had this great tolerance for each other's idiosyncrasies, and this nice camaraderie," Loy said. "It was the first time that married people had been pictured. Usually they got married and lived happily ever after, but you never saw them married."[54]

But eager as Wyler was to cast Loy, it was Sam Goldwyn who "romanced" her for the part.[55] Loy had appeared in a few Goldwyn films over the years, including *The Devil to Pay* (1930) and *Arrowsmith* (1931). He had great respect for the actress, and she was a familiar face at his and Frances's dinners and parties. When it came time to woo her for the relatively small part of Milly, Sam and Frances invited her to dine at their home. They talked about her upcoming wedding, her third, to the writer-producer Gene Markey as well as Loy's wartime work with the Red Cross, in which she had overseen a morale program that focused on entertaining the troops. Loy had massaged her Hollywood connections to put together shows and programs for the Red Cross, and she also appeared in many of the skits herself. Based in New York during the war, Loy relished not only the work but also the relative anonymity she had there, which allowed her to do things like ride unrecognized on the overnight train between New York and Baltimore.[56]

The discussion at the Goldwyns' long dining-room table circled back to *Glory for Me*. Some accounts characterize Loy as having been anxious about working with Wyler, worrying about his rumored penchant for multiple takes and a reported inability to communicate clearly with his actors. These accounts also suggest that Goldwyn, in his inimitable way, reassured her that Wyler wasn't a "sadist," just a "very mean fellow."[57] But Loy later said that she was familiar with Kantor's novel and eager to appear in the film, no matter how small the part. To compensate for the relatively small role, in fact, Loy's contract stipulated she would receive top billing.[58]

Fredric March signed on to the project around the same time, but he had his own reservations about the film. He had read Kantor's novel and appreciated its screen potential, but like Sherwood, he worried that the subject matter wouldn't be relevant by the time the picture made its way into theaters. And like Fred MacMurray, March hesitated because the part of Al Stephenson was part of an ensemble rather than a traditional feature role. But because he had recently lost the lead in Warner Bros.' *Life with Father*, he was looking for work. March had been a freelancer since his contract ended with Paramount during the war, one of the first actors to eschew ties to an established studio.

March's new agent, Leland Hayward, who also represented Loy, had been in talks with Goldwyn about his clients appearing in the screen adaptation of Kantor's book. The part of Al, a middle-aged father and husband who had been a bank executive before the war, seemed tailor-made for March, once described by a theater critic as "easily, manfully in command."[59] March had even pursued a career in finance at one time before he discovered acting. March had remained stateside during World War I, serving as a second lieutenant in field artillery and teaching equestrianism to soldiers. He spent World War II touring with the USO across five continents, where his initial attempts to perform in comedic skits fell flat. The troops preferred him as a serious actor, so March came up with a performance that included a stripped-down re-creation of the "transformation" scene from his Oscar-winning role in *Dr. Jekyll and Mr. Hyde* (Mamoulian, 1931), which he delivered without any special effects.[60]

Glory for Me would be March's third picture with Goldwyn and his first with Wyler. Just shy of fifty, March was on the other side of leading-man status, but Hayward was able to include a clause in his contract stipulating that he receive second billing only to Loy. Hayward's star clients would both be earning $100,000, but March would be on set for an additional two weeks, since his character had more scenes than Loy's. Wyler reached out to March not long after he signed onto the film. The actor's 1937 hit *A Star Is Born* was being shown at a theater on Hollywood Boulevard, and Wyler mentioned that friends of his had recently seen it. "They all said how much better than *The Lost Weekend* it was," Wyler wrote, favorably comparing March's portrayal of an alcoholic movie star to Ray Milland's lush in the Billy Wilder film, which had come out a year earlier. Wyler also reminded the actor that in *Glory for Me* he would be playing a sergeant who was returning after years of combat duty. "You should look very thin and hardened," wrote Wyler, more "K-ration diet . . . than the 21 Club."[61]

By early spring, the rest of the film's cast was in place. Dana Andrews's agent, Charles Feldman, had negotiated a new contract with Goldwyn several months earlier, and Andrews signed on for the part of Fred Derry, the flyboy whose return home is complicated by PTSD-like symptoms. Wyler had worked with a relatively green Andrews on *The Westerner* in 1940, and he had his doubts whether the actor could pull off a character who, in Sherwood's adaptation, had become pivotal to the story.[62] But Goldwyn insisted that the film's cast include as many of his featured players as possible. Teresa Wright was chosen to play March and Loy's daughter, even though Goldwyn had suspended the actress twice in recent years. Wright had turned down a role opposite Andrews in *The North Star* because of illness and because Goldwyn had committed her before she had even read the script. And when Wright, married to the writer Niven Busch, discovered she was pregnant in the fall of 1944, Goldwyn suspended her again, writing to her agent, "She has been and is now physically incapacitated."[63] But Wright's star, like Andrews's, had risen during the war, and her Oscar win for *Miniver*, nominations for *The Little Foxes* and *Pride of the Yankees* (Wood, 1942), and a buzzed-about performance in Alfred Hitchcock's *Shadow of a Doubt* (1943) ensured that she made approximately $15,000 more than Andrews on *Glory for Me*.[64]

The role of Fred Derry's wife, Marie, went to Virginia Mayo, a former vaudeville dancer whom Goldwyn had plucked from the stage of Billy Rose's Diamond Horseshoe club in New York City. Mayo had spent years as part of a popular comedy act called Pansy the Horse, in which she played a feisty blond who coaxed and berated an uncooperative Pansy, played by two men in a horse's outfit. In 1941, Goldwyn offered the dancer a fairly standard five-year contract: Mayo would receive $100 a week as well as six months of "grooming," which included acting lessons with a Goldwyn favorite, Florence Enright, and speech, voice, and dance classes. After a screen test, Goldwyn arranged for Mayo to receive daily facial massages to sculpt her face, which he told her was too full for the camera.

Mayo eventually graduated from being one of the "Goldwyn Girls": beautiful young actresses who appeared in the background of Goldwyn pictures, often musical comedies, and attended press events for the studio. The producer insisted on pairing Mayo with Danny Kaye, one of his top stars, and the two began working on the comedy *The Secret Life of Walter Mitty* (directed by Norman McLeod) around the same time that Mayo started work on *Glory for Me*. Goldwyn was taking a chance by offering the comedienne the mostly dramatic role of Marie. But it wasn't out of character for the mogul occasionally to be nice to his contract players. "Stern lecture, kind gesture" is how Mayo came to describe working with Sam Goldwyn.[65]

Hoagy Carmichael was cast in the supporting role of Homer's Uncle Butch. Carmichael's jazz-infused melodies in compositions such as "Moonburn" and "Heart and Soul" had played on the soundtracks of more than a few Hollywood movies since the 1930s. A slightly built composer and piano player whose flat, nasal voice conveyed the plainspokenness of his Indiana upbringing, Carmichael began to appear in front of the camera as well. But it wasn't until he held his own as Cricket, trading lines with Lauren Bacall's sultry Slim in *To Have and Have Not*, that casting directors began to see Carmichael as capable of providing more than just background color and melody. Although not a lead role, the character of Uncle Butch is central to *Glory for Me* because he owns the piano bar where the three servicemen reunite and continue to meet after their homecoming. Butch also serves as a neutral father figure for Homer, separate enough from his immediate family to withhold judgment but close enough to represent a safe haven when Homer needs to escape the pressures of home. Carmichael was hired at $22,000 for several months of work, which also included some offscreen piano lessons: Carmichael would be working with Harold Russell on "Chopsticks" for a scene in the film.[66]

One of Goldwyn's newest finds rounded out the *Glory for Me* cast of main players and their onscreen partners. Just twenty-two years old, the Alabama native Ann Steely was hired to play Wilma, Homer's girlfriend and next-door neighbor. Steely worked as a secretary after graduating from the University of Oklahoma, and she dreamed of becoming an actress. Her wholesome good looks—a heart-shaped face and gently sculpted cheekbones framed by soft brunette waves—concealed a determination that matched her surname. Her father had owned a movie theater in Siluria, a mill town near Birmingham, and appearances in student productions over the years had convinced Steely to pursue acting. Once Ann had saved enough money from her job taking dictation at an army induction center, she financed a trip to Los Angeles in 1944, where she signed with an agent, who arranged a meeting with Goldwyn.

As with Mayo, Goldwyn set about grooming Ann Steely. He rechristened her "Cathy O'Donnell," saying her winsomeness deserved an Irish-sounding name. Almost immediately, Goldwyn sent O'Donnell for voice lessons to rid her of a syrupy southern accent. She took acting classes at the American Academy of Dramatic Arts for a semester and won a small role in the touring company of *Life with Father*. The young actress's penchant for writing and reciting her own poetry raised some eyebrows in Hollywood, particularly on the set of *Glory for Me*. Soon after being hired by Goldwyn, she sent him a sample of her work entitled "Once I Found a Moonbeam," which began: "Once I found a moonbeam / I wound around my throat / And I hanged myself one stormy night / and that is why I float."[67]

Goldwyn took a brief break from overseeing preproduction details on the film to throw a small wedding party for Harold and Rita Russell. In January, the *Los Angeles Daily News* ran a story about Private First Class Robert Langstaff, a handless vet who married a WAC corporal named Ruth Spaulding and managed to place a ring on her finger with his hooks. In response, Goldwyn's publicity department decided it was a good time for Harold and Rita to get married.[68] Rita flew in from Cambridge on February 20, and a week later, the giddy couple arrived just before noon at Judge McKay's chambers in the Los Angeles courthouse. Bill Hebert, one of Goldwyn's PR men, had thought of every angle: Virginia Mayo and Steve Cochran, another Goldwyn contract player cast in the film, stood up for the couple. "Rita and I were practically reduced to playing bits at our own wedding," the groom recalled. Mr. and Mrs. Harold Russell and their party then traveled to the Beverly Hills Club, where Sam and Frances hosted a wedding breakfast. With rehearsals scheduled to begin in late March, Harold and Rita had just enough time to take a two-week honeymoon.[69]

Even without a wedding and a honeymoon to contend with, the months leading up to the start of filming in mid-April were a flurry of activity for Russell. Not long after his arrival in Los Angeles, Goldwyn had instructed Pat Duggan to set up acting classes for him with Florence Enright. For ninety minutes three times a week, Russell practiced how to walk, sit, and stand on camera. Enright also worked with Russell on his strong Boston accent, taking him through what Russell later referred to as "the whole pear-shaped vowel routine." When Wyler found out Russell was getting the Goldwyn treatment, he "hit the ceiling," recalled Russell. Wyler, who rarely displayed his anger, told Goldwyn, "I didn't hire an actor. I hired a guy to play a role." The lessons stopped.[70]

Goldwyn and Wyler had respect for each other, but they also had very different ideas about filmmaking. In 1950 during an interview for a magazine profile about Wyler, Goldwyn stopped a reporter who began a question, "When Willy made *Wuthering Heights* for you . . ." Goldwyn was polite but firm in his correction. "*I* made *Wuthering Heights*. Willy directed it for me." But on *Glory for Me*, Wyler was adamant on a number of points, such as preserving Russell's unstudied approach on camera. According to Russell, Wyler also issued a firm order during preproduction that whenever possible, veterans would receive preference on all positions on the picture.[71]

The cinematographer Gregg Toland doubtless would have been hired even if he had not served in World War II. Toland was part of the Hollywood group that John Ford had rounded up to work in the navy's Field Photographic Unit. Toland's wartime experience in shooting footage for a documentary about Pearl Harbor strengthened the on-set bond between him and Wyler. By 1946, Toland had made four movies with the filmmaker, and the pair had developed a tremendous mutual respect. The diminutive Toland was the only child of parents who divorced when he was quite young. He and his mother moved from Illinois to Los Angeles, where she made ends meet by cleaning the houses of film executives. His mother's connections may have led to his first job, at the age of fifteen, as an office boy at William Fox Studios. Although Toland was studying to become an electrical engineer at the time, his summer job at Fox exposed him to the motion picture camera, and he knew then that he had found his calling. Within several years, Toland was working as the assistant to an innovative cinematographer named George Barnes, who approached lighting and focus from a portraiture perspective. When Barnes left Paramount and began to shoot films for Goldwyn in the mid-1920s, he took Toland along. Goldwyn supported the cameramen in their ceaseless experimentation, which led to films like *The Dark Angel* (1925), with its expressive lighting and compelling camerawork.[72]

Toland won his first Academy Award for the diffused and haunting cinematography of *Wuthering Heights*. By then, he and Wyler had become an effective team, overcoming the initial tension that had developed on *These Three* a few years earlier. Wyler was used to telling a film's director of photography exactly what he wanted, which he did out of habit when he started working with Toland. Within a day or two, word got back to Wyler that Toland had requested to be transferred off the picture. Toland, who once wrote that the cameraperson was "the one person who is never idle" on a movie set, was used to collaborating with the director well in advance of the first day of shooting, breaking down the script and discussing every scene from both a photographic and dramatic perspective.[73] Once they talked, Wyler realized that working with Toland would have to be a cooperative endeavor. "You didn't tell him what lens to use, but what you wanted. And he would help you by suggesting the best way to photograph it," Wyler said. "(Gregg) had a feeling of how to use the camera to enhance the story," recalled Talli, "and Willy felt that was one of his valuable assets."[74]

The two men made an unlikely pair at first glance. Perhaps because of Toland's small stature (he stood only five feet, one inch), the quiet cinematographer commanded attention through his appearance, typically wearing neatly pressed slacks and a Harris tweed jacket on set. Wyler's clothing, on the other hand, was often rumpled and sloppy, and he inevitably pushed up his shirtsleeves at some point during the shooting day. And while Willy's eyes crackled with intensity, Toland's eyes behind his owlish glasses often looked tired despite the alert energy he projected. Some even described Toland as sickly; in 1948, in fact, he died suddenly from a massive heart attack at age forty-four. Goldwyn cried upon hearing the news, a testament to his deep affection for the cinematographer.[75]

Toland had already shot one picture for Goldwyn since returning from the war. *The Kid from Brooklyn* (McLeod, 1946) was a musical comedy that featured Danny Kaye and Virginia Mayo, but it didn't present much of a challenge for Toland. *Glory for Me*, on the other hand, would allow Toland to showcase some of the innovations he had perfected on *Citizen Kane* before the war. He had sought out *Kane* so that he could work with the film's director, Orson Welles, a twenty-five-year-old rebel from the theater world. Working with Welles, Toland tested out techniques that he and George Barnes had been working on for years, such as shooting on ceilinged sets and using newly developed, faster film to photograph a scene in deep focus. This technique, which Toland later called pan-focus, kept every plane of the image in focus, allowing the filmmakers to create complex and layered scenes using action in the back, middle, and foreground of a shot.[76]

Deep-focus photography and ceilinged sets would become important elements of *Glory for Me*'s visual design, and Wyler and Toland began working on ideas early in 1946. Shooting in black and white to add to the film's realism was another stylistic choice both men agreed on. While Toland was overseeing film tests for night shots, other pieces of the film's preproduction began to fall into place. Goldwyn traveled to the Long Beach Airport in January to inspect a hangar that was being considered for one of the film's earliest scenes. Perry Ferguson, the art director, had been hired to oversee set design, and he began drawing up a budget and a list of potential locations in and around Los Angeles that could stand in for places like the Stephensons' upscale high-rise apartment building.[77] Ferguson had worked on *Citizen Kane*, and like Toland, he had a relatively easygoing personality and was known for experimentation and innovation.[78] Ferguson's previous work on Goldwyn productions included *Ball of*

Fire (Hawks, 1941), *The Pride of the Yankees*, and *The North Star*, which meant he had already worked with Teresa Wright and Dana Andrews.

Working alongside Ferguson was the Broadway set designer George Jenkins, whose meticulous scene and lighting work on productions such as *I Remember Mama* impressed Goldwyn enough that he brought Jenkins to Hollywood. On *Glory for Me,* his first screen credit, Jenkins was assigned to draw elegant charcoal illustrations of the sets that would be re-created on the Goldwyn soundstages. His theater background as well as early training as an architect helped Jenkins achieve the realistic scale and authenticity that Wyler envisioned for the film. Later admitting that he wasn't as interested "in the externals of presenting a scene as I have been in the inner workings of the people the scene is about," Wyler clearly relied on Ferguson's and Jenkins's combined expertise.[79]

The fact that Wyler and his crew planned to shoot several scenes on location was as much a nod to the veterans' having been influenced by the documentary style of combat cinematography as it was to the postwar reality of limits on set-construction budgets. In April 1946, when *Glory for Me* was to begin shooting, the Civil Protection Administration, a governmental agency, had not yet lifted its wartime limit ($15,000) on what could be spent on construction materials for set design. This restriction, combined with an increase in the number of films in production, affected the availability of studio space as well as filmmakers' ability to shoot retakes after principal photography had ended. These limitations threatened to interfere with Wyler's penchant for multiple takes.[80]

Wyler's attention to detail extended to every aspect of *Glory for Me*'s preproduction. Goldwyn signed off on a $100,000 re-creation of a drugstore interior for scenes in which Andrews's Fred Derry resumes his prewar position as a soda jerk and sales associate at a local pharmacy. Some of the fixtures and merchandise were on loan from the Owl Drug Company, a California subsidiary of the Rexall chain, and once shooting started, four private detectives were added to the payroll to guard the products.[81] After the film opened, in November 1946, much was made in the press about the cast's costumes, mostly bought off the rack. During preproduction, the costume designer Irene Sharaff took Loy, Wright, and the other featured actors shopping in and around Los Angeles. Nicknamed the "Black Widow" for wearing head-to-toe black, the designer had worked on several films for Goldwyn.[82] Despite her personal monochromatic preference, Sharaff liked to costume actors in shades of red, orange, and pink. But on *Glory for Me* she adhered to Wyler's instructions that the actors' clothes be in muted shades of gray, white, and black so that they would photograph more realistically on the black-and-white film Toland would be using. Wyler told the cast to spend time wearing their wardrobe before filming to give the clothing a lived-in feel and help them get into their characters. Wardrobe test photos taken in March followed Wyler's instructions about makeup, too: the men in the cast were to go without, and the women were to wear only "street" makeup, similar to what they might use in their daily lives. The purpose, said Wyler later, was "so that we could really see our people, and feel their skin textures" in the finished film.[83]

A month before principal photography began, production reports and other studio paperwork began to refer to the film by a new title. Several months earlier, in December 1945, Lynn Farnol, a Goldwyn publicity man, had hired Audience Research, Inc. to test the title *Glory for Me* with moviegoers. Women gravitated toward sentimental options such as "Back Home for Keeps" and "Heart of Life," while men favored wartime references such as "When Daylight Comes" and "No More Bugles." When ARI came back with the news that the title of Kantor's book had scored the lowest among those suggested, the PR department decided to sponsor a studio-wide contest to rename the film. The Goldwyn employee who came up with an "acceptable" title would receive fifty dollars. It seemed as if everyone who worked at the studio took part. Miriam Howell, the assistant who had first met with Harold Russell, suggested several possibilities, including "Take Care of Them," which was inspired by General MacArthur's closing words on the occasion of the surrender by the Japanese to the United States. A waiter in the studio's dining room thought "Reflection Rebuffed" offered a provocative alternative. Many titles used the words "glory" or "home." A few oddities, like "Atomic Energy Seeped into Her Heart," acknowledged the bombing of Hiroshima. Finally, in a late-spring memo to the Goldwyn executives Pat Duggan, Marvin Ezzell, and Leon Fromkes, Farnol sent a short list of unattributed titles from the New York office. "One or two might strike your fancy," he wrote, and among the possibilities was the film's new title, *The Best Years of Our Lives*.[84]

In the midst of preproduction, Willy and Talli traveled to Washington so that he could receive the Legion of Merit. General Eaker, Wyler's former commanding officer, had recommended him for the award, which recognized Wyler's "extraordinarily meritorious conduct" while making *Thunderbolt*. Before Wyler agreed to receive it, however, he requested that Lester Koenig and John Sturges also be commended for their work on the documentary.[85] The Legion of Merit meant as much to Wyler as the Air Medal he had received for the missions he flew while making *The Memphis Belle*. But the commendation was bittersweet. He had lost his hearing in the process of making *Thunderbolt*, and as he prepared to direct his first postwar film, he couldn't help feeling anxious. Hearing aids were awkward and unreliable at best. Publicly, he dismissed the chore of dealing with his hearing loss as "a big bore," but privately, he worried that he wouldn't be the same director as he had been before the war. He noticed, for instance, that he often missed a word or two when in conversation with others. "And [if] it's the key word, then the whole sentence makes no sense," he later explained.[86] The Legion of Merit also reminded Wyler that *Thunderbolt* had yet to find a distributor. Monogram Pictures, a company known for distributing mostly low-budget genre films, had reached out to Wyler about *Thunderbolt* back in December 1945, but by the spring of 1946, nothing had come of that initial interest.

Still, Wyler had reason to celebrate. On April 2, Talli gave birth to a baby boy with dark hair and blue eyes. They named him William, after his father. The baby, whom they called Billy, looked like Willy. Billy had a sweet disposition, and the Wylers were thrilled. Talli later described it as one of the best days of their lives. "It was just wonderful," she said of Billy's joining his older sisters Cathy, who was seven, and Judy, about to turn four. "The family was complete."[87]

CHAPTER 4

Underwater Again

There were times during the shooting of the picture when I thought I was reliving all the miserable, agonizing days after I lost my hands.
HAROLD RUSSELL, *Victory in My Hands*

Robert Sherwood was back on the East Coast when he received a letter from Samuel Goldwyn. "You would have been thrilled if you could have seen the rushes this morning of Al's homecoming," Goldwyn wrote in late April of 1946. "I haven't been as moved by a scene in many years."[1]

Best Years was in its second full week of production on the Goldwyn lot. Most of the film's interiors were being shot in Studios 1 and 6, where the crew had constructed sets with muslin ceilings per Wyler and Toland's specifications. The muslin hid the lights and other technical equipment, and on film it gave the illusion that the two-dimensional rooms had actual ceilings, which enhanced the depth of each onscreen space as well as the film's overall authenticity.

The previous day's dailies were screened every morning at nine thirty, and on Wednesday, April 24, Goldwyn, Wyler, and many in the cast had assembled to watch a scene that Sherwood had based in part on Willy's first wartime reunion with Talli. The awkwardness that the Wylers felt at the Hampshire House in 1943 was captured in the initial scene between Al (Fredric March) and Milly (Myrna Loy) Stephenson. Al returns home to the couple's comfortably appointed, multiroom apartment, catching his entire family off guard with his early arrival. Milly has her back to the camera as she sets the table for dinner on the terrace. She straightens and then turns to look back through the doorway, passing through it and into the entryway, where she sees her husband. Al and Milly pause on opposite sides of the long hallway. The screen direction in the script describes the mood: "Their silence is strained, intense," before Al walks toward Milly and "seizes her, almost roughly in his arms."[2]

Wyler had discussed his and Talli's wartime reunion not only with Sherwood but also with the actors. "Willy never forgot the feeling that he had—he was just panicking," Loy said of Wyler's initially not being able to find Talli in the hotel. Loy also drew on her own wartime experiences with the Red Cross. "I had worked in the hospitals so much, and I had seen so many of these men who had almost had a traumatic experience because of their separation from their homes," she recalled. "The disconnected feeling of coming back, the fear of going home . . . because they had grown in some horrible way or some wonderful way, one way or another." Years later, Loy offered another perspective on why the film's opening scene between Al and Milly was so powerful: "They just can't wait to get into the sack."[3]

Tender scenes like Milly's reunion with Al were balanced with more humorous sequences, as when Milly and her daughter, Peggy (Teresa Wright), have to bring home Al and his new friend Fred Derry (Dana Andrews), both of whom have passed out from a night of drunken revelry. Fans of Loy's *Thin Man* movies would recognize the actress's expert timing as the foil to her inebriated husband, whom she must undress and put to bed, in one of the film's few scenes verging on slapstick. It had taken Loy years to build up enough confidence as an actress to let her guard down onscreen. When she was just starting out at MGM, Irving Thalberg, the studio's head of production, had given her some advice. "There's something between you and the audience. It's almost like a veil," Thalberg told her. "You must learn to take hold of that audience and just do with it what you want." By 1946, after more than two decades in the business, Loy knew when she needed to lower the veil. "You have to be true. If you're not, it shows. That camera's right there, looking right into your eyes, and you can't get away with anything."[4]

March's and Loy's scenes were some of the first to be shot, partly to limit the amount of time they were on the Goldwyn payroll. But even though the two stars commanded the highest salaries among the cast, there was little sense of a hierarchy among the actors on set. Wyler liked to rehearse extensively. The day before an important sequence, he would stage a morning table read, similar to a rehearsal for a theatrical production, and the cast would work through the scene. Wyler would share his thoughts about the characters' moods, and the actors would weigh in as well. "If we didn't agree with him, we'd discuss it back and forth till we got our sights lined up together," remembered Harold Russell.[5] Then Wyler would stage a run-through with the actors, usually allowing them to get comfortable with the scene in whatever way they preferred. Before shooting a scene, Wyler would do more rehearsals on set. "Each time we go through it, I try to make suggestions for improving it," Wyler wrote of his rehearsal preferences. "I have been called a perfectionist, but that hasn't usually been intended as a compliment. I do make a great many takes, when necessary, but there is always a reason."[6]

It wasn't uncommon for Goldwyn to stop by the set, and as Wyler began to run behind schedule, Goldwyn's visits became more frequent. "He knew he had a winner," recalled Russell of Goldwyn's feeling about *Best Years*. While Goldwyn rarely gave Wyler a hard time about spending money on the pictures they made together, he did harangue the director about sticking to the schedule. "Wyler was not one to pay much attention to time," Russell said. "He just went ahead and did the directing without too much regard to how many pages of script they covered each day." In one early scene with Russell, in fact, in which his character gazes out through the Plexiglas of a B-17's nose cone as dawn breaks through the clouds below, Wyler wasn't getting what he wanted from Russell. After the tenth take, Wyler could tell Russell was uncomfortable, and he didn't want to make the young man feel worse. Still, Wyler pressed him to go again. Finally, on the twentieth take, Russell gave Wyler the performance he wanted, leading Wyler to comment afterward that the discomfort for both men was worth it.[7] Occasionally, this kind of slowdown in production led to on-set arguments between Goldwyn and Wyler, who would huddle off to the side, the impeccably dressed Goldwyn becoming visibly angry while a rumpled Wyler maintained his composure. "Wyler was very quiet about it. Not only quiet, a determined type of anger," said Russell.[8]

Before filming, Wyler steeled himself for the friction that inevitably developed between him and Goldwyn during a production. In a letter to Lillian Hellman earlier that spring, he made a joke about it, referring to "occasional attacks of 'Goldwynitis.' I thought the war had toughened my skin, but it has made me less immune than ever."[9] Once production started, Wyler's Goldwynitis might manifest itself physically in migraines, stomach troubles, or excessive smoking on the set. But Talli, for one, thought the conflict between the two men served a greater purpose, giving Wyler "a peer" to argue with and with whom to work through difficult creative decisions. "I think all those fights, all those arguments, are very important to the making of the picture," she said.[10]

Despite the friction between producer and director, the *Best Years* set was generally a happy place. Russell, who had been warned by several people in Hollywood that Wyler could be difficult to work with, had anticipated a different mood once shooting began in mid-April 1946. "Everybody did exactly what Willy said. He was in charge, he was the director. When he said quiet, he meant quiet. But at the same time, it was positive," Russell recalled.[11] Loy went into the production with reservations about Wyler, too. She had done two Goldwyn films before *Best Years*, but she didn't know Wyler. Yet once production began, Loy and Wyler hit it off. "They all had sort of shared something," Teresa Wright said of Wyler, March, Loy, and the others who had gone away during the war.[12] Loy had always been politically aware—her father had been a state legislator in Montana, and her aunt had been a county treasurer there—and she became even more active during the war, when her Red Cross involvement led to a friendship with First Lady Eleanor Roosevelt and participation in the association to form the United Nations. Her on-set bond with Wyler prompted Fredric March to observe, "I can't believe the radar you two have going. You don't even need to talk."[13]

Willy and Talli's joy over the recent birth of their son, Billy, no doubt contributed to Wyler's happiness during the making of *Best Years*. More good news arrived with the start of filming. The discovery of an on-set solution to his hearing loss gave Wyler back his confidence. Early on during shooting, Wyler realized that he could sit beneath the camera and wear a headset whose cable fed into Richard DeWeese's sound-recording equipment. With an attached amplifier, Wyler could hear the actors' dialogue as DeWeese was recording it—straight from the on-set microphone. The device worked almost like a hearing aid—a medical device that Willy loathed—but because it was a piece of motion picture sound equipment, it filtered out any distracting, peripheral noise.

Missing out on side conversations and background utterances can put someone at a disadvantage in normal, everyday situations. Even on set, Wyler hated that he couldn't hear everything going on around him. But for the purposes of directing a scene, the "hearing aid-like thing" allowed Wyler to pick up exactly what the actors were saying and how they were reading their lines.[14] With the hearing problem taken care of, at least during filming, Wyler could fully involve himself in the rhythms of the production, with all of its trials and tribulations. Talli once described her husband's approach to a production as a complete immersion, as if he were descending into the depths of the ocean. As she later remarked of his *Best Years* experience, "He was underwater again."[15]

Production began on Monday, April 15, at the Long Beach Airport, where some of the film's initial scenes were shot, even though the production as a whole generally filmed out of sequence. Goldwyn had hired a group of technical advisers that included a Bank of America executive, an air force colonel, and an administrator from the Veterans Association, who were on hand to ensure accuracy in scenes involving Al's returning to work at a bank, any military matters, and veterans' issues.[16]

One of the first sequences filmed was in fact the movie's opening scene, beginning with a crane shot of a busy airport terminal. The camera tracks slowly into the crowd and settles on Fred Derry (Andrews) as he walks across the terminal, dressed in a uniform whose shoulder pins reveal him to be an air force captain. He approaches the ticket counter and tries to book a flight home to Boone City, the fictional midwestern setting of both MacKinlay Kantor's novel and the film. As an airline representative tries to find him a flight, another man approaches the counter. Dressed in a business suit and followed by an African American porter lugging a suitcase and a bag of golf clubs, the gentleman, a

Mr. Gibbons, interrupts Fred's transaction so that he can pick up the ticket his secretary reserved for him. As Fred reluctantly steps to the side, the porter puts Gibbons's luggage on the scale. When the ticket agent tells him that his luggage is overweight, he responds, "Oh, that's all right. How much is it?"

The scene, which lasts fewer than two minutes, deftly hints at the plight of the returning serviceman. The combination of Wyler's staging, Andrews's delivery and facial expressions, Gregg Toland's camerawork, and Sherwood's dialogue make it clear that Fred's wartime expertise and captain's privileges will carry little weight in a world where postwar socioeconomic distinctions and racial divisions seem relatively unchanged.

Other scenes shot during the production's first few weeks involved March, Russell, and Andrews as the three vets heading home to Boone City. After the film's release, Goldwyn's publicity department worked overtime to sell the story that Boone City was based on Cincinnati, Ohio. Stories about sending John P. Fulton, the film's special effects director, to take aerial photographs of Cincinnati backdrops were promoted in the film's press kit, and versions of those stories were then perpetuated in magazine articles and interviews. In reality, the second-unit photography of football fields, bleachers, hot dog stands, and other background locations was shot during February and March, before the start of principal photography, likely in and around Los Angeles. Indeed, the apartment house featured in exterior shots of the Stephensons' upscale high-rise was the Sycamore Apartments, located on the corner of Beverly Boulevard and North Sycamore Avenue, where the building still stands today.[17]

The night before his wardrobe test, Harold Russell received a telegram from Fredric March: "May you enjoy every minute of the picture. We are lucky to have you with us with your wonderful spirit."[18] But despite both his warm welcome to Hollywood and his experience in *Diary of a Sergeant*, Russell was gripped by nerves on the first day of filming. Some of his earliest scenes were with Andrews, who initially struck Russell as cold and standoffish. But it turned out that Russell wasn't the only one battling anxiety. Andrews, whose star turn in Otto Preminger's *Laura* had boosted his profile in Hollywood, still struggled with a lack of confidence in front of the camera. "I love acting and yet I'm not really a good actor, though I think I work harder at it than any other man in the business," he later confided to Russell.[19] They shared a scene on the second day of filming, and after the initial take, Wyler called Andrews over. The director hadn't worked with the actor since before the war, when Andrews had had a small part in *The Westerner*, with Gary Cooper. "What happened to you!" Wyler exclaimed with a glint in his eye. "You're a very good actor!" Andrews laughed and said, "Willy, thank you very much, but I've made 20 pictures since I first saw you."[20] Andrews eventually went out of his way to help Russell, running lines and rehearsing scenes with him throughout the shoot.

In addition to daily rehearsals and multiple takes, Wyler pushed for naturalness from his cast in other ways. Before production, he had instructed all the actors to learn their parts in the script from start to finish so as to understand their characters. Then they could put aside their character's arc and focus on individual scenes the night before each one was to be filmed. Because Sherwood and Russell had spent so much time together in the weeks after Russell's West Coast arrival, discussing for hours his experiences at Camp Mackall and later at Walter Reed, many of the details that made their way into Homer's dialogue and reactions came straight from Russell's life. But once in a while there was too much reality. During a scene in which Al, Fred, and Homer catch a ride back to Boone City in a B-17, not unlike the ones that Wyler flew in during the war, the three men peer out of the Plexiglas nose cone at the landscape below. While Boone City's exteriors may not have been shot in Ohio, Wyler needed the audience to believe that the characters hailed from a midwestern city. But when it came time for Russell to say Homer's lines about how small the cars appeared from the air, his Boston accent got in the way. Russell's original line was, "Boy oh boy. Hey, look at that. Look at those cars down there." With every take, Wyler could hear Russell dropping the *r* when he pronounced the word "car." Finally, after nine takes, Wyler changed Russell's line to, "Look at those automobiles."[21]

While switching the words in that line was a relatively minor change, Goldwyn was adamant that Wyler leave Sherwood's script intact. Before filming, Goldwyn had been very direct with the filmmaker about this, reminding him that these were the terms the producer had established with the screenwriter.[22] Somewhat disingenuously, Goldwyn later defended his position to Wyler, telling him that since Sherwood had not been paid for his services, it was the least he could do as the producer. In fact Sherwood *had* been paid for his work on *Best Years*, earning $100,000—the same amount as the top three highest-paid actors on the film.

Perhaps Goldwyn was alluding to Sherwood's follow-up work on the script in the weeks leading up to production. Unavailable to do rewrites in early 1946, Sherwood suggested that Goldwyn reach out to Howard Koch, who had won an Oscar for cowriting *Casablanca*. Koch did a quick polish after Czenzi Ormonde (*Strangers on a Train*) spent a few weeks on rewrites. Their work took place while Sherwood was in New York, where he had returned after the death of Harry Hopkins, the former secretary of commerce whom President Roosevelt had relied on for foreign policy advice. Hopkins died at the end of January, and his adult children had reached out to Sherwood, a close associate, about finishing the book that Hopkins had been working on about his time with FDR. Sherwood, who valued his wartime service to the president as a speechwriter, felt compelled to take on the Hopkins book, which was published not long after the release of *Best Years*. Still, the playwright regretted not being able to help Wyler and Goldwyn in the month or two leading up to production, and by March he was back on the project.[23]

Goldwyn had another reason for wanting Wyler to adhere to the screenplay. The producer and the director, along with Sherwood, had negotiated certain changes with the Production Code Administration (PCA), the industry's self-censoring entity, and Goldwyn did not want the release of *Best Years* held up by any last-minute objections from Joseph I. Breen, who oversaw the PCA. Goldwyn's independent colleagues David O. Selznick and Howard Hughes had battled with the PCA in the past and emerged at least satisfied that they had retained the integrity of films such as *Rebecca* and *The Outlaw*. Goldwyn had issued a statement shortly after the war ended that suggested he was willing to challenge the code's restrictions: "I think it is about time we all joined to do something about this awful millstone around the neck of the motion picture industry."[24] Still, on a project as risky as *Best Years*, Goldwyn was willing to negotiate with Breen.

The man whom *Variety* often referred to as the "Production Code Czar" was a devout Irish Catholic with a background in journalism and public relations. He had been hired by Will Hays, the head of the trade group called the Motion Picture Producers and Distributors of America (MPPDA). The MPPDA was formed in the early 1920s to give Hollywood a makeover after a series of celebrity scandals sparked public outrage. By the early 1930s, national groups such as the Catholic Church's Legion of Decency were once again threatening the industry with censorship. Its concern was due in part to a rise in onscreen representations of violence and vulgar language, which, thanks to the advent of sound film, could now be seen *and* heard by moviegoers. Earlier guidelines established in a Purity Code, known around the studios as the "Don'ts and Be Carefuls," were no longer sufficient. In the early 1930s, a revised Production Code was drawn up, and by 1934 the Hays Office (as the MPPDA was called) had established the PCA.

By 1946, Breen had accumulated tremendous power in Hollywood. In his late fifties, Breen resembled a kindly grandfather with his three-piece suits, wire-rimmed glasses, and neatly slicked-back white hair. He could pass for any number of Irish American patriarchs, writes Thomas Doherty, "perhaps a police captain looking forward to a cushy pension, or a ward politician with a lifetime of favors in his pocket."[25] Despite taking a leave of absence during the war to be general manager of RKO Studios for a year, Breen was dedicated to the PCA and took his job as enforcer of the code very seriously.

Wyler invited Breen to meet with him and Sherwood at Willy and Talli's house. On the last Saturday in March, two weeks before *Best Years'* principal photography was scheduled to begin, Breen pulled into the half-circle drive of the Wyler residence. He was there to discuss the PCA's objections to the script, which Sam Goldwyn had sent to Breen earlier that month. Goldwyn had waited until the last minute to submit the screenplay to the Breen Office, as the PCA was known, but Breen already knew about the project. Nearly nine months earlier, Goldwyn had sent him an advance copy of Kantor's novel with a note that said it would be the basis for Goldwyn's next film, to be scripted by Sherwood. Breen responded two days later, warning Goldwyn that "as now written, the story contains many unacceptable incidents, lines of dialog, and characterization" that would be in violation of the Production Code.[26] Most of Breen's objections to the novel had to do with references to sex and sexual infidelity, and those concerns carried over to the screenplay. On Monday, April 1, after meeting with Wyler and Sherwood, Breen sent an eight-page letter to Goldwyn detailing the lines, situations, and characterizations that he found most objectionable.[27]

Breen's letter began with a general suggestion about the kissing scenes: "These should not be prolonged, or lustful, and there should be no open-mouthed kissing," he advised. He also issued a blanket directive that the scenes involving the dissolution of Fred and Marie's marriage "should be reexamined and possibly rewritten" so that the film did not appear to condone divorce.[28] Conversely, Breen took issue with any scenes that revealed "the sacred intimacies of married life," pushing for twin beds in Al and Milly's bedroom. The remainder of the letter went page by page through the screenplay, pointing out objectionable lines of dialogue and potential problems, such as the evening gowns the characters Marie and Peggy were to wear in a nightclub scene ("The dresses . . . should not expose their breasts."). Among other things, Breen asked that all references to and scenes about alcohol be taken out "entirely," that Wyler refrain from including a toilet in any bathroom shots, and the word "bum" be removed, because it would be eliminated anyway by British censors when the film was released in England, where "bum" was slang for a person's backside.[29]

Nowhere in Breen's letter, however, was there any objection to politicized dialogue, such as Al's pointed speech to his banking colleagues about the importance of the GI Bill and giving loans to veterans whose only collateral "is in his heart and his hands and his guts—it's in his rights as a citizen." Most interesting, perhaps, is that Breen had no problem with Homer's hooks or how they might be shown onscreen, even though as recently as 1943, the media had avoided publishing images of wounded veterans or their injuries in reporting about the war. The focus of the PCA's concerns, as with most films it vetted, came down to sex and alcohol.

Wyler and Sherwood agreed to some of Breen's demands, such as omitting shots of toilets and deleting the word "bum." The Stephensons' master bedroom, however, retained its queen-size bed. Wyler and Sherwood also kept in certain scenes involving alcohol, particularly since Al's character develops a drinking problem as a way to cope with his difficult readjustment and disillusionment about resuming work at the Cornbelt Trust. And while Goldwyn had publicly criticized the code in the months following the end of the war, Wyler for the most part paid lip service, at least publicly, to its existence. "The only trouble with censorship on this picture was in explaining why we did things," Wyler said about having to make the case for certain scenes that showed Al drinking or hung over.[30]

It is difficult to know whether Wyler was merely trying to make nice with the Breen Office or whether he sincerely believed that some censorship of the industry was necessary. But perhaps he agreed with those who thought Breen's enforcement of the code challenged filmmakers in the best and most creative sense. "Breen was not the voice of [Will] Hays, Wall Street, the Legion of Decency, or the state censor," writes Leonard Leff. "Rather, he was the agent of ambivalence: he helped producers translate the 'dangerous' into the ambiguous and, on occasion, even into the subversive."[31]

In his April letter to Sam Goldwyn about *Best Years*, Breen pointed to the advance reaction of mainstream magazines like *Time* and *Life* to the soon-to-be-released adaptation of James M. Cain's novel *The Postman Always Rings Twice*. Breen hinted at the critics' objections to *Postman*'s supposed explicitness, making the case for why Goldwyn should heed the PCA's suggestions on the *Best Years* script.[32] But when *Postman* hit theaters during the first week of May, in the midst of *Best Years'* filming, several critics, such as Bosley Crowther, said just the opposite: "Without illustrating any of the bluntly carnal scenes of the book, the authors, actors and director have suggested sensual tensions thoroughly."[33] Teresa Wright believed this power of suggestion to be one of the strengths of *Best Years*. Describing the first breakfast scene between Al and Milly, in which Milly carries a tray into the bedroom to serve Al breakfast in bed, Wright referred to it as the "morning after scene." In the sequence, shot during the first month of production, Al puts the tray aside and pulls Milly into a passionate embrace. "To me it's one of the most erotic scenes that I can imagine," said Wright. "I think it's a perfectly beautiful married love scene."[34]

Wright shot one of her most difficult scenes during that first month of production while March and Loy were still on the call sheet. In the scene, Peggy lashes out at her parents when they confront her about her romantic feelings for Fred, who is still married to Marie (Virginia Mayo). Peggy has returned from a double date with the couple, a date that she had orchestrated in order to "stop being silly" about her growing feelings for Fred. She knocks on the door to Al and Milly's room, where the couple is getting ready to turn in for the night. When Peggy declares, "I'm going to break that marriage up!" Al confronts his daughter. "So you're going to break this marriage up. Have you decided yet how you're gonna do it? You're gonna do it with an ax?" Telling her father that it is none of his business, she accuses her parents of forgetting what it is like to be in love. Wright was struggling with the line, which sounded ridiculous to her, given Peggy's backstory as a mature, responsible twenty-one-year-old who has been working at a local hospital and, in Wright's mind, "doing things beyond her years," as so many young women had had to do during the war. "How can even in the heat of anger she talk like a stupid, spoiled fourteen year old?" Wright asked Wyler on the set. Wyler admitted that he could see it from Wright's point of view. But he also explained the line was necessary because it led to Milly's speech about her and Al's marriage, a moment that deepens their own relationship.[35]

Wyler nonetheless called Sherwood to discuss a dialogue change, and shooting paused while other lines were considered. Finally, Wyler agreed with Sherwood that the original line should stay, and the actors took their places on the bedroom set for another take. After Wright said her line, March responded in a ragged voice: "You hear that, Milly? I'm so old and decrepit, I've forgotten how it feels to want somebody . . . desperately." During one take, Loy placed her hand on top of March's, a subtle but powerful gesture and the kind of improvisation that Wyler often encouraged, particularly from an experienced actress like Loy.

"Everything's always been so perfect for you," Wright stammered, tears welling up in her eyes.

"We never had any trouble," Loy said as a slight smile played across her lips and she gazed up at March. "How many times have I told you I hated you and believed it in my heart?" The exchange between the long-married couple, prompted by Peggy's outburst, would become one of the most authentic moments in the film.

The sequence ends with Peggy breaking down in tears and throwing herself across her parents' bed as Milly goes to console her and Al quietly slips out of the room. Years later, Wright recalled Wyler's generosity as a director. "There are times you must say something," she said of speaking out about the problematic line. "Somebody else might have said, 'Look, you're going to have to say it because she won't have the line.' So you do it, but you don't do it with the same sense [that] somebody has listened to me, and he agrees with me. But there isn't an alternative [line], so you do it with as much as you can put into it." Interviewed even later, when Wright was in her early seventies, she told one of Wyler's biographers that the line finally made sense to her: "The older you get you realize that sometimes intelligent people can say the most unintelligent things, especially if it has to do with their own love affair."[36]

Lighter moments came in Hoagy Carmichael's sequences, which were filmed during the first half of production. As Homer's Uncle Butch, Carmichael didn't have many scenes, but his character's saloon was essential for all three veterans. The setting figures largely in a pivotal moment of conflict between Al and Fred that was scheduled to shoot later. The saloon also functions as a place for Butch to counsel his troubled nephew in a relatively risk-free environment. As the two sit together at Butch's piano, the older man offers some gentle advice to Homer about his responsibility to his family and to his girlfriend, Wilma, plucking a melody among the keys as he and Homer sit side by side.

Scenes such as this allowed Carmichael to flex both his acting and musical chops. During breaks between takes and shot setups, Carmichael would work with Russell on his piano playing, supplementing the lessons that Goldwyn had arranged before production. "Teaching a guy with no hands to play the piano is no small thing," recalled Russell. "But he was so quick and sincere about it. Knew just how he wanted to go about it."[37] Carmichael got so caught up in working with Russell that he designed an attachment that Russell could use with a golf club so that he could still enjoy time on the course. Carmichael even got the studio's machine shop to make a prototype. The musician, who had appeared in only four films by the time he shot *Best Years*, also offered acting tips to Russell, ostensibly trying to help the younger man relax on set. "Hey, Carmichael!" Wyler yelled when he overheard one such exchange. "What the hell do you think you're doing? I'm the only one around here who talks to the actors!"[38] And when Carmichael suggested during filming that some aspects of his barkeep character weren't "dignified" enough for his fan base, Wyler became exasperated with the crooner. Referring to the set for Al Stephenson's workplace, Wyler said, "What do you want us to do, Hoagy? Move your piano into the bank?"[39]

As the *Best Years* production headed into its second month, something else besides the occasional tension between Wyler and Goldwyn threatened to disrupt the set's relaxed mood. Dana Andrews, the accomplished actor who became something of a mentor to Russell, was battling alcoholism, and one day he simply didn't show up to work. Ironically, the cast was in the middle of shooting some of the film's earliest scenes, including those of Milly and Peggy driving Al and Fred home after a night of drinking and celebrating their homecoming at Butch's Place. In one scene, they pull up to the apartment building where Fred's wife, Marie, has moved. Up to this point in the film, he has yet to find Marie, who, according to Fred's family, has taken a job at a nightclub to make ends meet. Wyler had begun shooting the scene the previous evening, but when Loy, March, and Wright returned to the set the next morning, Andrews was nowhere to be found.

Despite Andrews's recent success in films such as *State Fair* and *Laura*—or perhaps because of it—he turned to alcohol as a way to cope and to prop himself up during times of doubt. Not long after *Best Years* was released, in fact,

Andrews read a newspaper article by Tennessee Williams entitled "A Streetcar Named Success," which detailed the playwright's inability to enjoy his good fortune after the success of *The Glass Menagerie*. Andrews underlined several sentences in the piece and at the bottom of the article wrote, "I know what he means."[40] Norman Lloyd, a fellow actor and friend who considered Andrews a quintessential American actor for that time period, marveled at his friend's ability to consume large amounts of alcohol without appearing to be drunk. What Andrews did struggle with, however, was the morning-after hangover.[41] The crew members whom Wyler had dispatched to find Andrews discovered him passed out at a nearby motel. They brought him back to the set and served him cup after cup of coffee in an effort to sober him up.[42]

Wyler called for the actors to take their places on the Goldwyn backlot, where the scene was being shot in front of a mockup of the front entrance to the Grandview Arms, the apartment building where Fred's wife, Marie, was living. Wright took her place behind the wheel of a four-door sedan, a Buick that Wyler insisted on using to make the scene as realistic as possible. Andrews was in the passenger seat, and Loy and March were in the back. Wyler was perched near Toland's camera, his headset plugged into the sound recordist's equipment. When Wyler called, "Action," the camera's lens hovered mere feet from Wright's face as she drove the car into frame. The characters said their good-byes as Fred got out of the vehicle. The script called for Andrews to be unsteady on his feet, which in reality he was. He was then supposed to stumble back to the car after ringing the buzzer to his wife's apartment and getting no answer. As Andrews ducked down to lean into the car window and deliver his next line, he bumped his head on the roof of the car. "Hey, that's good. I like that," said Wyler, and he instructed the actor to do the scene again, keeping in the bit about hitting his head on the car roof.[43] The cast did take after take as the morning grew late.

"He will do a scene over and over and over again, and I think sometimes he doesn't know exactly what he wants—in opposition to some directors I know that do know exactly what they want, and their minds aren't malleable to accept something that might even be better," Andrews once said of Wyler. "I think that he's waiting to see what develops. And when he gets it, he knows immediately."[44]

Teresa Wright sat through each take, delivering her lines and cringing every time the hungover Andrews had to hit his head on the car. "On about the 25th take I'm saying, 'Oh god,'" Wright recalled. "By [then] Dana was not going to complain about it, but he was just hitting harder and harder."[45] Having made multiple films with Wyler, she had mixed feelings about the director's technique. She loved his European charm, his intelligence and wit, and she knew she had given some of her finest performances under his "attentive" direction. But years later she questioned what people often described as his inability to put into words exactly what he wanted an actor to do in a scene, resulting in the need for multiple takes. "I'm not sure if he was actually unable to articulate what he wanted, or if he simply did not want to impose himself or a certain idea on the actor. . . . He was interested in creating an effect on film." Wright also wondered whether he didn't have something of a "sadistic" streak that drove him to push his actors as he did with Andrews in the filming of the car scene.[46]

One day Wyler finally pulled Andrews aside on the set. He spoke matter-of-factly about the actor's drinking and his resulting absences. Next time, he told Andrews, call in sick. "You don't have to call me. Just call in [to the studio] and say you're sick. And then we'll just shoot around you. You don't have to worry about that. We'll get you another day," said Wyler, as if it weren't a big deal and Goldwyn wasn't already yelling at the director for being so many pages behind on the picture. Andrews was struck by the director's kindness. "I mean the *way* he did it. No criticism or anything. Just do me a favor," Andrews said later of the casual way in which Wyler dealt with the actor's drinking. "I never had another drink while we did that picture."[47]

In May, the *Best Years* crew prepared to shoot a lengthy sequence that established Fred's lingering war trauma and brought him and Peggy together in one of their first intimate encounters. In the film, the scene follows the one in which Milly and Peggy drive Al and Fred home after their drunken celebration at Butch's. Peggy deposits a passed-out Fred on her own bed and relocates to the living-room couch for the night. Hours pass, and Peggy is awakened by the sound of talking coming from her room. She finds Fred sitting up in bed, his face covered in sweat, in the middle of a nightmare about the fire that took the lives of some of his fellow bombardiers. With his eyes open, he panics, saying, "She's on fire. She's on fire!" Peggy sits on the bed next to him and tries to wake him up. Finally, she reaches over and covers his eyes with her hand. "It's all right, Fred. Go back to sleep," she says firmly. She pushes him down on the bed and tries to encourage him to return to sleep, but Fred begins to cry. She places her hand on his shoulder as she tells him that he has nothing to be afraid of. "All you have to do is go back to sleep," Peggy says, wiping Fred's sweaty face and caressing his forehead as he continues to weep.

Wyler and Toland had discussed the scene during preproduction. Once filming began, they allotted time for daily rehearsals that allowed the actors to fine-tune their gestures, expressions, and dialogue. Wyler generally disliked breaking up the rhythm of scenes with unnecessary edits in postproduction, which meant that most scenes had to be filmed in a single take that could last several minutes onscreen. It was a technique that the French film critic André Bazin later identified as part of Wyler's "invisible style," a style that is less about a particular set of techniques than a sense that each film requires its own cinematic language. Wyler's penchant for long, uninterrupted takes was "democratic," Bazin wrote not long after the release of *Best Years*. "All [he] wants is that the spectator can (1) see everything; and (2) choose as he pleases. It's an act of loyalty toward the spectator, an attempt at dramatic honesty."[48] This type of long take meant that the actors had to hit their marks and have their lines down cold. If any of the players made a mistake, Wyler would call for another take, from the beginning of the scene.

The shooting of Fred's nightmare lasted the better part of a week that May. It was an important sequence in the film, the first indication that Fred is struggling mentally. Nightmares are a common symptom of war trauma, and audiences of the time would have recognized this. In the final cut of the film, the sequence runs about five minutes, with the bulk of the action taking place in only three shots. The final one, in which Peggy sits on the bed and soothes Fred in her no-nonsense, almost stern manner, lasts nearly two minutes. Wyler made Wright and Andrews do that particular shot again and again, letting Fred's nightmare build to a terrifying crescendo that was enhanced by Toland's high-contrast lighting and tight cropping. The mounting terror that Fred relives in his nightmare is matched by Peggy's gradual realization that it is up to her to break the awful spell. Andrews's stark vulnerability in the scene needed to be offset by Wright's quiet but commanding presence, and Wyler pushed his actors until he felt that they had captured the subtle mix of moods.

Wright had watched Andrews struggle during the production, but the shooting of this particular sequence seemed different. "He gave a really wonderful, sensitive performance that amazed everyone," she said.[49] According to some, it was even Andrews's idea to have a hungover Fred, in the "morning-after" scene, hurriedly check his wallet upon realizing that he is in a strange woman's bed. Telling Wyler that Fred had probably been rolled a few times, the actor suggested the sly bit. "Wyler said to try it and boom, that was it. We printed that," Andrews recalled. The coda to the intense nightmare sequence later reportedly earned plenty of guffaws from male audience members.[50]

Demanding as Wyler could be with his actors, he was equally exacting with the crew on his films. In a follow-up scene to Fred's nightmare, Peggy prepares breakfast the next morning in the Stephensons' kitchen. As Fred drinks coffee at the kitchen table, Peggy stands at the stove, making scrambled eggs. Wyler's composition of the actors in different parts of the frame allows for both a shared awkwardness and an unexpected intimacy. Without saying too much about Fred's night terror, they acknowledge that it happened, which creates a bond between them. Simultaneously, they are still strangers who know very little about each other. As Wright played the scene, she went through the motions of whisking the eggs in the frying pan. Richard DeWeese, who was recording sound, got Wyler's attention. DeWeese was picking up the scraping noise of the fork in the pan, which was competing with Wright's dialogue. Wright spoke up, saying that she thought the cooking noises added more realism to the scene, but DeWeese protested. Wyler sided with Wright. The director's consideration of details such as this "spoiled" Wright for working with less attentive filmmakers, she later recalled. "If you had a scene where you were supposed to be quiet, Willy would tell sound, 'She's going to be quiet, and you'll just have to catch it.'"[51]

Goldwyn had budgeted seventy-two days for the *Best Years* production, but by the end of May, which marked the picture's halfway point, Wyler was running several script pages behind. An agitated Goldwyn arrived on set and began giving the filmmaker advice. Wyler's response to this and other unannounced visits by Goldwyn was usually the same. He would come up with reasons to put off filming a scene, and key members of his crew, such as Toland and DeWeese, would also stall. Goldwyn would eventually leave the set, but on this day, he yelled out to Wyler as he left, "You're too many pages behind schedule!" Wyler would occasionally lash out after conflicts with the producer, as he did one morning when he returned to the set after a meeting in Goldwyn's office. "This goddammned picture. Goldwyn wants it produced by Sam Goldwyn, directed by Sam Goldwyn, acted by Sam Goldwyn, and seen by Sam Goldwyn," ranted Wyler.[52] But on the day that Goldwyn accused the filmmaker of being behind schedule, Wyler kept his cool. "Okay, Sam. How many pages?" he said quietly. "Let's just tear them up and we'll be right back on schedule!"[53]

Midway through production, however, Goldwyn and Wyler seemed to agree on one thing. Both men began to worry about the film's ending.[54] Sherwood's script united all the major characters at Homer's wedding to Wilma, but Wyler, especially, thought a scene of Fred confronting his war trauma in an abandoned B-17 bomber might bring greater closure and make a stronger impact on the audience. Goldwyn and Wyler reached out to Sherwood in New York, and the writer sent another nineteen pages containing new scenes and a revised ending. The writer was aware that the production was running behind schedule, and he cautioned Goldwyn and Wyler, "I consider it vitally important that the story must be rounded off and not ended too abruptly just because it is already over length."[55] But Wyler continued to vacillate about the film's final scene. Perhaps worried that the director might take matters into his own hands, Goldwyn fired off a memo to Wyler, reminding him of the "pledge" that Goldwyn had given to Sherwood about not making changes to the script without consulting him first: "I feel that it is distinctly unfair to him to make any changes without consultation, particularly when you know that he is willing to cooperate in every way, even today if necessity should arise, and has in fact already done so."[56]

Sherwood was willing to cooperate—up to a point. A week later, in early June, Wyler again reached out to the screenwriter. "I want to make one last effort to sell you on the idea of coming here for a few days in order that you may see the film we have shot so far," Wyler telegrammed. "I sincerely believe that you will agree that the picture creates a great amount of expectancy and that after seeing it you will have considerably less difficulty in writing something that will meet this expectancy." Sherwood had scripted the scene of Fred confronting his recurring nightmare in an abandoned B-17, and months earlier Wyler had located an airfield in Ontario, California, where hundreds of bombers sat waiting to be scrapped. But in the script, Sherwood included only the barest description of the scene, deferring to Wyler's wartime experience to make the scene come alive with authentic detail and dialogue. "Naturally I will do everything I can with the scene in the B-17 but frankly I am terribly worried that the last part of the picture may be a let-down," Wyler's telegram continued. "Sorry to sound a little desperate but perhaps we here are not completely clear on all your ideas and you know that telegrams and telephones are no substitute for talking things over."[57]

Sherwood was by then caught up in his own project, the book he had inherited after Harry Hopkins's death, which would offer one of the first intimate looks inside Roosevelt's wartime administration. Politely but firmly, Sherwood told Wyler he would not be coming to Los Angeles.

For the time being, Wyler was on his own.

CHAPTER 5

Fade on Kiss

Willy Wyler and Gregg Toland wanted the picture to have the look of an American newsreel. They wanted it to have the feel of a live newspaper article.
TERESA WRIGHT

In early March 1944, William Wyler was in Washington, DC, on a brief leave from the army air force after the successful release of *The Memphis Belle*. Dressed in his uniform, which was adorned with the gold oak leaf insignia denoting his recent promotion to the rank of major, Wyler waited in the taxi queue outside the Statler Hotel. He was behind a man in civilian clothes, and as a cab pulled up, an army officer cut the line in front of the civilian and took the taxi. The civilian, whose name was Michael Lynch, turned to Wyler and muttered something along the lines of, "That's just like those goddamned Jews." Wyler's reaction was immediate. "I'm one of those goddamned Jews," he said as he reflexively drew back his arm and punched Lynch in the face.

The incident was quickly reported to Wyler's commanding officers at army air force headquarters, and there was talk of a court-martial. Punching someone was bad enough, but the fact that Wyler had struck a civilian while wearing his uniform made it a punishable offense. "It was quite bad," Talli recalled. "I felt they might exile him to some island for the duration of the war."[1]

The military bureaucracy was predictably slow in getting a report together. On May 1, as extensive preparations were underway in southern England for Operation Overlord (D-Day), which was set to begin on June 5, Wyler received a confidential report about the incident. Official documents informed him that under Article of War 104, Wyler's conduct, which occurred "without legal provocation," was considered "unbecoming an officer and a gentleman" and therefore serious enough to be tried by court-martial. The report condemned Wyler's behavior, describing his actions as revealing "a lack of self control which is inconceivable on the part of an officer of your grade and experience." He was reminded that his behavior also reflected poorly on the military. Wyler replied immediately: "I hereby agree to accept punishment under the Article of War 104." Two weeks later, he received notice of his official punishment, which had been reduced to a reprimand. Wyler again responded quickly, alerting the army that he had received the official notice, accepted the decision, and would not appeal it.[2]

"I guess he had friends high enough in the service," said Talli years later.[3] But while Wyler's connections had saved him from serious consequences, the official reprimand went into his military file and kept him from receiving any additional promotions and medals due him by the time he left the service.

Like many of Wyler's wartime experiences, the altercation in front of the Statler Hotel inspired a scene in *Best Years*. In Sherwood's script, an incident takes place between Homer and a customer at the drugstore where Fred has reluctantly resumed his prewar job as a soda jerk. The customer, a middle-aged man, approaches the counter and orders a sandwich from Fred. While he waits, he opens a newspaper to the front page. The above-the-fold headline cautions, "Senator Warns of New War." Homer enters the drugstore and approaches the counter to chat with Fred. The customer, who is also in the frame, stares openly at Homer, who greets him good-naturedly. The man moves a couple of seats closer to Homer as they begin a conversation. "It's terrible when you have to see a guy like you sacrifice himself. And for what?" he says with disgust. Homer challenges the customer's statement, and they begin a conversation that quickly escalates. Homer defends America's involvement in the war, while the customer declares, "The Germans and the Japs had nothing against us. They just wanted to fight the Limeys and the Reds. And they would have whipped them, too, if we didn't get deceived into it by a bunch of radicals in Washington."

Wyler began shooting the soda counter scene on Monday, June 10, just a few days after his anxious cable to Sherwood about the bomber sequence. The six pages of dialogue-heavy script took three full days to film, with Wyler scheduling plenty of rehearsal time for the actors. Peggy McIntyre and Mickey Roth, two young actors playing a teenage couple sitting at the counter for part of the scene, appeared with Dana Andrews and Harold Russell in the lengthy sequence. They were joined by Ray Teal, who was cast as Mr. Mollett, the belligerent customer. Teal had been in the service during the war, and he was also a seasoned bit player.

The drugstore set included fixtures (a back bar and soda fountain) and merchandise that the studio had borrowed from the Owl Drug Company, part of the larger Rexall chain. Some of Andrews's rehearsal involved perfecting his ice-cream-scooping and sundae-making skills. In addition to pages of dialogue, the scene required Russell to spoon a rich chocolate sundae into his mouth, which he did with gusto. One of the first things that Samuel Goldwyn had said to Russell when he arrived in Hollywood was that he needed to lose weight in order to photograph well on camera. "I was constantly thinking and worrying about food," remembered Russell. "During the entire time I was in Hollywood, I don't remember enjoying a single meal."[4]

The schedule for the shooting of the drugstore altercation was the same on each of the three days. The actors began with rehearsals while Gregg Toland devised a way to block and shoot the conversations and the action. Toland instructed the camera crew to lay dolly tracks for the complicated sequence, which ends in a fistfight between Mollett and Homer. Shooting commenced after an hour or so of rehearsals, and each day concluded with rehearsals of the next day's shots.[5]

Filming began with the sequence's initial shots, in which Fred makes sundaes for the teenagers. With the exception of a take or two ruined by Mickey Roth's furious gum chewing, filming of these shots went relatively quickly.[6] Wyler took his time with some of the other shots, such as when Mollett sits at the counter and opens the mocked-up newspaper. Sherwood's script for the sequence was very pointed about the camera's picking up the paper's "screaming" headline. The final version of the script indicated the headline should read, "Crisis in Middle East—U.S. Warned International Unity Threatened by Foreign Aggression."[7] It is unclear at what point the headline changed, but by mid-June, when shooting of the sequence began, the headline had lost its international focus. Instead it referred to Washington and a "new war."

As Sarah Kozloff and others have observed, the revised newspaper headline hints at the festering political divide between the country's rabid anticommunists and the defiant liberals who opposed them. Unbeknownst to Wyler, the FBI had begun investigating him nearly a year earlier, in the fall of 1945, around the same time that the House Un-American Activities Committee (HUAC) became a standing, or permanent, committee. Its nine congressional members, first led by Edward J. Hart (D-NJ), were charged with investigating potential threats to the liberties protected by the US Constitution. Wyler's involvement with Sherwood and Goldwyn on *Best Years* was tracked via newspaper clippings, and his FBI file noted that in 1941, Wyler was on the board of the charitable organization Russian War Relief, which members of HUAC later claimed was a "satellite front of the Communist Party."[8] In the fall of 1947, Wyler helped form the Committee for the First Amendment with his friend and fellow filmmaker John Huston and the screenwriter Philip Dunne, and Myrna Loy became one of the dozens of Hollywood insiders who made up the committee.

The soda counter conversation and the subsequent fight between Homer and Mollett took the most time to rehearse, block, and shoot. The printed take of the shot at the beginning of the conversation, when Homer acknowledges Mollett with a good-natured hello, may be the most authentic moment in *Best*

Years. Homer's easygoing way with the stranger not only represents the kinds of daily interactions that the handless Russell faced in real life, but also most likely resonated with many injured or struggling vets who were regularly forced to finesse similar social situations.

Wyler took his time in filming a series of shots that included several specific lines of dialogue. In Sherwood's final draft of the script, Mollett's line "And they would have whipped them, too, if we didn't get deceived into it by a bunch of radicals in Washington" ended with "by a bunch of radicals *and Jew-lovers* in Washington."[9] It was a pointed reference to the bigotry that Wyler had witnessed two years earlier in front of the Statler Hotel, and it spoke to the larger intolerance that Wyler, Sherwood, and others felt was taking hold in postwar America. Joseph Breen had objected to the line and "demanded" it be removed from the script in April when he had previewed the screenplay. A week into production, Sherwood defended the line to Goldwyn in a letter: "Without the anti-Semitic insult, the scene is somewhat ambiguous. I feel strongly that this word should stay in." Toward the end of the letter, Sherwood added, "The vast majority of people would applaud our courage in coming right out with it." Goldwyn allowed the line to be left in the script.[10]

When it came time to shoot that exchange between Homer and Mollett, Wyler instructed Toland to film two versions, one with and one without the phrase "Jew-lovers." They shot several takes of both, and the script clerk indicated that they printed the best take that included "Jew-lovers" and put a hold on the best one without the phrase.[11] It was the latter shot, the one mentioning only the radicals in Washington, that made it into the theatrical release of *Best Years.*

In the sequence's finale, an agitated Homer follows Mollett to the cash register after Fred demands that Mollett pay his check and leave. The script describes the action: As Homer asks Mollett, "Look here, mister. What are you selling, anyway?" he is to approach the customer and get increasingly "outraged" as Mollett replies, "Again, I say, just look at the facts," and continues to insist that Homer lost his hands in a war that could have been avoided. As Mollett begins to walk away, Homer reaches out with his right hook to stop him, holding it against the customer's chest as he recounts watching hundreds of his crewmates go down with a sinking ship. Mollett is unmoved. "That's the unpleasant truth," he tells Homer, but before he can finish the rest of his sentence, Homer rips off Mollett's American-flag lapel pin and throws it to the floor. Mollett stops talking as Homer sputters, "If only I had my hands," and rears back as if to land a punch. Mollett reaches out to defend himself, grasping at Homer's hooks. Fred, who has moved into the background of the shot, is framed between the men as they struggle momentarily. In a separate cutaway shot, Fred jumps over the soda counter. He thrusts himself between the men in the next shot, telling Mollett to take his hands off Homer, who is pushed out of frame as Fred finishes the punch that Homer started. The force of it propels Mollett backward, sending him crashing through one of the drugstore's glass display cases.[12]

Sherwood was very particular in certain parts of the final script, indicating in some detail how a scene should look or how an actor should behave. In other sections he was much less specific, and the fight scene was one such instance. Sherwood left the details of the scene's action to the director, writing only, "Fred and Mollett fighting." The fight sequence involved extensive choreography, and Wyler worked closely with all three actors to block the scene during rehearsals. It was one of Russell's more challenging moments on film, since it required him to remember several lines of dialogue for each shot as well as to simulate becoming angry and to initiate a fistfight. Andrews and Teal had had enough experience with fight scenes to be able to pull off their moves in relatively few takes, and a double stood in for Teal when it came time for the actor to crash through the glass display case. The spectacular shattering of the case was made possible thanks to special-effects "glass" made out of spun sugar so delicate that it had to be packed in dry ice to keep it from melting between extensive breaks in filming.[13]

Wyler saved other onscreen confrontations for the midway point in the production, perhaps knowing that he would get more authentic performances out of his actors the longer they were in character. Although many of the scenes at Butch's bar had been shot by early June, Wyler delayed the filming of some of the key close-ups and two-shots between Fred and Al in a particularly confrontational sequence. Al, newly aware of Peggy's feelings for the married soda jerk, arranges to meet Fred in a booth at Butch's. Once there, Al gets right to the point. "Are you in love with Peggy?" he asks, and it is clear from March's delivery that Al is not happy about the potential relationship. After a moment, Fred answers yes. The conversation is terse and not especially lengthy, with relatively long pauses, and it ends with Fred offering to break things off with Peggy.

Wyler and Toland agreed that the scene's inserts should be lit and framed to enhance the tension between the characters. The tight over-the-shoulder shots were sparsely lit, with only a single light illuminating each actor's face as he spoke. With his sharp features and thin face, Fredric March looks especially dramatic and menacing. This was a far cry from the actor's demeanor off camera, when he would clown around with other members of the cast, for example, telling Russell to keep his attention-grabbing hooks out of camera range when it was March's turn to deliver his lines in their scenes together. As Fred, Andrews was appropriately wary in his close-ups opposite March, delivering his lines with a feigned offhandedness. The actor set his jaw, effectively conveying Fred's underlying anger and emotional pain. The filming of the confrontation corresponded with March's final days on the *Best Years* set, and Wyler made sure to get several takes of each shot in order to avoid having to do expensive reshoots later in the summer.

The entire sequence at Butch's showcased deep space and deep focus, the cinematographic techniques that Wyler and Toland favored. Deep space employs action in every plane of the image (fore, middle, and back), and deep focus keeps all three planes in sharp focus simultaneously. In May they had filmed the group shots, which included Butch (Carmichael) and Homer playing "Chopsticks" on the piano, a bit that had been teased throughout the film as Homer mentioned the piano lessons he was receiving from Butch. The intense, private conversation between Al and Fred was edited into the middle of the sequence, which concludes with a carefully composed shot of Al, Butch, and Homer at the piano in the foreground. In the far background, Fred stands in the bar's telephone booth, ostensibly calling Peggy to end their relationship. Writing about the scene two years later, the French film critic André Bazin praised not only the composition of the sequence but also its pacing. Recognizing Wyler's awareness of his audience, Bazin observes that the sequence's dual actions—the piano duet, a minor catharsis for the troubled and aimless Homer, and Fred's phone call to Peggy—are both necessary to "recharge the flagging attention of the audience," which might have lost interest if the camera focused exclusively on one character or the other. Bazin adds that while Orson Welles, another Toland collaborator, tended to use deep space as an "aesthetic end," Wyler made sure the technique remained "subordinate to the dramatic needs of the *mise en scène* and especially the clarity of the narrative." In that way, the audience can remain engrossed in the drama of the scene.[14]

Wyler used the technique of composing in depth to similar effect in the sequence featuring the wedding of Homer and Wilma, also filmed during the second half of production. The extended sequence became the movie's finale, but in the third week of June, Wyler was still undecided about how to end the film. He waffled between the wedding and another compelling sequence, yet to be shot, of Fred confronting his war trauma in the cockpit of a B-17 destined for the scrapheap. The filming of the wedding sequence came first, if only to take advantage of March and Loy before they wrapped their involvement with the project.

Russell didn't need to dig too deep for inspiration during the sequence: he and Rita were still newlyweds. But Russell did struggle a bit in trying to connect with his costar Cathy O'Donnell. On paper at least, the pair seemed well matched, neither one having had much acting experience. Yet O'Donnell was nearly a decade younger than the thirty-two-year-old Russell, and he felt the age difference. "She was lovely to look at, young, unspoiled," he said later, "but she was more like a bobby-soxer than an actress."[15] O'Donnell's penchant for writing poetry, some of which she gave to Goldwyn, made her an easy target for the other actors. During breaks in filming, they ribbed her good-naturedly about the hobby and her tendency to daydream. It was this quality, which she conveyed onscreen with longing looks and searching eyes, that Wyler showcased in her scenes with Russell.

One person was especially captivated by O'Donnell. Wyler's forty-five-year-old brother Robert was often on the set of Willy's films. His job description wasn't always clear, although he did some writing on *Detective Story* (1951) and *The Big Country* (1958) and served as associate producer on seven other films directed by Willy in the 1950s and 1960s. Whatever Robert's role, his on-set presence seemed to be important to his younger brother, and some have said it eased Willy's anxiety during production.[16] Robert got to know O'Donnell, who was more than twenty years his junior, on the *Best Years* set. They began a serious relationship, which was something of a surprise to Willy and Talli, given Robert's bachelor life. In 1948, while O'Donnell was still under contract to Goldwyn, she and Robert Wyler decided to wed. The producer was furious, thinking it would interfere with his plans for O'Donnell's career. The couple defied Goldwyn and eloped to Las Vegas.[17]

Wyler budgeted five days to shoot the wedding scenes, which ran eight pages in Sherwood's final draft of the screenplay. The sequence brought together most of the cast, including the child actors who played Homer's younger sister and her neighborhood playmates. Most of these youngsters had been in other movies and had more onscreen experience than Russell and O'Donnell combined. Russell couldn't stand them, referring to the children as an "insufferable mob" of "miniature monsters." He watched during rehearsals as mothers coached their children during the shots that featured them serving as attendants in the wedding, surrounding Hoagy Carmichael's Butch, who plays "The Wedding March" on the Parrishes' piano, or preceding Wilma down the stairs and into the living room. "They battled fiercely just to see which brat would have the privilege of singing out of tune and maybe getting a laugh," recalled Russell.[18]

The sequence provided closure for four of the characters, uniting Homer and Wilma in marriage and reuniting Peggy and Fred. Once again Wyler and Toland used deep space and deep focus to bring together both couples in the same master shot, the main image that establishes the action. The wide shot includes Homer, Wilma, and the minister in the foreground and to the right of the screen, with Fred, as best man, facing the couple and turned slightly away from the camera on the left side of the image. The Stephensons stand with the other wedding guests in the background of the shot, with Peggy just to the left of her parents as they all watch Homer and Wilma recite their vows. The Stephensons are framed in deep focus between Fred on one side and the bride and the groom on the other. As the couple promises lifelong fidelity, Fred turns his head to gaze at Peggy.

Teresa Wright enjoyed shooting these later sequences. The disruptions created by Andrews's drinking had stopped, and she felt more at ease in their scenes together. She had a lot of affection for Fredric March, too, who appeared with her in the sequence and was originally supposed to be in the final shot of the film with her and Andrews. "Freddie had a tremendous love of life and a tremendous honesty and authority," she said later. "We all loved and enjoyed him so much that it just embellished our scenes with him."[19]

The dramatic impact of the wedding scene works like the confrontation sequence between Al and Fred at Butch's, both heightening and diffusing the tension by incorporating two actions within the same space. In the establishing shot of the wedding, the audience's attention is directed toward Homer and Wilma as they commit to each other in front of their family and friends. The turning of Fred's head as he gazes toward Peggy distracts viewers from the bride and groom and raises the stakes in Peggy and Fred's story: will the emotion and happiness of Homer and Wilma's wedding prove strong enough to reunite Fred and Peggy?

Wyler used the sequence to showcase Wright, giving her close-ups when she returns Fred's gaze and reacts to the emotion of the wedding. Toland lit the shots beautifully, using additional lights to illuminate the tears glistening in Wright's eyes. As he had with Greer Garson's emotional final scenes in *Mrs. Miniver*, Wyler monitored the filming of these shots carefully, calling for multiple takes when Wright's eyes overflowed with too many tears.[20] Wright's wardrobe in the sequence is also effective, with the white-trimmed, scalloped neckline of her dress providing a kind of frame for her face. The wide-brimmed straw hat she wears echoes the framing effect and provides something of a symbolic halo. Given Peggy's occupation as a nurse's aide and her compassionate treatment and acceptance of the war-ravaged Fred, the symbolism seemed apt.

Wyler didn't rush Homer and Wilma's exchange of vows, and he even chose a take in which Russell stumbled over his lines, adding greater realism to that occasionally anxious part of any wedding ceremony. It was the only indication of nerves on Homer's part. Sherwood specifies in the script that Homer is "quite possibly the least visibly nervous person in the room," and in another note he indicates that Homer should steady Wilma's trembling hand before he places the wedding ring on her finger.[21]

Wyler shot many takes of the moment when Homer nudges the ring onto Wilma's finger, in part because Russell kept dropping the band as he tried to maneuver it with his hooks. Sherwood's screenplay makes much of the moment: "Everybody is watching fearful that he will drop [the ring]."[22] Another note dictates that the cinematographer "go to CLOSE SHOTS" throughout the filming of the wedding ceremony but "especially at this moment." Sherwood identifies ten characters who should be featured in these close-up shots, but during filming

Wyler cut the list to just two, instructing Toland to film a series of reaction shots of Milly (Loy) and Homer's mother (Minna Gombell), which would be cut into the wider group shots of the other guests. Sherwood's screen direction indicates these wider shots as well: "There is an almost audible sigh of relief on all sides."[23] The wedding is absent from MacKinlay Kantor's novel. Sarah Kozloff believes that Sherwood added it to the script after being inspired by the real-life wedding of Robert Langstaff, the disabled veteran who married Ruth Spaulding, a women's army corps corporal, in January 1946.[24]

Perhaps the most moving moment in the wedding sequence comes at the end, but it doesn't involve the bride and groom. As guests press toward the couple to congratulate them after their kiss, Fred goes instead to Peggy, who remains apart from the other well-wishers. Sherwood's screen direction describes Fred walking "like a somnambulist" before he takes Peggy in his arms and kisses her "fiercely." Andrews did in fact play the shot as Sherwood indicated, but other aspects of the film's final moments were changed during the last day of shooting. Sherwood's final script has Fred making a speech to Peggy after their kiss, telling her how difficult their future will be together: "You know what it'll be, don't you, Peggy? It may take us years to get anywhere. We'll have no money, no decent place to live. We'll have to work, get kicked around." Writing about the moment in her analysis of *Best Years*, Kozloff aptly describes it as a "backwards, bitter proposal."[25] Nonetheless, Peggy beams through Fred's dour speech, responding, "We'll be together," before Al breaks in with the final line of the film, teasing, "Hey, buddies—whose wedding do you think this is, anyway."[26]

This particular part of the wedding sequence was filmed over two days, June 24 and June 25, and they were the last days devoted to scene 301. The production was eight days behind schedule, but Wyler took his time. If the scene between Fred and Peggy was to be the film's final image, then it had to strike just the right emotional note for the audience. Wyler instructed the actors to perform the scene as written, but over the course of fourteen takes, he played around with the sequence, trying it with and without Peggy's line as well as Al's final joke. After some deliberation, a new scene (301A) was scripted, which omitted all dialogue but Fred's speech. Toland filmed the scene four times. On one take, Peggy's wide-brimmed hat fell off her head as she and Fred shared a final kiss. Wyler spoke to the script clerk on *Best Years*, who wrote in the notes, "PRINT . . . fade on kiss."[27] Although a decision about the film's ending wouldn't be made for another three months, Wyler had just directed the final shot of the film.

The second half of *Best Years*' production schedule featured several of the movie's most dramatic scenes, but the on-set mood remained relatively upbeat. From time to time invited guests would stop by, lightening the mood even more. At one point, General Curtis LeMay visited Goldwyn's studio. LeMay had met

Wyler overseas when the general was in charge of the Third Bombardment Division during the later part of the war. LeMay had begun his military career as a flying cadet, and in the late 1930s he was one of the pilots who flew B-17s to South America for the first time. LeMay's soft-spoken nature belied his reputation as an intense, highly skilled airman. He had ended his time in the war, in fact, by flying a B-29 Superfortress nonstop from Japan to Chicago, a trip that set an airspeed record.

Wyler appreciated LeMay's no-nonsense attitude, and when the general came through Los Angeles that summer, Willy and Talli threw a party in his honor. The Wylers invited the film's cast to attend, and on the day LeMay came to the set, he posed with the film's leads on the Goldwyn soundstage housing the set for Butch's Place. March, Wright, Loy, and Wyler squeezed in around LeMay in one of the booths. Sy Bartlett, another old friend of Wyler's, joined in the group photo. Russell and Andrews sat cross-legged on the floor in front of the booth, and Hoagy Carmichael leaned into the shot from behind. Danny Kaye, who was shooting *The Secret Life of Walter Mitty* next door for Goldwyn, scooted into frame just before the photographer clicked the shutter.

It was finally time for Wyler to shoot the sequence of Fred wandering among row upon row of abandoned Flying Fortresses. Wyler had considered the sequence for the film's finale because it provided closure for Fred's story in a way that was as hopeful as the wedding scene but less predictable as an ending. It was also the scene that Wyler had written to Sherwood about in May, asking for more details and for more suggestions about how to shoot it than were in the final version of the script. Although Sherwood had seen battle during World War I, he deferred in this instance to Wyler, who had not only flown on B-17s during his time with the Ninety-First Bomber Group but also, like Fred, experienced war trauma.

In Sherwood's April version of the screenplay, Fred climbs into the fuselage of a bomber and begins to relive the air battle that inspired the nightmare he had while staying overnight in Peggy's bedroom earlier in the film. Sherwood scripted an aural reenactment of the air battle, with Fred in conversation with his copilot, right and left waist gunners, and a ball turret gunner as they fly a bombing mission somewhere over the North Sea. Dialogue among the "characters" runs more than two pages. The tone of their conversation is casual, even good-natured and joking in parts, as the men go about their jobs. Then, as the battle heats up and the situation becomes at first serious and then dire, their frantic voices compete with the sounds of flak and machine-gun fire.

The scripted sequence reveals Sherwood's typical attention to detail, and yet the screen direction, though pointed, indicates that the scene's power will come from multiple sources. "All of this scene requires music and highly imaginative pictorial treatment," Sherwood explained within the script. And while he offered suggestions for the music (a military song in a "weird, minor key" or a repeated "theme" from earlier scenes featuring the three vets), Sherwood left the sequence mostly in Wyler's hands.[28]

The filming of the sequence was spread out among the remaining two months of production. In late June, a week or so after the wedding scene was completed, Wyler spent a couple of days on location with Andrews, Toland, and a small crew. They were about thirty-five miles from the Goldwyn Studios, in Ontario, California, where the municipal airport had served as an aircraft training and operating base for the army air corps during the war. By 1946, the airport had become a "bomber graveyard," one of five centers throughout the country (mostly in the Southwest) where military aircraft were stored, scrapped, or sold after the war. Row upon row of decommissioned B-17s, P-38s, and other aircraft ended up there, and some would later provide parts for prefabricated houses, something a character tells Fred will happen as he walks among abandoned planes while waiting for a flight out of Boone City.

The on-location filming went relatively quickly. Toland's crew tracked Andrews moving among and reacting to the abandoned aircraft, some of which had already been stripped of their propellers, engines, and other parts. The most complicated setup involved a moving crane shot of Andrews, with the camera gradually tracking from eye level up to a bird's-eye view of the entire airfield. The dynamic shot simulated Fred's perspective as he stares at the countless rows of abandoned planes, which seemed to stretch beyond the horizon.

The shots of Fred climbing inside the fuselage of one of the empty B-17s were filmed on Stage 6 and on the back lot of Goldwyn Studios. Using a B-17 nose cone and a bombardier's cabin that Goldwyn had purchased for the film from a stunt pilot named Paul Mantz, Wyler rehearsed the sequence's most dramatic moments, when Fred relives the doomed air battle from his nightmare. The set decorator Julia Heron dressed the interior of the cabin and nose cone to suggest their abandonment: the nose cone's Plexiglas was smudged with dirt and debris, and cobwebs crisscrossed the cabin's interior. Toland's team lit the sets to suggest shafts of daylight piercing through a haze of spiderwebs and dust.

Although Wyler could be exacting in the handling of his actors, he deliberately told Andrews very little about what he wanted the actor to do in the scene. When it came time to film the shots of Fred sweating through his traumatic memories, Wyler let the actor find his way through the scene. "Dana realized that his character would be the still part of this panorama," writes Andrews's biographer Carl Rollyson of the sequence, which wouldn't achieve its full power until the individual shots had been edited together and layered with sound effects during postproduction, much as Sherwood indicated in the original script.[29] Still, it was up to Andrews to convey Fred's trauma as he relives the doomed mission that killed his crew. Unlike the earlier nightmare sequence, which Andrews shared with Teresa Wright, this series of shots would rely on the actor's facial expressions rather than dialogue to communicate Fred's terror. Throughout several takes, Andrews played the scene quietly, letting the camera take in his clammy face, deadened eyes, and clenched jaw. Toland shot Andrews from the front, the camera slowly tracking in on his face. Another setup captured Andrews from behind, the camera's slow approach toward the hunched figure suggesting the menace of a horror movie. "The world comes to him, so to speak, in the crucial seconds of his crisis," Rollyson writes of Andrews's subdued portrayal, "when he seems to have nowhere to go, with no job and no beloved. He is in the graveyard of his own hopes."[30]

The sequence concludes when Karney, the salvage foreman, interrupts Fred's flashback by demanding he get out of the plane. The stocky character actor Pat Flaherty, a veteran of World War I, filmed his shots with Andrews on location at the airfield in Ontario. Toland composed the initial shot of Karney from Fred's perspective, framing the foreman within the triangular hatch of the nose cone. Flaherty's gruff delivery of the lines, "Hey bud, what are you doing up there?" and "Hey, you!" jolts Fred back to the present. Flaherty's character is all business, and it is clear from his dismissive attitude that he doesn't hold "bomber boys" like Fred in high esteem. "Reliving old memories, huh?" Karney sneers, but Fred's reply is optimistic: "Or maybe getting some of them out of my system." From Karney, Fred learns about the salvaging of aircraft parts to build new houses, and their encounter leads to a job for Fred and, more importantly, a reason to remain in Boone City.

Andrews didn't record the dialogue flashbacks for the bomber sequence until mid-August, after the conclusion of principal photography. The majority of the layered soundscape that Sherwood sketched for the scene, with atonal music playing underneath the conversation among Fred and his crew, was cut from the final film. But in late June and mid-July, when Andrews filmed the bomber boneyard sequence, Wyler intended to edit the scene as indicated in Sherwood's screenplay. Despite the more obvious catharsis provided by the film's wedding scene, Wyler was considering the bomber sequence with Andrews as a possible ending for *Best Years*. The way the sequence brought together Fred's coming to terms with his war trauma and finding work by repurposing the very machines that contributed to this trauma conveyed to Wyler a subtle sense of optimism that struck him as potentially more authentic than the wedding's characteristic jubilation.

After a one-day break for the July 4th holiday, production on *Best Years* resumed on the Goldwyn lot. The hands-on producer was now less a presence on the set because he was dividing his time between *Best Years* and *The Secret Life of Walter Mitty*, which was being shot simultaneously. The romantic comedy featured Danny Kaye in the title role as a daydreaming publisher of pulp novels who gets mixed up in a spy ring. Goldwyn had chased the multitalented performer for years, and in 1943 finally succeeded in signing him to a movie contract. It was Goldwyn's idea, in fact, to lighten Kaye's naturally dark hair to make him more photogenic after multiple screen tests led to comments about his potentially "sinister" (1940s code for "Jewish") appearance.[31]

Virginia Mayo was Kaye's costar in *Mitty*, a part she was juggling along with her role in *Best Years*. With her background in vaudeville, Mayo was comfortable playing the mysterious blond whose zany chance encounter with Walter Mitty results in a series of madcap adventures. Working with Kaye, though, was another story. Decades later, Mayo compared her costar's frenetic energy to that of Robin Williams, but she disliked Kaye's condescension. She thought he was difficult to work with, and she hadn't completely forgiven Kaye for helping send her down to the chorus on *Up in Arms* (Nugent, 1944) because he didn't think she had the comedic chops to play opposite him.[32]

For nearly eight weeks, Mayo split her days between the two films, dashing among the soundstages on the Goldwyn lot and preparing intensely at night and on her rare days off. Goldwyn was taking a chance by casting Mayo in the dramatic role of Marie, and the actress worked overtime to prove to him and to Wyler that she was up to the challenge.

Mayo shared most of her scenes with Dana Andrews, and several of the screen couple's lines were among the content flagged by Joseph Breen. Early on, Breen indicated that the character of Marie had the potential to be offensive. She and Fred had married quickly before he headed off to war, and she later took a job in a nightclub. He cautioned Goldwyn that particular attention should be paid to Mayo's wardrobe, to which Goldwyn's publicity head, Pat Duggan, responded, "The costuming of Marie will be adequate and in good taste."[33] An exchange between Fred and Marie that suggested both had been unfaithful during their separation was also problematic. "I suppose you're gonna tell me you acted like a saint with wings!" Marie says during a heated confrontation. "No, I didn't. So what?" Fred responds, to which Marie retorts, "So what! We're even." This dialogue became a source of repeated back-and-forth between Goldwyn and Breen. On June 21, more than two months into filming, Breen again highlighted the section in Sherwood's screenplay and wrote, "This must be changed." The lines were kept as is.[34]

Another of Breen's objections concerned a nightclub sequence featuring Fred and Marie on a double date with Peggy and a beau. In addition to the usual warnings about drinking and sexual innuendo, Breen's office flagged a scene in which Marie and Peggy share a conversation in the club's powder room. "Please see that the door is marked 'Ladies Lounge,'" Breen wrote of the shot that had Marie making a joke about the "Ladies" sign on the door of the restroom. "You know, I pay *no* attention to the sign," she says smirkingly to Peggy as they pass through the door. Breen's objection to the sign left Pat Duggan scratching his head. "Is there any reason why 'Ladies Lounge' must be used instead of 'Ladies'?" he wrote in reply. "The point of Marie's line is lost completely if the sign on the door is Ladies Lounge."[35] Although Breen never answered Duggan's query in writing, the sign on the door remained as it was in Sherwood's final draft.

The nightclub sequence turned out to be Mayo's greatest challenge while making *Best Years*. Three of the ensemble's actors were responsible for pages of chatty dialogue that had to be delivered while dancing on a nightclub set crowded with extras. Within the film, the scene is meant to give Peggy a glimpse into the fragile state of Fred and Marie's union. Although Peggy invited the couple to join her and her date as a way to convince herself that Fred was better off with his wife, Peggy ends the evening convinced that she needs to "break that marriage up." Midway through the evening, Marie invites Peggy to join her in the ladies' room, where she offers Peggy unsolicited advice about her hairstyle and coolly appraises her date's marriage potential. All the while, Marie and the less glamorous Peggy touch up their faces in front of a large, decorative mirror.

Wright later described the scene as "a Gregg Toland mirror shot" that was "technically . . . quite interesting."[36] Toland had become known for such shots, most notably of an elderly Charles Foster Kane (Orson Welles) walking past two mirrors on opposite sides of a long hallway in order to create a "hall of mirrors" visual effect in *Citizen Kane*. At first glance, the stylized powder-room shot seemed to violate Wyler's authentic vision for *Best Years*. And Toland worried about the shot as they were setting it up, a process that took nearly two hours. "I thought we might be getting arty and trying to prove how damn clever we were instead of playing a scene," the cinematographer later confided to Lester Koenig, the film's associate producer.[37]

Perry Ferguson and George Jenkins worked with the rest of the small art department to transform Goldwyn's Studio 4 into a popular nightclub of the day. Unlike most of the film's sets, the nightclub did not have a muslin ceiling, which left room for Toland's camera to rise and dip without restriction during the crowded dance-floor sequences. Filming began in early August and ran for a couple of days. Shooting had to be interrupted fairly often to accommodate the changes in lighting for different segments of the sequence. Mayo continued to rehearse during breaks, and she was especially anxious about the powder-room sequence with Wright, an accomplished dramatic actress. When Wyler called them to the set, they took their seats in front of the large mirror. Louise Franklin, an African American actress who had danced and sung in several films in the 1930s and 1940s, played the role of the ladies' room attendant. Although Wyler had had to abandon the documentary *The Negro Soldier* during the war, he remained committed to making the most of opportunities in his films to reflect on race relations in the immediate postwar era. In this sequence, viewers learn even more about Peggy and Marie by the way they acknowledge (or ignore) Franklin's presence.

Mayo composed herself before the first take, adjusting her satin evening gown as she ran her lines silently. As she tilted her head to adjust her earrings, she caught a glimpse of movement in the rafters above the set. There, high above the soundstage, perched Danny Kaye. The performer had sneaked over from the *Mitty* set and was there to tease Mayo, who he knew was anxious about her scene with Wright. But despite Kaye's pulling faces at her and occasional calls of "Cut" from Wyler when their dialogue overlapped, Mayo and Wright had relatively little trouble performing the scene. "I worked very hard on the timing," Mayo recalled. "I had to apply lipstick and cosmetics in between bits of dialogue."[38] Wright had fewer lines than Mayo, but her reactions to Marie's nonstop chatter, particularly the commentary about Fred's job prospects and marriage in general, were crucial. As Sarah Kozloff observes, composing the scene in front of a large mirror was a way to capture both women simultaneously without the distraction of cutting back and forth.[39] It is another example of what André Bazin describes as Wyler's "democratic" style of filmmaking, allowing viewers to edit a deeply composed shot themselves and form their own opinions about the characters without the camera directing them where to look.

After nine takes, Wyler felt he had what he needed. Years later, Wright reminisced about shooting the powder-room scene, saying, "It was just fun watching Virginia because she's extremely good in that scene. It was a wonderful chance for her to show what really made [Marie] tick."[40] And although Toland had worried about the potential artiness of the mirror shot, he decided otherwise after watching a rough cut of the sequence. "Willy was right," he later said. "It worked for us."[41]

Harold Russell's last big scene in *Best Years* was filmed over several days in mid-July. He shared the scene, which takes place in a kitchen, with Cathy O'Donnell, and it appears toward the end of the movie, immediately following the scene at the soda counter with the belligerent customer. The kitchen sequence begins at night, with Homer dressed in a robe and pajamas and rummaging in the refrigerator for a late-night snack. Suddenly Wilma is at the back door, and he lets her in. She tells him that her parents are sending her away, and she makes one final attempt to convince Homer that she loves him. He takes her upstairs to his room, wanting to demonstrate for her exactly what their nighttime routine will be should they marry.

The wedding scene, which the actors had filmed the previous month, may have offered a satisfying resolution to the veterans' stories, but the kitchen sequence is the film's emotional core. It answers the deeper question that had plagued disabled veterans like Wyler and Russell: am I still desirable? Sherwood scripted the scene carefully, including very specific screen directions about the characters' expressions and interior states as well as indications for the lighting and set design.

One of the film's most important sequences, it featured the production's least experienced actors. Wyler channeled any anxiety he might have been feeling into rehearsals with Russell and O'Donnell. Despite the film now being ten days behind schedule, Wyler worked with the two actors for nearly an hour and a half on the first day, running through lines and the various bits of business that had to occur simultaneously. Russell's biggest challenge was not the juggling of lines and action, however. For dramatic effect, Homer's limitations in using and removing his hooks, as shown in the scene, were more extensive than they were in Russell's real life. Unlike the character, for instance, Russell did not need assistance to remove the harness that secured his prostheses to his elbows. Having to act as if he couldn't do certain things was difficult for Russell, if only because he had spent so much time relearning basic skills like opening a drawer or pouring himself a drink. It was also challenging to try to accomplish these tasks differently from how he had taught himself.[42]

In one of the sequence's first shots, Homer opens the refrigerator door, picks up a bottle of milk, closes the door, and removes the milk bottle's lid. Russell struggled to perform the scene to Wyler's exacting specifications, repeating the action over the course of nine takes. The holdup with the shot was less about Russell's inability to remove the bottle's lid than about performing the task the way Wyler thought it should be done for the camera. They shared a similar experience during an earlier scene that took place in a woodshed behind the Parrish house. "I was going to get hold of the door handle to open the door [and] I didn't do it the way he wanted," Russell explained to Wyler's biographer. They retook the shot multiple times, trying different ways of turning the doorknob. Finally, the director laughed and said to Russell, "Imagine me telling a guy who has a pair of hooks how to open a doorknob with a hook."[43]

Sherwood's screen direction called for strong emotion from both Homer and Wilma throughout the sequence, which begins in the Parrish kitchen and ends with Wilma tucking Homer into bed in his room on the second floor. The script indicates that Homer is by turns embarrassed to be seen in his pajamas and dreading a confrontation with Wilma: "He knows that she is going to get to subjects personal to them both—that the scene which he had tried to dodge is coming up anyway." Sherwood was also specific about Homer's response to Wilma after she tells him that she is going away. His lines—about wanting her not to be tied down, to be free—needed to be said as if "he has to tear the words out of his soul" as sweat beads across his forehead.[44]

For her part, O'Donnell needed to convey a mix of longing and fear, particularly once Homer invites Wilma to follow him upstairs. "She is terribly scared, but she is fighting with everything she's got to reveal no trace of it," wrote Sherwood. Once in the bedroom, and as Homer begins to walk her through his bedtime routine, Sherwood's screen directions indicate a shift in Wilma's demeanor: "As he talks, Wilma listens with absorbed interest. Her fear evaporates in the face of Homer's courage."[45]

This particular sequence is one of the few places in the screenplay that includes specific directions about the lighting for the scene. Sherwood indicated that light should come into the room as if from a street lamp and that it should fall across Homer's face as he settles himself in bed. The sequence as a whole involved complex lighting setups to capture the mix of moods. The scene begins with limited lighting to simulate a dimly lit kitchen at night and then shifts to a high-contrast mix of light and shadow as the couple ascends the staircase to Homer's bedroom. This highly dramatic style of lighting was more commonly associated with films noir and horror movies of the period. An interesting stylistic choice for such an intimate scene, it seems to acknowledge the complicated feelings of both characters in such a delicate situation. The lighting scheme shifts again once Homer and Wilma enter his bedroom. The use of light and shadows underscores Wilma's fear and Homer's vulnerability at the beginning of the bedroom scene before shifting back to a less dramatic mood as Homer goes to sleep after Wilma departs.[46]

Wyler was patient with Russell and O'Donnell throughout the filming of the sequence, aware that he was asking a lot of the most inexperienced actors in the *Best Years* ensemble. While O'Donnell struggled to convey a certain amount of impatience with Homer during the kitchen conversation, Russell downplayed his emotions too much in an effort to express Homer's reticence and vulnerability. "Not acting," scribbled the script clerk on take after take. The sequence ends with the couple's kiss, a chaste but tender moment shared after Wilma buttons Homer's pajama top and straightens the bedspread after he is tucked in for the night.

That kiss had been flagged by the Breen Office on the censors' first pass through the screenplay. In Sherwood's original shooting script, the scene ended with a fade-out as Wilma leans over Homer, who is already in bed, and kisses him goodnight. This was unacceptable as written, the fade-out hinting at the possibility that sex would follow. "Before the fade-out . . . it should be clearly indicated that Wilma is about to leave the room," Breen wrote.[47] Shooting the scene required multiple takes to capture a kiss that might be acceptable to the censors. The first four attempts were "too l-o-n-g," according to notes made by the script clerk. Finally, on the fifth take, the actors delivered.[48]

As for where to place the fade-out, Wyler didn't have to worry about that until he and the longtime Goldwyn editor Daniel Mandell began working through the footage. Principal photography on *Best Years* wound down as the summer of 1946 came to an end. Most of the film's footage had been completed by the second week in August, except for a handful of retakes such as close-ups of Fred in the bomber graveyard sequence. The film's two assistant directors, Bert Chervin and Joe Boyle, handled many of these assignments as Wyler moved into postproduction. Pickup shots for background scenes of street action and for exterior shots of locations such as the Parrish home, an actual residence at 1125 West 20th Street in Los Angeles, were also completed in mid-August.[49]

As the *Best Years* cast and crew worked on the film's final few scenes that summer, they may have been aware of a new release from RKO making its way into theaters. Certainly, Goldwyn paid attention to *Till the End of Time*, another drama about homecoming, which beat *Best Years* to the screen by four months. Coincidentally, *End of Time* was adapted from *They Dream of Home*, a 1944 novel written by Teresa Wright's husband, Niven Busch.

End of Time was produced by Dore Schary, who had recently become production chief at RKO, the same studio poised to distribute *Best Years*. Directed by Edward Dmytryk, *End of Time* focuses on three marines returning from the war and features a trio of what were then young up-and-coming actors: Guy Madison, Robert Mitchum, and Bill Williams. Dorothy McGuire plays Patricia, a war widow and Madison's love interest. In contrast to the story in *Best Years*, the film's veterans are friends at the start, and all served in the same branch of the military. And while Williams plays a former boxer who returns from the war with missing limbs, like Homer in *Best Years*, in real life Williams was not disabled.

Each of the men in *End of Time* struggles with reintegration in different ways. The good-looking Madison, who had little acting experience but plays the story's main character, Cliff, is adrift and feels misunderstood at home. When he tells his mother, "I've got so much to talk about I don't know where to begin," she brushes him off, not unlike some of the supporting characters in *Best Years*, saying, "Don't talk about it, Cliff. I know you don't want to talk about it." Mitchum's William Tabeshaw returns home seemingly okay but with an injury that required him to have a metal plate implanted in his head. Williams's Perry Kincheloe struggles the most visibly, feeling bereft after the loss of his legs leaves him unable to resume his boxing career.

While *End of Time* has its flaws, its inclusion of Pat, a war widow, as Cliff's romantic interest gives the film some unexpected depth. Her character is showcased in an especially moving sequence in which Pat and Cliff, on a date at a local ice rink, come upon an African American serviceman in distress. Shaking from nerves, the veteran tells the couple that he is on a three-week furlough from a nearby hospital and "afraid to go home," a scene reminiscent of Harold Russell's real-life experience while on a break from Walter Reed. Pat gives the serviceman a pep talk, encouraging him to return to his family and telling him not to be ashamed of his war-related tics, saying, "Let them look."

Two other movies released around the same time also tackled postwar trauma, but in very different genres. Paramount's *The Blue Dahlia* (Marshall, 1946) features Alan Ladd as a returning bomber pilot who finds his wife (Veronica Lake) in the arms of another man. When Joyce (Lake) turns up dead, Johnny (Ladd) is a suspect. With its gritty subject matter and dark story line, scripted by Raymond Chandler, *Dahlia* offers a classic example of film noir, a genre that began to take hold in Hollywood as the war ended. While Johnny's lingering war trauma is only hinted at, more is made of that of his friend Buzz (William Bendix), a veteran whose violent outbursts are linked to combat. In early drafts of Chandler's script, Buzz was Joyce's killer, but the navy objected and the script was rewritten.[50]

MGM featured two of its top stars (human and canine) in *Courage of Lassie* (Wilcox, 1946), a family drama about a dog—played by Lassie but called Bill in the movie—pushed into wartime service on the front lines. A young Elizabeth Taylor is Kathie, who loses Bill after he is hurt in an accident (unbeknownst to her), taken to a pet hospital, and then sent to a military training center. Bill goes into battle overseas, and his time on K-9 duty takes its toll: he turns vicious and becomes a killer. A traumatized Bill escapes while returning home from the front. He eventually reunites with Kathie, who must fight to clear Bill's name so that he can be rehabilitated.

Of these three, *End of Time* received the most consistently positive reviews and did the best at the box office, earning RKO just under half a million dollars.[51] At the very least, the success of these films signaled that audiences were ready for stories about characters dealing with postwar trauma. Only time would tell whether these same viewers would be willing to pay higher ticket prices to watch *Best Years*.

CHAPTER 6

Pure Emotional Dynamite

You've captured what the screen needs so badly, reality. Give the customers everyday life and they'll eat it up.
THEATER MANAGER TO SAMUEL GOLDWYN

While William Wyler was overseeing the process of assembling a rough cut of *The Best Years of Our Lives*, Sam Goldwyn read a recent magazine article about veteran instability. It was written by Lyle M. Spencer, a former army officer who had served overseas in the information and education division. Spencer argued that the idea that most veterans were psychologically unstable had been "greatly exaggerated." The problem, he proposed, was a lack of knowledge, a "public misunderstanding" about veterans in general. Once this was rectified, by spotlighting those veterans who were doing well (i.e., most of those who served), the misunderstanding would be "overcome."[1]

Was Goldwyn having doubts about the film? Robert Sherwood had given voice to similar concerns a year earlier, when Goldwyn first reached out about the project then called *Glory for Me*. Sherwood was hesitant to commit himself to a film that might only add to the public perception of veterans as unstable and ill suited to postwar life. Wyler, himself a disabled veteran struggling to adjust, helped convince Sherwood that the film could do just the opposite by telling the story of each veteran's challenging readjustment with candor and compassion.

In the spring of 1946, as Wyler began principal photography on *Best Years*, his friend John Huston was immersed in a project focused on "psychoneurotic" veterans. During the war, Lieutenant Huston had made documentaries for the Signal Corps, and his last assignment focused on the treatment of veterans at Mason General Hospital on Long Island. By early 1946, Huston, like Wyler, had moved back into feature filmmaking and was prepping *The Treasure of the Sierra Madre*, a gritty western noir featuring Humphrey Bogart alongside

Huston's father, Walter. He was also trying to secure a general release for the documentary he had made a year earlier at Mason General, which he was calling *Let There Be Light*. Organizers of a documentary film festival at the Museum of Modern Art (MoMA) in New York had chosen *Light* as one of the festival's highlights, and Huston was in talks with Arthur L. Mayer, an independent distributor, about releasing the film to a general audience.

Mayer and his partner Joseph Burstyn had begun distributing foreign films, including *Open City* (Rossellini, 1946) and *Paisan* (Rossellini, 1946), shortly after the end of the war. *Light*'s straightforward, black-and-white images and the sensitive treatment of its subjects, veterans dealing with "acute" cases of war trauma such as "battle neurosis," were in line with the kind of films that Mayer and Burstyn wanted to release.

Huston was allowed fairly unrestricted access to the veterans undergoing treatment, and his cameras captured a range of men being treated with hypnosis, participating in occupational therapy, and speaking one-on-one with psychiatrists. "The guns are quiet now. The papers of peace have been signed. . . . In faraway places, men dreamed of this moment. But for some men, the moment is very different from the dream," intones Walter Huston over images of men on stretchers being carried off ships. "Others show no outward signs, yet they too are wounded."[2]

Light is a compelling and poignant document of the eight- to ten-week treatment offered at the army hospital in 1945. The vulnerable men who agreed to appear in front of Huston's cameras demonstrate a remarkable inner strength and self-awareness in working through their psychological issues. But as the army repeatedly blocked Huston's attempts to release the film, the director began to suspect that the portrayal was too revealing, too contradictory, in his words, of the military's "'warrior' myth, which said that our American soldiers went to war and came back all the stronger for the experience. . . . They might die, or they might be wounded, but their spirit remained unbroken."[3] In April 1946, just as *Best Years* began filming, Huston planned to show the film to a select group of friends and film critics in advance of MoMA's documentary film festival. He arranged a private screening at the museum, but several hours before the event, military police seized the print.[4]

In 1945, when Huston was beginning to plan for *Light*'s potential distribution, army brass told him that the signed releases he had obtained from veterans in the film were not valid in peacetime. As the military continued to thwart his efforts to release *Light*, Huston came to the conclusion that they wanted to suppress the film. A few contemporary historians who have delved deeper into the situation suggest, among other possibilities, that one reason for the military's reluctance might have been because *Light* shows African American and white soldiers receiving treatment together. This minimal move toward racial integration reportedly irritated higher-ups, who seemed proud of the army's segregated military.[5] One psychiatrist working at the hospital while Huston was filming maintained that the filmmaker wanted to portray the soldiers as "weak-willed" for the purposes of his film, and that the military "suppressed" the film because of this slant.[6] Others have pointed to the film's focus on a single method of treatment—hypnosis via an injection of sodium amytal, which Wyler himself received (with disastrous results). By 1946 this treatment, as well as the practice of sending veterans to a military hospital such as Mason General, situated in an isolated location away from patients' loved ones, had proved less effective than other methods of rehabilitation.[7]

Whatever the reason for the army's decision, it was final. In the summer of 1946, Mayer threw up his hands over the saga, telling a dejected Huston, "I am beaten." More than three decades passed before *Let There Be Light* was allowed to be screened publicly; it was shown at the Cannes Film Festival in 1981.[8]

Wyler almost certainly knew about his close friend's battles over *Let There Be Light*. In fact, Wyler was dealing with similar distribution difficulties regarding *Thunderbolt*, his final wartime documentary. In July, around the time when Mayer was informing Huston that he was unwilling to continue battling the army over *Light*, a brief news item ran in *Variety*. "Efforts to sell William Wyler's THUNDERBOLT have failed," wrote Florence S. Lowe. "Film is said to be a beauty, but too long and not now timely."[9]

By the end of August, when *Best Years*' cast and most of its crew had moved on to their next projects, Wyler and his longtime editor, Daniel Mandell, began working through the rough cut that Mandell had put together during principal photography. *Best Years* was Wyler and Mandell's seventh film together, but it was their first since Wyler returned from the war. The director and the editor had met at Universal when Mandell was assigned to work with Wyler on *Counsellor at Law* in the early 1930s, and when Wyler did *These Three* for Goldwyn in 1935, he recommended that the producer hire Mandell.

Short and wiry, Mandell often credited his earlier career as a teenage acrobat for the subtle sense of timing that came to define his editing style. Having been a performer, he said, gave him an understanding of how audiences reacted to things, and he seemed able to anticipate those reactions in the editing room.[10] He and Wyler shared a respect for the audience. Despite their successful collaborations, Mandell considered Wyler one of the more challenging filmmakers to work with. "It's more difficult to cut a film for Wyler," Mandell later explained. "He would print three takes and in many cases he'd want you to use a piece of each take, and then soundtracks from something else in another take; and sometimes it wasn't easy to get from one take to the other without making an obvious cut."[11]

Over the years, the editor came to admire Wyler's attention to detail. "He's a good director because he points out things," said Mandell. "All those little things make the difference between a good picture and a great picture." Mandell's editing on Wyler's *The Little Foxes* earned him his first Academy Award nomination, but his favorite Wyler project was *Wuthering Heights* (1939). Mandell liked to tell the story of how Wyler's slight change to a line reading made a difference in how the audience felt about Isabella, played by Geraldine Fitzgerald. The line, which referred to Merle Oberon's willful main character, was written, "If Cathy dies, I might begin to live." Fitzgerald first read the line as, "If *Cathy* dies, I might begin to *live*," but Wyler suggested she shift the emphasis on subsequent takes to draw more attention to her own character. The line became, "If Cathy dies, *I* might begin to live."[12]

Although Gregg Toland stayed out of the editing room, he, Wyler, and Mandell had worked closely during production, sharing ideas and conferring about the rough assembly that Mandell put together during principal photography. By the end of production, in August, Wyler had shot just under 350,000 feet of film negative. Every few weeks or so at the end of a shooting day, he and Mandell would gather to watch the footage that the editor had cut together. Sometime in late July or early August, Goldwyn had asked Robert Sherwood to fly out from New York to see the first cut while the actors were still available for retakes. It wasn't typical for a Hollywood producer to invite a screenwriter to weigh in on the rough cut of a film, but Goldwyn wasn't a typical producer. He had tremendous respect for Sherwood and stayed true to his promise that nothing would be changed in the final version of the *Best Years* screenplay without the writer's approval. Sherwood liked what he saw and returned home, content to let Wyler and Goldwyn sort out any remaining decisions.[13]

The rough cut ran just under three hours. Wyler and Mandell had sifted through the multiple takes of every shot and pared the cut to approximately 15,500 feet of film. Although Sherwood was happy with this version, Wyler continued to tinker with the editing. Goldwyn was still overseeing both *Best Years* and *The Secret Life of Walter Mitty*, which generally kept him out of the editing room, much to Mandell's relief. Goldwyn could be impatient and excitable, which often led to miscommunication. "He'd actually tell you one thing thinking that he was telling you something else. You almost had to carry a crystal ball with you to know what he meant," said Mandell years later.[14]

The most pressing problem during *Best Years*' editing phase had to do with the narrative's continuity. Wyler wanted to make sure that each couple's story stayed "alive" within the larger narrative, which required more intercutting among the sequences than was in Sherwood's original script.[15] In the end, Goldwyn agreed to the changes. Wyler also spent extra time on the editing of a scene between Homer and Wilma in the Parrish woodshed. The sequence involves Homer shooting a rifle for target practice in the woodshed behind the Parrish home. Wilma arrives and tries to engage him in a conversation about their relationship.

When reviewing those takes in the editing room during production in July, Wyler wasn't satisfied with what he saw. He spent an additional day reshooting the scene with Russell and O'Donnell. Back in the editing room, Wyler turned to Lester Koenig, whom he had worked with on *The Memphis Belle* and *Thunderbolt*. Koenig had become such a trusted colleague during the war that Wyler had hired him as his assistant director on *Best Years*. "I think we got the wrong take. She's a little too possessive in this take. Don't you think so?" Wyler said of O'Donnell in the scene. Koenig agreed. Wyler's solution was to print all the takes of O'Donnell reacting to Russell and then decide whether one of the alternates was better than the take that Mandell had included in the rough cut. In the end, said Mandell, Wyler chose "the very first take that was shot on the first day" of filming for that particular sequence.[16]

Wyler was a stickler for getting the "right" shot, even if it meant reshooting a scene. But while working with Mandell on the scene in which Fred first visits the drugstore where he worked before the war, Wyler realized that the best take of Andrews drew attention to someone else, too. During production, Wyler had decided that seven-year-old Cathy Wyler and four-year-old Judy Wyler could appear in the film as extras in this scene. Wyler's direction for his daughters was clear: pretend to be looking at the prop candy on the drugstore shelves and keep your backs to the camera, which would focus on Andrews as he walked by the girls. In the editing room, Wyler decided that the best take of Andrews included a shot of Cathy facing the camera. "We were told by my father to be looking at a candy display, but I had this big crush on Dana Andrews," Catherine Wyler recalled later. "If you know exactly where to look, you'll see this little girl with her mouth wide open and watching Dana Andrews as he walks by."[17] Wyler himself appears to be in the background too, trying to distract Judy.

In September, the rough cut was ready to be scored. Goldwyn had approached Bernard Herrmann, who had written the scores for Orson Welles's *Citizen Kane* (1941) and *The Magnificent Ambersons* (1942). While today Herrmann may be best known for his later collaboration with Alfred Hitchcock on the effectively dissonant score for *Psycho* (1961), Herrmann's work in the 1940s was innovative but still symphonically oriented, a style that Goldwyn envisioned for *Best Years*. But Herrmann was tied up in New York for the fall. Alfred Newman, Goldwyn's former music director, then suggested Hugo Friedhofer, who had done the score for Goldwyn's *The Adventures of Marco Polo* several years earlier. Trained as a cellist, Friedhofer had begun his career in the 1920s as a member of orchestras that accompanied silent films playing at movie theaters around San Francisco. By the end of the decade, as movies began to "talk," Friedhofer pivoted into composing and arranging. In the summer of 1929, Friedhofer moved his young family to Los Angeles, where he began to score movies for Fox and later for Warner Bros.[18]

Despite being American born, Friedhofer spoke German, as did Wyler. They also shared an appreciation for chamber music, even though Wyler didn't really listen anymore because of his hearing loss. The curmudgeonly Friedhofer and the more gregarious Wyler discussed possibilities for *Best Years*' score in detail before Friedhofer set to work on it in September. They agreed that its melody should make use of folk themes, and its sound should conjure feelings of Americana similar to the music of Aaron Copland. For *Best Years*, Friedhofer took inspiration from Copland's spare aesthetic. "The influence was largely inspiring in my weeding out the run-of-the-mill Hollywood schmaltz," said Friedhofer, who steered clear of the kind of "mood music" created by "harp glissandos, harmonicas, celesta," and other "impressionistic" sounds often associated with sweeping Hollywood scores of the time.[19]

Friedhofer worked on the score into October. Midway through the process, he, Wyler, and Emil Newman, who was conducting the score for *Best Years*, had dinner together. Taking a break from the days' work, they had food brought into one of the dressing rooms in the Writers' Building on the Goldwyn lot. Seemingly out of the blue, Wyler turned to Friedhofer and told him he thought the music he had composed was "all wrong." Wyler continued, "I think we have put music in all the places that don't need music, and we have left music out of all the places we do need music." Friedhofer counted to ten before he said anything. Then he reminded Wyler how much planning they had done and how thoroughly they had discussed the score's American themes and folk influences. Thinking he was sealing the deal, Friedhofer "got real classical" on Wyler, saying, "Remember what Rimsky-Korsakov said to Stravinsky in relation to the music of Debussy. He said, 'You know, it's very dangerous to listen to that kind of music because you might wind up liking it.'"[20]

Wyler continued to dislike the score. The director's hearing loss made listening to certain sounds almost painful and might have been to blame for his dissatisfaction with the soundtrack. Wyler's disability particularly affected his hearing of lower frequencies like those in instrumental compositions. "He said that it sounded like it was all a muddle," recalled his daughter Catherine.[21] It would take time—and the recognition of the Academy of Motion Picture Arts and Sciences, as well as praise from a fellow veteran—for Wyler to finally appreciate Friedhofer's score.

On October 17 an unsuspecting audience was treated to a sneak preview of *Best Years* at the United Artists Theatre in downtown Long Beach. Wyler and Mandell were there, along with Sam and Frances Goldwyn and a team of people from the studio. The group was most concerned about the film's length.

With a running time of more than two and a half hours, *Best Years* was nearly twice as long as the average feature film in 1946. The audience stayed with the picture, though, and their applause could be heard in the lobby after the final scene of Fred and Peggy's kiss. Wyler, Goldwyn, and the others gathered outside the theater while waiting for the audience to complete their feedback cards. Of the 314 cards returned, more than 200 ranked the picture as "excellent," "very good," "wonderful," and "best ever." George Gallup's Audience Research Institute (ARI) provided Goldwyn with more detailed information.

By 1946, Gallup had become a household name, having introduced the idea of polling citizens during the 1936 presidential election. In the 1940s he created the ARI and struck an exclusive deal with RKO, the distributor of *Best Years*, to determine filmgoers' likes and dislikes. Gallup's results for *Best Years* revealed the preview audience's favorite and least favorite scenes and cast members. Surprisingly, none of the viewers commented on the fact that Al and Milly's son Rob, played by a newcomer named Michael Hall, leaves for school the day after Al's homecoming and effectively disappears from the movie, a narrative hole that never seemed to bother Sherwood or Wyler.[22]

Gallup provided a highly technical, eight-page "Preview Profile Chart" mapping out viewers' interest levels for each of the film's major scenes. Dana Andrews, who at the time had the "highest marquee value," was an audience favorite, as was Teresa Wright. Hoagy Carmichael and Virginia Mayo tied for least favorite. The initial homecoming scenes struck a chord with the audience, and while they also found the group scenes at Butch's Place entertaining, scenes of drinking and drunkenness were considered less appealing.[23]

The ARI concluded its report with the audience's reaction to the length of the screening. "In view of the unusually long running time of *The Best Years of Our Lives*, it might be expected that a number of people would think that it dragged," an ARI executive wrote to Goldwyn. "When queried after the picture, however, two-thirds of those seeing it stated no part of it dragged."[24]

In "How Long Should a Movie Be?," published a year earlier in the *New York Times Magazine*, the film critic and screenwriter Frank Nugent wrote about a trend toward longer running times in Hollywood. In 1944, wrote Nugent, twenty-three films were longer than two hours, and four clocked in at more than two and a half hours. That year also registered the highest box-office total in fifteen years, which was "more than sufficient to overcome the loss of [revenue from] four million men now seeing their movies overseas." Nugent made note of successful longer-than-average films such as *The Birth of a Nation* (1915) and *Gone with the Wind* (1939), whose screenings were elevated to "events" in part because of the higher admission prices that were charged (which in turn contributed to their higher box-office earnings). Goldwyn planned to adopt a similar pricing strategy for *Best Years*. Twentieth Century–Fox's Darryl Zanuck, however, disputed Nugent's theory: "There is no such thing as a trend toward longer pictures. There definitely is a trend toward bigger productions." He was referring not only to the type of films being made but also to the postwar increase in production costs for lumber and other construction materials. But perhaps the anecdote that the producer David O. Selznick shared with Nugent answered the film critic's question best. Selznick had recently released *Since You Went Away* (Cromwell, 1944), which runs 171 minutes. Selznick told Nugent that when he was producing *David Copperfield* (dir. George Cukor) for MGM in 1935, he queried the studio's president, Nicholas Schenck, about the length the film should be. "What do you mean, how long can you make *David Copperfield*?" Schenck reportedly replied. "How long is it good?"[25] (The film eventually came in at around 130 minutes.)

Riding high after *Best Years'* first preview, Goldwyn prepared to host several private screenings for industry friends and press. He was also putting the final touches on the film's official opening, planned for the following January at the Pantages Theatre, an RKO movie palace on the corner of Hollywood and Vine with red velvet seats and ornate, art deco fixtures. Wyler was likewise buoyed by the well-received Long Beach preview, and he met with Goldwyn to suggest they move up *Best Years'* release so that it could qualify for the 1946 Academy Award nominations. To do so, they would have to screen the film in New York and Los Angeles before the end of the year.

Although the director and producer were no longer butting heads on the film set, they were at odds over the film's authorial credit and publicity. For his last film with Goldwyn, Wyler expected to receive the screen credit "A William Wyler Production" and to have his name featured prominently in all advertising. Wyler considered *Best Years* his most personal film to date and would later admit that he identified with Fredric March's Al: "I wasn't a kid anymore, had no problem of getting a job, but did have a problem re-adjusting to civilian life."[26] Goldwyn had provided, within the film's publicity materials, a hierarchy of whom to promote. In descending order, the list was himself, Sherwood, Wyler, and the stars. As Goldwyn told an interviewer years later, the films he made with Wyler were Samuel Goldwyn productions. Wyler had simply directed them for him. In late October, Wyler went as far as to gripe about the situation to the reporter Sheila Graham, who mentioned his frustration in her syndicated column, "Hollywood Chatter."[27]

Goldwyn was not swayed by Wyler's rather public attempt to shame the producer into sharing screen credit for *Best Years*. After all, Goldwyn had agreed to have Wyler's name appear last in the film's opening credits. But Goldwyn did trust the filmmaker's instincts about the movie. He agreed that if they waited to open the film until January 1947, it risked being forgotten by the time year-end awards were handed out. Goldwyn arranged to fly to New York with Frances and a print of the film, which he ran for a real estate investor named Robert Dowling, who owned the first-run Astor Theatre in Times Square. Goldwyn had staged an invitation-only premiere at the Astor in 1937 for *The Hurricane*, directed by John Ford. *Gone with the Wind* had made its New York City premiere there two years after that, and Alfred Hitchcock had opened *Spellbound* at the Astor in 1945. Dowling was impressed enough by *Best Years* not only to book it for the premiere but also to give Goldwyn what for him was an unprecedented deal: 40 percent of the film's ticket sales during its initial run there.[28] *Best Years'* premiere was set for the evening of Thursday, November 21, on Thanksgiving. Its Los Angeles premiere, at the Beverly Theater on Christmas night, would be equally festive.

Goldwyn spent the month between the Long Beach preview and the New York premiere overseeing more test screenings. These were invitation-only events, but Goldwyn still solicited feedback from his guests, who received elegant ecru reply cards at the end of each screening. One side was stamped and addressed to Samuel Goldwyn at the studio, and the other side asked two questions: "How did you like *The Best Years of Our Lives*?" and "Which individual players did you enjoy the most?"[29] Guests who saw the film at Goldwyn Studios included *Glory for Me*'s author, MacKinlay Kantor, as well as his wife and the columnist Hedda Hopper. Kantor praised the film, telling the *New York Post* that he had "no reservations" about the movie. "I would have given the rights free just for the satisfaction of having such a picture made from my work—any novelist would," said Kantor, and he continued to promote the picture in print and on the radio.[30] Hedda Hopper went a step further, citing *Best Years* as her choice for the Best Picture Academy Award. "It is democracy at work," Hopper wrote in a November column that ran in advance of the film's East Coast opening. "Harold Russell who uses hooks for hands is outstanding."[31]

Russell, however, would not be at the film's New York premiere, nor was he scheduled to fly out for the Christmas opening in Los Angeles. Keeping Russell and Cathy O'Donnell under wraps before the film's wide release in early 1947 was all part of Goldwyn's extensive publicity campaign for *Best Years*. Every manager of a theater scheduled to screen the film after its Astor premiere received a pamphlet entitled "Circular on Procedure," which spelled out exactly how to promote the film, including the directive that Russell and O'Donnell should be promoted only after the film opens "and not before": "After the picture has been seen, publicity on Harold Russell and Cathy O'Donnell has a new meaning."[32] Pat Duggan, Bill Hebert, Lynn Farnol, and other members of Goldwyn's executive team had been working behind the scenes on the film's promotion since the end of principal photography. It was Goldwyn's custom to start selling a film as soon as production ended, and he would often ask Daniel Mandell to cut together a "sizzle reel" of the film's best scenes to show to exhibitors.

In the case of *Best Years*, Goldwyn focused a good portion of the production's $500,000-plus publicity budget on an elaborate print campaign handled by the advertising firm Foote, Cone and Belding. The campaign got off to a rocky start, however, with an advertisement invoking a Bible verse meant to remind audiences that a Samuel Goldwyn picture always started with a great screenplay adapted from a prestigious source. The two-page spread, which ran in the October 21 issue of *Life* magazine and the October 28 issue of *Time*, featured an illustration of March and Loy alongside other stills from the film. Entitled "Living and Loving," the extensive copy opened with the phrase, "In the beginning was the word." The ad mistakenly attributed the verse to Genesis instead of the Gospel of John.

Readers' letters started pouring in. Many writers simply wanted to point out the mistake, and the majority of the letters were cordial and even humorous. Others expressed stronger feelings, such as the press agent for B'nai B'rith, whose letter took Goldwyn to task for invoking the Bible to sell his latest movie. In a postscript, Shalom Borscht concluded, "Furthermore, I ain't going to see your Goddammed picture." And if there was any doubt that the average person living in 1946 America was unfamiliar with what a "Goldwynism" was, the Reverend William H. Hunter, head of the First Presbyterian Church in Tunkhannock, Pennsylvania, put that to rest. "Can it be that this is just another attempt to uphold the tradition you are touted to have for burbling your words?" he asked.[33]

Goldwyn's initial response to the advertising mishap was to do nothing. He left it to the advertising firm and the magazines to handle any printed corrections and responses to the letters. But as the number of letters climbed to two hundred, Pat Duggan began answering some of the more irate missives on Goldwyn's behalf, thanking the letter writers for their interest and encouraging them to see the movie anyway.[34]

Less controversial were the advertisements that stuck to the movie itself, such as the string of vivid red billboards featuring the disembodied heads of five of the leads (Loy, March, Andrews, Wright, and Mayo) that dotted the landscape across several cities in New Jersey. Between October 1946 and March of the following year, Goldwyn spent just under $365,000 to promote the film in top magazines. More than three hundred stills of the actors and scenes from the film were placed in *Life*, *Time*, *Look*, and *Redbook* before the New York premiere. Dana Andrews was given strict instructions to discuss only *Best Years* in interviews and not to mention *Boomerang!* (dir. Elia Kazan), which he was currently filming for the producer Darryl Zanuck. Other Goldwyn stars such as David Niven were told to work in plugs for *Best Years* during any and all interviews.[35]

Most of the film's stars were also involved in tie-ups, or promotions involving specific brands and products timed to the movie's opening. Some, like Virginia Mayo's advertisements for Chesterfield cigarettes, swimwear, and gloves, were in keeping with the actress's *Best Years* portrayal of Marie as a woman who smoked and enjoyed the latest fashions. Others were less pointed, like Teresa Wright's modeling of Manikin hosiery in *Vogue* magazine and appearing in ads for Lipton Tea. As Goldwyn's top star, Dana Andrews had the most tie-ups, promoting toothpaste, cereal, and a line of sportswear. He and Wright posed with General Electric televisions and even appeared in an ad for Berland diamond rings. Considering how their characters' relationship blossoms while Fred is still married to Marie, the Berland diamond ring promotion may have caused a few raised eyebrows in the Breen Office. Goldwyn's publicity team even lined up a deal for MacKinlay Kantor, having him promote Scripto pencils in connection with *Best Years* as the secret to his writing success.[36]

It seems nothing was off-limits when it came to promoting *Best Years*. When Mayo's beloved dog, Dinky, accompanied her to a photo shoot, ingested some rat poison, and died before the New York premiere, the Goldwyn team discussed it internally as a possible publicity opportunity. "It seems to us that you could get a hell of a break out of New York," wrote Lynn Farnol to Bill Hebert, "if you arranged for some youngster to present her with a pup as she was leaving the opening of the picture."[37] This, however, never came to pass.

Less than a month before the premiere, while Goldwyn was focusing on the film's promotion, Wyler was still tweaking *Best Years'* final edit. He sent Goldwyn a list of twelve scenes to be reedited. For example, he wanted to shorten a close-up in the bedroom scene between Homer and Wilma in which she fastens the buttons of his pajama top. Wyler thought the action of Wilma smoothing out the collar of Homer's pajamas forecasted her acceptance of his condition and lessened the drama of the scene. "It makes Homer's speech about his hands unnecessary and the suspense should be saved for the moment where he says, 'You didn't mind?'" Wyler wrote in a memo to the producer. He was also concerned with Fred's line about his salary, in which he tells Marie, "My last job paid $32.50 a week, but I can live on less." Wyler worried that the line would elicit "both laughter and resentment among many people all over the country." In the year since Sherwood wrote that line, the cost of living in the United States had increased substantially as consumers rushed to buy previously rationed goods and businesses raised prices after governmental controls were lifted. Wyler also singled out the film's final shot, which at the time still contained Al's line of dialogue ("Hey buddies, whose wedding do you think this is, anyway?") over the close-up of Fred and Peggy kissing. "At this point people aren't even listening, just waiting for the lights to go up," Wyler wrote.[38]

After Wyler's additional edits were made, the film was about 700 feet shorter than the cut shown at the Long Beach test screening, bringing its running time to just under 170 minutes. Joseph Breen previewed the print and issued *Best Years* certificate number 11972, but his office included caveats about two lines of dialogue, one mentioning "nailing Old Glory to the top of the pole," and the other, uttered by Marie the morning after Fred's return, "I feel just like a bride."[39] Goldwyn's office assured Breen that the deletions would be made. *The Best Years of Our Lives*—Wyler's twenty-third feature film, Goldwyn's sixty-fifth independent production, and the last film they would make together—was ready for its New York premiere.

Willy and Talli set off for New York by train, arriving at Grand Central Station on November 7, where they were met by a small press contingent that had been arranged by Wyler's personal publicist, Mack Millar. Millar was highly respected and well connected, and Wyler had hired him in the late 1930s, around the time he made *Wuthering Heights*. "At that time directors didn't get much attention, so if Willy ever wanted to get his name in the paper, he had to have someone doing it because the studio was not going to do it," Talli recalled.[40] In the two weeks before the premiere, Willy and Talli caught up with old friends like Lillian Hellman, who would be accompanying them to the event at the Astor. They stayed in a suite at the Hampshire House, the same hotel overlooking Central Park where Willy and Talli had met up during the war, which in turn had inspired the tender reunion scene between Milly and Al Stephenson. Willy did some interviews for the film, perhaps getting in another dig at Goldwyn when he told *Film Daily* that the quality of films could be improved in Hollywood "if many more directors were given a freer hand in production."[41]

On the evening of November 21, Willy and Talli donned evening clothes and made their way to the Astor. Hellman, dressed head to toe in black, joined them there. The film's title was spelled out above the theater marquee in brilliantly illuminated letters. The names of the film's stars—Loy, March, Andrews, Wright, and Mayo (in that order)—were also in lights. "Samuel Goldwyn Presents" appeared above the stars' names, while Wyler's name was nowhere to be found.

The National Broadcasting Company's newsreel cameras recorded the arrivals of the Wylers and some two hundred other guests. Virginia Mayo glittered in a dazzling white dress with a low neckline and entered the theater with Hoagy Carmichael. Danny Kaye was there with his wife, Sylvia Fine, and Dana Andrews arrived with his wife, Mary. Myrna Loy's opera-length satin gloves peeked out from a sophisticated mink cape. Despite Goldwyn's insistence that Harold Russell and Cathy O'Donnell stay "under wraps" until after the premiere, O'Donnell attended the Astor screening, posing with Loy and the other cast members for photos before the film. Adding an extra bit of glamour to the evening were the Duke and Duchess of Windsor, who attended as guests of Sam and Frances.[42]

Robert Sherwood was also at the premiere, looking uncomfortable in his tuxedo, among all the Hollywood notables. Once the screening got underway, he ducked out of the Astor and walked seven blocks north to the Alvin Theatre, where Ingrid Bergman was appearing as the lead in *Joan of Lorraine*, a drama about a group of actors putting on the play *Joan of Arc*. Sherwood's Playwright's Company, which he had formed with Maxwell Anderson, Kurt Weill, Elmer Rice, and John F. Wharton, had premiered the production earlier that week. Sherwood's leaving the premiere of *Best Years* had nothing to do with how he felt about the film. In fact, he had written to a friend a week earlier saying that if *Best Years* became a success, it would be due in part to the Goldwyns. "Sam backed me up in everything I wanted to do in the development of the story. And so, I may add, did Frances," Sherwood wrote, acknowledging Mrs. Goldwyn's key role in the picture. After all, it was Frances who had found the *Time* article that ultimately inspired the film. The real reason that Sherwood left the Astor, he told another friend, had to do with all of the hoopla surrounding the premiere. "I couldn't take the ermined crowds at that opening," Sherwood admitted. After standing for a while in the back of the Alvin Theatre to watch Bergman, he left the show and stopped at a newsstand to buy early editions of several newspapers as he headed to the *Best Years* premiere party.[43]

"Pure Emotional Dynamite," declared the headline above the film's review in the *Hollywood Reporter*. "This is it," wrote Jack D. Grant. "The post-war film drama we have long expected."[44] The *Reporter*'s enthusiastic review kicked off a deluge of positive—even ecstatic—notices for the film. "When Samuel Goldwyn said recently that *The Best Years of Our Lives* . . . represented his outstanding achievement as a Hollywood producer, he spoke nothing but the truth," wrote Kate Cameron in the *New York Daily News*. Calling *Best Years* the best Hollywood movie since the war's end, Cameron wrote glowingly about Sherwood, Wyler, and the film's cast, singling out Virginia Mayo for her "arresting" performance and correctly predicting that it would boost Mayo's profile "sky-high in Hollywood." Cameron did criticize one "alien" scene but didn't identify it. Perhaps she was referring to Homer's confrontation at the soda counter with the customer who suggested the Russians were the real enemy, which months later another reviewer complained about as unnecessary and obviously written by "message-sender Sherwood."[45] Cameron wrote something similar about the anonymous problematic scene in her review, describing its content and tone as a "left-over from Sherwood's O.W.I. experience in the war" with "no artistic place" in the story.[46] (The Office of War Information conducted extensive news and propaganda campaigns at home and abroad.)

In the *New York Times*, Bosley Crowther called *Best Years* a "thrilling exception" to the hundreds of Hollywood movies released in 1946 that were lacking in social thought. His review went on to praise the entire film, but spotlighted Harold Russell's portrayal as Homer. "It is in the extraordinary performance of this young man in a startlingly candid role . . . that much of the clear illumination of a veteran's isolation and anguish is achieved," wrote Crowther. He credited the film for providing through its interwoven stories and characters a "broad cross-section of the so-called 'veteran problem' today." Interestingly, Crowther noted that the one "major area" related to veterans' issues *not* covered by *Best Years* was the case of the psychoneurotic, a comment that seemed to ignore Homer's moments of anguish, such as when he shoves his hooks through the window of his family's woodshed, and, more obviously, Fred's recurring nightmare and his climactic catharsis in the nose cone of the abandoned bomber.[47]

More praise for the film appeared in another section of the *Times* in the same Sunday edition as Crowther's review. Dr. Howard A. Rusk had overseen medical services at a barracks in St. Louis during the war. He had a special interest in helping disabled and wounded servicemen, and he developed a rehabilitation program that addressed a patient's physical and mental health through exercise, talk therapy, and vocational training and education. Every branch of the military adopted Rusk's program, but after the war, he met with some resistance in promoting it within the medical community. A friendship with the *Times'* publisher, Arthur Sulzberger, who found relief from his crippling arthritis thanks to Rusk's emphasis on rehabilitation, led to Rusk writing a weekly column for the newspaper. The weekend following *Best Years'* premiere, Rusk called the picture "a training film for all of us" and lauded its "significant" portrayal of the problems faced by many veterans. "Its message is even more important for the veteran's family, the general public, and particularly the hundreds of thousands of non-veterans who suffer from physical disabilities," wrote Rusk. Like Crowther, he noted that despite "a score" of movies and books about the subject, "they have failed to achieve the same clarity, insight and understanding" seen in *Best Years*.[48]

Goldwyn and Wyler had been somewhat worried about the film's length possibly deterring potential audiences, so the film's promotional materials tackled the issue head-on. Banners billing the picture as the first three-hour movie since *Gone with the Wind* traded on the prestige of that film, which had been adapted from a best-selling novel and was then the highest-grossing film in Hollywood. And while several reviewers did mention the film's running time, it was often in the context of not letting its length scare away moviegoers from seeing the film. "Most of three hours seems not too long," wrote Howard Barnes in the *New York Herald Tribune*, noting that the film "moves with variety and insistency to its climax." And as another reviewer observed, "The show is overly long, but to cut any one of the scenes would require an artistry unknown in Filmtown."[49]

For a few critics, however, the film's length was just one of its problems. Terry Ramsaye, the noted film reviewer for the *Motion Picture Herald*, wrote: "'The Best Years of Our Lives' is a long title for a long picture about a long story full of long thoughts. They will cry over it, every little while." And while he seemed to appreciate the film's "documentary quality," Ramsaye faulted some of the actors' "unimpartial speeches," which sounded "exactly like a collaboration of Archie MacLeish and Mr. Sherwood."[50] Under the subtitle "Goldwyn's Longest," John McCarten's review for the *New Yorker* took a similar stance. Although McCarten praised the film's dialogue for its "down-to-earth" quality, he leveled a one-two punch that skewered both the film's length and its connection with another "prestige" picture. "Before the drama has finally resolved itself, the spectator is inclined to suspect that he's watching the longest picture *anybody* ever made, but this, of course, isn't true, since Goldwyn's epic is by no means as interminable as Selznick's 'Gone With the Wind' and a couple of others," McCarten wrote.[51]

In James Agee's column in the *Nation*, he expressed his conflicted assessment of the film in a detailed review that seemed to dedicate more inches to the film's flaws than to its high points. He didn't like the film's "misfired" title, its plot contrivances, or its tendency to "dodge . . . its own fullest meanings and possibilities." But he admired the film's "hot flashes of talent" and the "remarkably real and mature" affair between Fred and Peggy. "The movie has plenty of faults, and the worst of them are painfully exasperating," Agee wrote, "yet this is one of the very few American studio-made movies in years that seem to me profoundly pleasing, moving, and encouraging."[52]

Another less-than-positive review came from a rather surprising source. Although it is unclear whether Lillian Hellman shared her thoughts about the film with Wyler at the time, she did speak about it on the record while he was still alive. "I don't like *Best Years* as much as other people do," she told the biographer A. Scott Berg, who was interviewing her for *Directed by William Wyler*, a documentary coproduced by Wyler's daughter Catherine in the mid-1980s. "It's a slightly over-sentimental picture, but it's a wonderfully made picture, and I think very moving, really," Hellmann continued. "It was everyone's predicament, obviously."[53]

Wyler addressed this type of criticism a few months later during an interview. "Sometimes a hypersensitive critic accuses me of overreaching myself dramatically, of going corny. But this I am sure of, that going slightly too far is less of a crime then not going far enough," he said. "Nothing is more wasteful than to play a scene at less than its maximum effect, and to play a whole picture that way is fatal."[54]

Still, the majority of *Best Years'* reviews were very positive. One unexpected benefit of all the praise came in the form of a telegram from the military. The army air force was finally willing to release *Thunderbolt*, Wyler's shelved documentary about P-47 Liberators. Unlike the military documentaries made during wartime, however, which tended to omit or downplay onscreen credits for direction, photography, and so on, General Carl Spaatz contacted Wyler about the possibility of using his name to promote *Thunderbolt*. Wyler responded to his former commanding officer in mid-December, giving Spaatz the okay to include his name on the final credits as long as collaborators such as Lester Koenig also received recognition.[55]

The Best Years of Our Lives opened in limited release immediately after the Astor's Thanksgiving-night premiere. As was the custom, prestige pictures like *Best Years* were roadshowed, or screened in New York, Los Angeles, Chicago, and other major cities, for a limited time before a wider release throughout the country. Roadshow screenings featured reserved seats at higher-than-average ticket prices, which were about fifty cents at the end of 1946. Tickets to see *Best Years* on Christmas and New Year's in Los Angeles, for instance, were priced at $1.20 and $1.80. In some cities, reserved seats cost as much as $2.40.[56] Raising the admission price was a common roadshow element, one that Goldwyn's fellow independent producer David O. Selznick was implementing at the same time for *Duel in the Sun*, an epic western that was also in limited release to qualify for the Academy Awards. Yet the entertainment press targeted Goldwyn for the practice, and more than a few reporters commented on "the Goldwyn gouge," especially after it was announced in early 1947 that this aspect of the film's release would remain in place throughout the year in key cities "for deluxe pre-release engagements" of *Best Years*.[57]

Perhaps a few of these reporters were taking sides in the ongoing feud between the film's producer and its director, since some ads continued to promote *Best Years* without using Wyler's name. Wyler had his supporters, such as Archer Winsten, who wrote in the *New York Post* that *Best Years* was "a picture on which the cunning hand of a great director is everywhere apparent."[58] Wyler's publicist Mack Millar wasn't afraid to complain to Goldwyn's executive team about their boss. "Every time [Goldwyn] opens his mouth, he puts his foot in it. . . . Someone ought to tell him—he might get more respect [in New York]," Millar fumed to Bill Hebert.[59] The *Hollywood Reporter* also took Goldwyn to task, writing that credit for the film's success belonged to Wyler, Kantor, Sherwood, and the cast. "There should be some way, some means of muzzling Goldwyn," wrote the publisher W. R. Wilkerson of the "space-grabbing" producer.[60]

None of this negative press seemed to faze Sam Goldwyn, however. In mid-December he and Frances prepared to sail to England on the *Queen Elizabeth*. They would be overseas for three weeks, through the Christmas and New Year's holidays, while they visited their son Sammy, who was working for J. Arthur Rank's film company.[61] The elder Goldwyn would also be negotiating *Best Years'*

"Pearl Harbor came to my rescue": William Wyler in uniform. Courtesy of the Wyler family.

Sam and Frances Goldwyn, 1960. Frances discovered the *Time* magazine article that inspired Sam to hire MacKinlay Kantor to write the novel *Glory for Me*, which eventually became *The Best Years of Our Lives*. Keystone Pictures USA.

Charles McGonegal, a World War I veteran, and Harold Russell, both bilateral hand amputees, 1947. McGonegal's training film *Meet McGonegal* gave Russell hope and inspired him to "star" in *Diary of a Sergeant* for the War Department. Everett Collection.

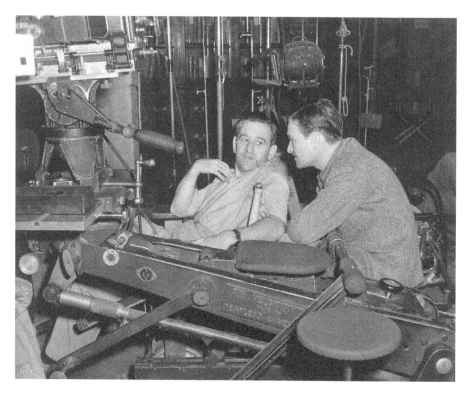

Wyler and the cinematographer Gregg Toland on the set of *Best Years*, their fifth film together, 1946. JT Vintage / Glasshouse Images.

Wyler clowning around on location while shooting *Best Years*. Everett Collection.

Fredric March, Myrna Loy, and Wyler discussing a scene on the set of the Stephensons' apartment. Note the realistic height of the doorways, designed to enhance the film's authenticity. Courtesy of the Wyler family.

Peggy Stephenson (Teresa Wright) consoling a traumatized Fred Derry (Dana Andrews). Cineclassico / Alamy Stock Photo.

*Cast of Best Years
with General Curt LeMay
plus Sy Bartlett & Danny Kaye*

The cast of *Best Years* taking a break from filming scenes at Butch's Place to visit with General Curtis LeMay (*between Wright and Loy*) and the screenwriter Sy Bartlett (*far right*). Danny Kaye (*seated below Bartlett*) often hung out on the set during breaks from *The Secret Life of Walter Mitty*, also filming on the Goldwyn lot. Courtesy of the Wyler family.

Wyler with Andrews and Perry Ferguson, one of the film's art directors (*foreground*). Andrews, an alcoholic, stopped drinking midway through the shoot out of respect for Wyler. Alamy Stock Photo.

Virginia Mayo, best known for her comedic roles before *Best Years*, liked to joke that her dramatic turn as Marie won Wyler his Best Director Academy Award. Samuel Goldwyn Company.

The aftermath of the drugstore fight between Homer and a customer, partly inspired by Wyler's wartime altercation outside a Washington, DC, hotel. Alamy Stock Photo.

As Fred Derry, Andrews wandering among a row of junked propellers in a bomber "graveyard" on location in Ontario, California, a scene that Wyler at one time considered for the film's ending. Courtesy of the Wyler family.

Wilma (Cathy O'Donnell) confronting Homer (Russell) in the Parrish kitchen. Lighting, composition, and music create a mix of moods that invokes melodrama, film noir, and even horror. Everett Collection.

Homer and Wilma's wedding sequence, which includes one of *Best Year*'s most memorable deep-focus shots, drawing viewers' attention to the tension between Fred (Andrews) and Peggy (Wright). Everett Collection.

Goldwyn, Russell, and Wyler posing with five of the film's nine Academy Awards, which include Goldwyn's Irving G. Thalberg Memorial Award and Russell's honorary Oscar. Alamy Stock Photo.

Russell, the head of AMVETS, meeting with President John F. Kennedy in 1961 to share a pamphlet that the organization produced to encourage legislators to fund the USS *Arizona* Memorial at Pearl Harbor. Photograph by Abbie Rowe, White House Photographs; John F. Kennedy Presidential Library and Museum, Boston.

London opening and general release in the spring of 1947, a deal made much easier thanks to the film's tremendous reception stateside.

Just before the Goldwyns' departure, Sam received a glowing review of the film from General Omar Bradley. Goldwyn's office had arranged a private screening for Bradley and others in Washington in late November. Howard Rusk, the medical doctor who had praised the film in his *New York Times* column, mentioned to Goldwyn that Bradley had been impressed by the film.[62] Goldwyn knew that a public comment from Bradley, a World War II general then heading up Veterans Affairs, would add much to the film's prestige. He pestered Bradley's office for something in writing, which finally arrived a week before he and Frances left for England. Bradley began by telling Goldwyn how struck he and his chief assistants were by the film's honesty and its relatability. "Multiply these three [characters] by the many millions of veterans who have come home and you will begin to understand not only the meaning of the movie but the meaning of our democracy to them," wrote Bradley. "I cannot thank you too much for bringing this story to the American people," he continued. "You are not only helping us to do our job, but you are helping the American people to build an even better democracy out of the tragic experiences of this war."[63]

With Goldwyn in London, Wyler was able to relax and enjoy the film's West Coast premiere, which was scheduled for Christmas night at the Fox Beverly Theatre. Even a torrential rainstorm didn't discourage Gregory Peck, Orson Welles and Rita Hayworth, Walt Disney, Lucille Ball, Jean Arthur, Gary Cooper, and other famous guests from attending. Before the premiere's 8:30 p.m. start, the deluge of rain was so forbidding that guests' cars could not pull up to the curb in front of the theater. The chief of police was pressed into service to carry some of the attendees from their cars to the lobby.[64]

Weather aside, the night was memorable for Wyler. While the tremendously favorable response to the film at the New York premiere had been "all that we could have expected and more," the Los Angeles premiere meant more to him because it was an audience of his peers. Eighteen months earlier, a newly deaf and thoroughly defeated Wyler wasn't sure whether he would ever direct again. Now he was being celebrated for making a film that was both deeply personal and nearly universal in its appeal. Wyler's happiness carried over to the post-premiere party at the Brown Derby, which lasted into the early hours of the morning.[65]

Meanwhile, Harold Russell was back in Cambridge and finishing up the fall semester at Boston University. Goldwyn's plan to keep Russell "under wraps" and away from the New York premiere ("until the critics stumbled over me") had worked. "I went to bed on Thursday just another guy and woke up Friday to find I had become more or less famous," Russell recalled. Goldwyn had already arranged for a private screening on the BU campus in late November. Fredric

March and Robert Sherwood attended the event with Russell, who was feted by the university's president, faculty, and other invited guests. On December 8, Goldwyn flew Russell out to Los Angeles so that he could appear on Louella Parsons's radio show for a three-minute segment. Bill Hebert and Lynn Farnol had been worried that Parsons, whose influential gossip column appeared in William Randolph Hearst's conservative newspapers, might take issue with the film's liberal politics. Instead, she loved the picture. Russell and Parson's brief interview was a success and another effective plug for *Best Years*.[66]

On the final day of 1946, Russell received a lengthy telegram from Wyler. Explaining that he hadn't reached out to Russell earlier because he didn't quite know how to express what he felt for him, Wyler wanted Russell to know how well received his performance and the film overall had been so far. "Last night the people who saw the picture were among the most gifted and knowing movie-makers and their sincere tributes made it as great a day for me as the day when I first saw you in 'Diary of a Sergeant,'" Wyler wrote. "It should be a source of great satisfaction to you that by your example you are going to help so many men find a way out of their own problems."[67]

The Best Years of Our Lives continued to earn accolades and set records at the box office at the start of the new year. The New York Film Critics chose the film as the best picture of 1946, and the Hollywood Foreign Correspondents Association (now the Hollywood Foreign Press Association) likewise made the film its top pick. The association, which gave out the Golden Globe awards, presented Russell with a Special Achievement Award at its ceremony in late February. Although the Golden Globes were only in their fourth year, the awards and the foreign press's impact were increasing in importance. In fact, several articles in the trade papers had begun to comment that foreign films in general were "taking over" Hollywood, citing the fact that the British actor Laurence Olivier's *Henry V* had been chosen by the National Board of Review as its top picture of 1946. (*Best Years* came in third.) And in 1947, the Golden Globes ceremony took place at the Hollywood Roosevelt Hotel in a room bigger than the one used the previous year. Goldwyn, who had returned from London in early January, was on hand to accept the Golden Globe for the film.[68]

The film's box office continued to soar as more awards and nominations were announced. *Box Office Digest* predicted that the film would earn nearly two and a half times its production budget of $2.1 million. In Boston, where the film had been playing at the Esquire Theatre in the Back Bay neighborhood, advance admission prices and reserved seats did not deter crowds from waiting in long lines even into its fourth week of play. Similar scenarios were playing out around the country, with a few theaters in Los Angeles instituting round-the-clock screenings to meet demand. One local theater manager felt the need to call in the police to manage the crowds queueing up for evening shows and to handle the overflow between screenings. "Turnaway so great could have sold last show at least twice," he telegrammed Goldwyn.[69]

The most exciting news in early 1947 was the announcement of that year's Academy Awards nominations. *The Best Years of Our Lives* received eight nods, including ones for best picture, best director, and best screenplay. Fredric March was nominated for best actor, and Harold Russell for best supporting actor. Daniel Mandell and Hugo Friedhofer received nominations for the editing and the score, and the film earned a nod for sound recording, too. The lack of recognition for Loy, Wright, and Mayo was considered an oversight by some. But perhaps the biggest surprise was Gregg Toland's snub in the Best Cinematography category. Going forward, Goldwyn, who had cultivated Toland's career and had tremendous respect for the innovative director of photography, made sure to add Toland's name to the film's advertising whenever possible.[70]

The year 1947 brought a few changes to the Academy Awards. For starters, the ceremony would be held in a different location, moving from Grauman's Chinese Theatre to the much larger Shrine Civic Auditorium in downtown Los Angeles. The academy also made a change to its voting rules. For the first time, members of the guilds for acting, writing, and directing also had to be members of the academy in order to vote in that year's competition. Studio heads demanded that their employees join the academy, whose membership nearly "doubled overnight," according to one report. The change nonetheless decreased the number of people voting for that year's awards, from approximately 9,000 in years past to around 1,600.[71]

On the evening of March 13, sixteen searchlights crisscrossed the front of the Shrine Auditorium and beamed into the evening sky as nominees, presenters, and other Hollywood personalities began arriving. Thousands of fans cheered from the rows of bleachers set up outside the auditorium. The venue could hold 6,700 guests, so the academy had decided to sell a portion of the balcony seats to the public. Ticket sales were sluggish, however. As the ceremony's start drew closer and some seats remained empty, behind-the-scenes staffers began handing out tickets to servicemen milling around outside the auditorium.

Harold Russell had flown to Los Angeles a day earlier, having just come from being a guest of honor with Cathy O'Donnell at a special screening of the film in Washington, DC. The event, called "Enable the Disabled," was a benefit put on by the Washington Committee for National Civilian Rehabilitation, and it preceded the film's official Washington opening by a day. First Lady Bess Truman was the committee's honorary chairperson, and Russell, his wife, Rita, and O'Donnell attended a tea in the East Room of the White House before the evening premiere.[72]

Rita Russell had a fear of flying, so Harold brought a Boston University classmate named Harry McLatchy to California as his guest for the Academy

Awards. Unlike his visit to Los Angeles when Goldwyn had put him and his brother Leslie in a rather bare-bones apartment for the duration of the *Best Years* production, Russell now received the star treatment. He and McLatchy luxuriated in their three-bedroom suite at the Garden of Allah Hotel on Sunset Boulevard.

Shirley Temple, then eighteen years old, presided over the evening's earliest awards, a group of special Oscars given for unique contributions to the film industry. Laurence Olivier received one of the gold statuettes for his work as a multi-hyphenate actor-director-producer on *Henry V*. Ernst Lubitsch was recognized for his body of work as a director, which by 1947 included such hits as *Ninotchka*, *The Shop Around the Corner*, and *To Be or Not to Be*. Temple, the veteran child actor, gave a pint-size statuette to young Claude Jarman Jr. for his moving debut performance in *The Yearling*. That successful film may have been *Best Years'* biggest competition; the *Los Angeles Times* had predicted it would win best picture. Perhaps no one was more surprised than Harold Russell when Temple announced him as a recipient of a special award for "bringing hope and courage to his fellow veterans" as Homer in *Best Years*. Dressed in black tie and smiling from ear to ear, Russell walked onstage to receive his statuette. "This is the proudest and happiest moment of my life. I wish to sincerely thank Mr. Wyler and Mr. Goldwyn and all the other wonderful people who helped me so much in the picture," Russell told the cheering crowd. Then turning to Temple, he said, "Shirley, I'd like to accept this trophy in the name of all those thousands of disabled veterans who are laying in hospitals all over the country."[73]

Not long after, Billy Wilder walked onto the stage to announce the recipient of the Best Director award. Wyler was up against David Lean (*Brief Encounter*), Robert Siodmak (*The Killers*), Clarence Brown (*The Yearling*), and his Liberty Films partner Frank Capra (*It's a Wonderful Life*). Capra and Wyler had begun production on the same day in April 1946, and they had sent each other telegrams to mark the occasion. "Last one in is a rotten egg," wrote Wyler, while Capra ribbed, "My first day was easy but do you know they're using sound today."[74]

Billy Wilder opened the envelope and smiled as he leaned toward the microphone. "*The Best Years of Our Lives* was the best directed picture I have ever seen," he said before revealing the winner as "the champ, Willy Wyler." Wyler pumped Wilder's hand enthusiastically as he accepted the gold statuette from his friend and fellow filmmaker. "I'm deeply grateful and very happy that the picture was liked so much. Thank you," Wyler told the audience in his lightly accented English. As Talli later observed, "The last movie he made before the war and the first movie he made after the war got him two Oscars, one on each side."[75]

Despite the *Los Angeles Times'* prediction that *The Yearling* would sweep the awards, it was *Best Years* that continued to be recognized throughout the night.

The film received Oscars for screenplay, score, and editing, but none of the recipients were on hand to collect their awards. Robert Sherwood was in New York, and Wyler accepted on his behalf. Hugo Friedhofer was already working on the score for his next project, and Daniel Mandell was tied up with editing his next Goldwyn feature. While the Oscar was a nice surprise for Friedhofer, the composer considered his nomination the greater thrill because it had been decided by his peers. But the award seemed to finally convince Wyler, who had never loved the film's score, that perhaps it wasn't so bad after all.[76]

A feeling of euphoria began to spread among the *Best Years* contingent as they waited to hear the outcome of the remaining awards. In the Best Actor category, Fredric March was competing against Laurence Olivier (*Henry V*), Larry Parks (*The Jolson Story*), Gregory Peck (*The Yearling*), and Jimmy Stewart (*It's a Wonderful Life*). March was appearing on Broadway in Ruth Gordon's play *Years Ago*. That evening's performance had just ended, and March and the rest of the cast were gathered offstage, listening to the radio broadcast of the ceremony, when March's name was announced as the winner. In Los Angeles, a breathless Cathy O'Donnell accepted the award on his behalf.[77]

In the Best Picture category *Best Years* was up against *The Razor's Edge*, *The Yearling*, *Henry V*, and *It's a Wonderful Life*. Produced by Darryl Zanuck for Twentieth Century–Fox, *The Razor's Edge* was considered the favorite, in part because at the time, independent producers such as Goldwyn didn't have the voting might in the academy that studios had. Like Goldwyn, Zanuck had campaigned hard for his film. Eric Johnston, who had taken over the MPAA from Will Hays, presented the nominees and their clips. When it came time for *Best Years'* snippet, the audience watched as Dana Andrews wandered among the abandoned planes in the bomber graveyard. When Johnston announced Samuel Goldwyn as the winner, the jubilant producer "danced up the aisle with a big smile on his face," according to a member of his team. The Best Picture nod marked Goldwyn's first win, after six previous nominations. Goldwyn was generous with his thanks, reading a list that began with MacKinlay Kantor and ended with Harold Russell. He thanked Wyler after Robert Sherwood, crediting the filmmaker for "the greatest direction I have seen for a motion picture so far." Goldwyn, whose linguistic flubs had become so celebrated as to warrant an entry in the dictionary, finessed his list of names until the very end, when he thanked Hugo, not Hoagy, Carmichael. As Goldwyn exited the stage, Jack Benny, the night's emcee, quipped, "I thought Hugo Carmichael was great, too."[78]

Goldwyn was called back to the stage to receive the Irving G. Thalberg Memorial Award. The honorary award was named for the late MGM unit producer who had passed away a decade earlier at just thirty-seven years old. Nicknamed the "Boy Wonder," Thalberg had revolutionized the Hollywood studio system with his ability to combine smart scripts, dynamic casts, and efficient and talented production crews to create critically and commercially successful films as diverse as *Mutiny on the Bounty* (Lloyd, 1935) and *A Night at the Opera* (Wood, 1935). Thalberg's namesake award honored producers whose work was consistently high in quality. Donald Nelson, the head of the War Production Board, presented the award to Goldwyn, who had been very close to Thalberg and was reportedly inconsolable upon the younger man's death. After sharing a few words that conveyed his affection and respect for Thalberg, an emotional Goldwyn closed by saying, "You could not honor me, give me any greater honor, than give me this award tonight, and I thank you from the bottom of my heart."[79]

One of the final categories of the evening was the award for best supporting actor. Harold Russell had been nominated alongside Charles Coburn (*The Green Years*), William Demarest (*The Jolson Story*), Claude Rains (*Notorious*), and Clifton Webb (*The Razor's Edge*). The academy's board members reportedly had decided to award Russell the honorary Oscar he had received earlier in the evening because they thought his performance deserved recognition, which he probably wouldn't receive as a nonactor competing against veteran performers such as Rains and Webb. Anne Revere, who had won the Best Supporting Actress award a year earlier for her role in *National Velvet*, took the stage to announce the winner. When she said Russell's name, the audience erupted as if at a sporting event. The shock of the announcement took Russell back to his training as a paratrooper. "It reminded me of that terrible moment long, long ago, when the jump-master had booted me out of the plane," he later recalled. Shaking from nerves, he made his way to the stage for a second time that evening. "Thank you very much. Two in a night is just too much!" was all he could manage. With a final thank you to the crowd, he walked into the wings and was quickly surrounded by a cheering mob. An exuberant Goldwyn, tears in his eyes, kissed him on the cheek.[80]

In the end, the only nominated category that *Best Years* didn't win was for sound recording. At that time, it was customary for the award to be accepted by the head of the studio's sound department rather than by the actual sound technicians. Gordon Sawyer, who "lost" that Oscar to John Livadary for *The Jolson Story* (Columbia), nonetheless enjoyed a brief moment onstage when he accepted Daniel Mandell's editing Oscar on Mandell's behalf. Virginia Mayo, who, like her female costars Loy and Wright, had been overlooked by the academy, still took credit for the film's Oscars sweep: "I always said that I won Willy Wyler his Best Director Oscar because nobody believed that Virginia Mayo could play a dramatic role."[81]

Harold Russell remembered many things about that night, but two incidents in particular stood out. After his award for best supporting actor, when well-wishers swarmed him backstage, an unknown gentleman took Russell into a nearby dressing room, locked the door, and made him knock back two shots of whiskey. Before that, however, Cary Grant had gotten Russell's attention as he came offstage to pose for press pictures. The dashing Grant had most recently made *Notorious* with Ingrid Bergman, and the film had been nominated for two Academy Awards, including a nod for Claude Rains in the category that Russell had just won. As flashbulbs popped, a mischievous Grant leaned over and whispered to Russell, "Where can *I* get a stick of dynamite?"[82]

CHAPTER 7

It's All the Same Fight

Some of my best work is in this picture, and I get real gratification from believing I contributed to an understanding of the times we lived in.
WILLIAM WYLER

After the Academy Awards ceremony, Samuel and Frances Goldwyn made their way from downtown Los Angeles to Peter Rathvon's mansion on Beverly Grove Drive. An attorney and businessman, Rathvon had taken over as president of RKO during the war, and he lived in a sprawling house overlooking Benedict Canyon that used to belong to the actor Charles Boyer. Rathvon's house boasted a retractable glass roof over the back patio, which on this particular night was open to reveal the Hollywood lights shimmering in the distance.[1]

More than fifteen hundred guests were expected to attend, including Willy and Talli Wyler. Even though Willy's hearing loss made it difficult for him to enjoy crowded events, he was in good spirits at the party and still riding the euphoric wave that had taken hold as Oscar win after win was announced for *Best Years*. Wyler and Goldwyn managed to avoid each other during the festivities, though they had posed together for photographs at the ceremony. In one picture, the two men appear happy and smiling, but Harold Russell is strategically positioned between them as a buffer. A columnist had reported that Goldwyn and Wyler had "kissed and made up" at the end of 1946, but both were still simmering over the tensions surrounding the production and promotion of *Best Years* as well as the accretion of slights (real and perceived) that had built up after working together for more than a decade.[2] *Best Years* was Wyler's final film under contract to Goldwyn. He had become a partner in Liberty Films eighteen months earlier, and he was done with Goldwyn's seeming inability to acknowledge his contributions to *Best Years*. Goldwyn viewed Wyler's leaving as a personal affront.

Life went on for both men after the Academy Awards. Goldwyn turned his attention back to the film's release, which now could be advertised with billboards, posters, and print ads hurriedly redesigned to reflect the film's seven Academy Awards. Harold Russell's honorary Oscar and Sam's Irving G. Thalberg Memorial Award brought the total to nine, allowing Goldwyn to trumpet a record-setting number of wins, which he did enthusiastically. A header proclaiming "Winner of nine Academy Awards" was added to many posters and advertisements, and illustrations of Academy statuettes were airbrushed into existing designs. "Free" advertising in the form of enthusiastic reviews continued to pour in. Popular magazines such as *Reader's Digest*, *Family Circle*, and *Modern Screen* all sang the film's praises, but perhaps the most unusual rave came from the women's magazine *Go*. "Hollywood has taken the bull by the horns and evinced some interest in the woman's ability to make a mature choice," wrote Thyra Samter Winslow of the film. A novelist and *New Yorker* contributor who had also written scripts for romantic comedies, Winslow saluted the film for setting a precedent, particularly through the characters of Homer and, most especially, Wilma. No doubt referring to the climactic scene when Wilma confronts Homer in the Parrish kitchen, Winslow wrote, "If a girl knows what she wants, she'll go after it, whether it's a job, a career or a man."[3]

More publicity came a few days after the Oscars on March 15 when Hedda Hopper scored "the radio scoop of the year" by having a few of the film's stars (Dana Andrews, Harold Russell, and Cathy O'Donnell) appear on her show, *This Is Hollywood*, to perform a truncated version of the film. The actors worked from a Goldwyn-approved twenty-one-page script that began and ended with Homer and Wilma's wedding. After *Best Years* won the Best Picture Oscar on March 12, CBS radio began plugging Hopper's coup immediately.[4]

By early April, *Best Years* was entering its twentieth week at New York's Astor Theatre, where it had premiered the previous November. At the time, the *Hollywood Reporter* noted that the film's weekly box office "continues to hover around $40K, often hitting above that mark."[5] One ad in the *Chicago Times* featured a photo of the Woods Theater manager, Jack Belasco, whose face was superimposed on the illustrated body of a man welcoming crowds of patrons into a theater lobby. "Meet Jack Belasco, the man with 834,562 friends . . . happy patrons who have seen 'The Best Years of Our Lives' now in its 22nd week."[6] The film was in its third month at the Beverly Theatre in Los Angeles and was also still showing or beginning its run at several other movie houses around the city. Goldwyn had spent just over $80,000 in Los Angeles since the beginning of 1947, promoting the film in newspapers, on the radio, and in twenty-four-sheet posters displayed on local billboards. But as one of his executives observed, the film had grossed $575,000, or approximately seven times its Los Angeles ad budget. "Both Metro and Selznick have spent far more than we did to obtain a comparatively negligible gross," the Goldwyn executive reported.[7] He was referring to David O. Selznick's *Duel in the Sun*, which had cost a rumored $8 million (approximately four times as expensive as *Best Years*) and was also beginning its wide release that spring. Unlike *Best Years*, *Duel* had failed to win an Academy Award.

Another matter that required Goldwyn's attention had been brewing since before the Academy Awards, when the Goldwyn executives Bill Hebert and Lynn Farnol became aware of a shift in MacKinlay Kantor's feelings about the film. Interviewed on a radio program one morning in January 1947, Kantor was asked whether he wasn't proud of having written the book on which the Academy Award–nominated film was based. "I am proud that at least one person seems to know it, and that's you," Kantor replied. Although the novelist stood by his initial pronouncement that the film was "a great picture," he wasn't happy that few people seemed to know he had written the source material, in part because the book's title, *Glory for Me*, was not included on the film's posters. Instead, the credit line often read, "Based on a novel by MacKinlay Kantor." *Best Years'* multiple Oscar wins seemed to aggravate the situation, and Kantor's agent reached out to Goldwyn about changing the posters. As the weeks went by and no change occurred, Kantor became more vocal and less complimentary about the film, telling one interviewer that the film's title ("What does it mean?" asked Kantor) "crimped" sales of *Glory for Me*. Set to produce *Gun Crazy*, which he cowrote with Dalton Trumbo, Kantor continued to badmouth the film until Goldwyn finally took matters into his own hands, giving a no-holds-barred interview about the situation. "There's nothing wrong with Kantor that wouldn't drive a psychiatrist crazy," the producer fumed, offering another Goldwynism. He went on to say that Kantor wrote the original screenplay for the film, but it wasn't any good. "As a matter of fact, his book was bad, too. And you can quote me on that."[8]

After the Oscars, Willy and Talli began to prepare for a three-month trip to Europe, which would coincide with the wide release overseas of *Best Years*. Taking a trip together after Willy finished a film had become something of a tradition for the couple, a way to "make up for lost time," according to the filmmaker.[9] Cathy, Judy, and baby Billy, who had just turned one, would stay behind in Los Angeles with Talli's parents. The trip would mark Talli's first visit to Europe.

Before they left, however, Wyler had to deal with the dissolution of Liberty Films. The company had taken out an advertisement shortly after the Oscars to announce Lester Koenig's joining Liberty as an associate producer on "future" Wyler productions "in recognition of his contribution to *The Best Years of Our Lives*."[10] But even then the situation at Liberty was tenuous, and by April the news went public that the independent company formed by Wyler,

Frank Capra, George Stevens, and the producer Sam Briskin shortly after they returned from the war had been acquired by Paramount Pictures.[11]

It's a Wonderful Life, Capra's first feature for Liberty, had received mixed notices after its initial release, in December 1946. Reviewing the film for the *New York Times*, Bosley Crowther described it as "a bit too sticky for our tastes."[12] Manny Farber, using the derogatory term "Capracorn" for perhaps the first time, wrote that the filmmaker "lights with more cinematic know-how and zeal than any other director to convince movie audiences that American life is exactly like the *Saturday Evening Post* covers of Norman Rockwell."[13] Released at the end of 1946, Capra's *Wonderful Life* went head to head at the box office with Wyler's *Best Years*, which had cost around a million dollars less. Although Capra beat out Wyler for the Golden Globe for best director, *Wonderful Life* failed to win any of the five Academy Awards for which it was nominated. With motion picture attendance dropping from a 1946 weekly peak of eighty million viewers to just over sixty million a week the following year, the market forecast didn't look promising for independent companies like Liberty. And while *Wonderful Life* earned a respectable $3.3 million, it wasn't enough to save Liberty.[14] Capra and Briskin wanted to sell the company, while Wyler was keen to wait. Stevens initially was against the idea of selling but eventually changed his mind.

The deal with Paramount gave Wyler stock in the company worth $750,000 and a maximum fee of $150,000 a picture in exchange for five films. "They assured us we would have the same independence as before, which didn't turn out to be true," Willy told a biographer years later. Instead, Paramount retained final subject and budget approval on each of the partners' films.[15]

After the Academy Awards, Harold Russell did not return to Boston University to finish his business degree. But neither did he take a position in Goldwyn's New York office, as one newspaper reported.[16] And he had already gone on record as saying he wouldn't be making any more films, because nothing could top his experience with Wyler on *Best Years*.[17] Instead, he promoted the film by touring with it around the country. Months earlier, Goldwyn's team had asked Russell to put his life on hold for the first half of 1947. He would be giving speeches on behalf of organizations such as the Red Cross and the American Legion. His talks wouldn't be about the film itself. Instead, Russell was given relatively free rein to speak about whatever he wanted to as long as it didn't reflect negatively on the film or on Goldwyn. "By an amazing coincidence," Russell recalled, "it turned out that *Best Years* was just about to open or had just opened wherever I went."[18]

Still, Russell tried to make the most of each engagement. Nearly two years after his honorable discharge from the army, he was struck by how divided the country seemed. At Walter Reed in ward 32, his fellow disabled veterans had come from different backgrounds. Often they did not share the same socioeconomic status or the same religious beliefs, and occasionally they represented different races and nationalities. And yet they bonded over what they had in common, what Russell described as "a splendid and inspiring spirit of comradeship." Russell wanted to emphasize this point in his talks, to point out the irony that as a nation, "we had been willing to battle hatred and intolerance in every far corner of the globe, yet we were unwilling or afraid to battle them right here at home."[19]

But the thirty-two-year-old, new to public speaking, wasn't ready to get too political on Goldwyn's dime. Instead, Russell invoked his Hollywood experience, observing that the cast and crew that had come together to make *Best Years* represented different backgrounds, nationalities, and political views. "Yet they had been able to fuse themselves successfully in a common enterprise, to submerge their differences in order to help create something that was fine and beautiful and true," Russell observed.[20]

Russell's life on the road soon became routine. Upon arriving in each city or town, he would be met at the train station by local Goldwyn representatives and press. At his hotel, he would hold a press conference before touring a hospital (military or otherwise) and having lunch with members of a local veterans group like the newly formed AMVETS. A radio interview would often follow lunch, and then he would appear that evening as the guest speaker at a banquet for charity. He frequently departed the same night, taking another train or occasionally catching a flight to the next city on his itinerary. In the end, the experience was sobering. "Few Americans really understood or were aware of the full price of war, and no amount of words or statistics, no matter how eloquent or impressive, would have any real effect," said Russell.[21]

Around the same time, a number of new reviews and editorials began appearing about *Best Years*, suggesting that the film contained communist propaganda. In April, William Markham reviewed the film for *Plain Talk*, an anticommunist journal, and criticized several scenes for their anticapitalist bias, such as the one near the beginning of the film when Dana Andrews's character, Fred, makes a rich businessman look bad for not giving up his airplane seat. *Best Years*, concluded Markham, was a "vicious and dangerous film."[22] In "An Oscar for Falsehoods," the *Tulsa Tribune*'s Richard Lloyd Jones described the film along suspiciously similar lines, calling *Best Years* a "masterpiece of subversive half-truths" that received its Academy Awards because of "organized pressure from all the organized leftist wings." Using language similar to Markham's, Jones called the film a "vicious picture . . . a humanly moving story prepared to serve as a convoy for a political tract deliberately falsifying American democracy and its attitude toward our soldiers."[23]

Conversely, the screenwriter Abraham Polonsky reviewed *Best Years* for a new leftist journal called the *Hollywood Quarterly*. Polonsky was open about his membership in the Communist Party, and he thought Wyler and Sherwood could have done *more* to promote a socialist agenda within the film. "Author and director bowed and passed," he wrote, although he praised the film's "human" characterizations as "a landmark in the fog of escapism, meretricious violence, and the gimmick plot attitude of the usual movie."[24] In the *Daily Worker*, John Ross leveled a similar charge against the character of Al, who just seemed "off" rather than effectively critical of his bank's cautious attitude toward giving loans to veterans lacking collateral, making the film's "social satire" of the banking industry "nonsense."[25] These and other mentions were flagged by Goldwyn's team, who discussed whether they deserved a response. After the Americanization Committee of the Veterans of Foreign Wars wrote to Goldwyn about Markham's piece in *Plain Talk*, he was urged by his team to respond publicly to one or all of the charges of promulgating communist propaganda.

But it wasn't until John Lechner, executive director of the Motion Picture Alliance for the Preservation of American Ideals, named *Best Years* to a list of recent films promoting communist propaganda that Goldwyn decided to respond. Walt Disney, the writer-director-producer Leo McCarey, and other well-placed conservatives had created the organization in 1944, and the list compiled by Lechner included the romantic comedy *Margie* (King, 1946). "I defy this man to prove that [*Best Years*] has been adjudged communistic in any way by the House Un-American Activities Committee," Goldwyn stated. (The congressional committee had resumed its investigation of communist "infiltration" in Hollywood.) Goldwyn also issued a challenge to Lechner, offering to make "a sizable donation" to a "recognized" charity if he could prove his claims. "I demand that he either prove them or shut up," Goldwyn fumed. Not long after, the MPAPAI board of directors announced Lechner's resignation.[26]

Best Years was just one of several films in the mid to late 1940s that explored important social issues of the time. *The Lost Weekend* (Wilder, 1945) dealt with alcoholism; *Crossfire* (Dmytryk, 1947) and *Gentleman's Agreement* (Kazan, 1947) addressed anti-Semitism; and *Pinky* (Kazan, 1949) dealt with racism, to name just a few that would later be labeled "social-problem films." As daring as *Best Years*, these films and their makers were in some cases punished for bringing such bold statements to the screen. Others may have been found guilty by association. Roman Bohnen, who played Fred's impoverished father, Pat Derry, in *Best Years*, was a cofounder of the Actors' Laboratory Theatre. In 1948, Bohnen and several others in the theater group were subpoenaed to come before the Tenney Committee, a HUAC-like panel in the California state senate.[27] Wyler and Robert Sherwood had sensed an escalation of this kind of fear and cynicism back in 1946 when they began working on the *Best Years* script, and they had tried to address it in different ways, as with the character of Mr. Mollett, who confronts Homer at the soda fountain. "I'm convinced I wouldn't be allowed today to make *The Best Years of Our Lives* as it was made a year ago," Wyler said in October 1947.[28]

But for the time being, Willy turned his attention to *Best Years'* overseas release. In late May, he and Talli prepared to leave Los Angeles for their European tour. Still forbidden to fly by his doctors, Willy arranged for them to travel by train to New York, where they would board the *Queen Elizabeth* for England. Their three-month itinerary included stops in France, Italy, Switzerland, Luxembourg, and Belgium, where Willy would receive an award for the film at the inaugural World Festival of Film in Brussels. Accompanying them on the ship was a brand-new Buick convertible purchased by Willy. He and Talli planned to tool around Europe in the automobile, a commodity in short supply on the war-ravaged continent. In England they spent time with Laurence Olivier and Vivien Leigh as well as the director Carol Reed and his soon-to-be wife, the actress Penelope Dudley-Ward. Willy and Reed, who had become good friends during the war, were happy to see each other again. Rationing was still in place in most of Europe—agriculture was slow to recover on the devastated continent. The food in Paris, as elsewhere, was lackluster. Decades later Talli remembered the city's yellow bread, a consequence of the lack of wheat.[29]

In addition to attending the Belgian film festival in June, where *Best Years* won for best scenario and Myrna Loy was recognized with the award for best female performance, the Wylers visited the set of Fred Zinnemann's *The Search*. The film was a Swiss-American coproduction featuring Ivan Jandl, a non-English-speaking Czechoslovakian boy who plays an Auschwitz survivor searching for his mother across Europe. Zinnemann was shooting on location amid the ruins of postwar Germany; the production would then move to Zurich, where filming would continue on a soundstage. Zinnemann shared Wyler's drive to portray authenticity on the screen, and Wyler enjoyed being able to watch his colleague at work. Wyler was also a fan of *Shoeshine* (De Sica, 1946), *Open City*, and other recent films of the postwar Italian neorealist movement, which favored nonprofessional actors, location shooting, and a black-and-white aesthetic.[30]

In Berlin, Wyler had the opportunity to watch *Best Years* at a theater where it was shown with German subtitles. He was pleased with how it came out. "You got the impression it was about German soldiers," Wyler said later of the universality of the story. He had intended to watch only one reel, but he wound up staying through the entire film. Wyler was less impressed with people's attitudes in the city itself, telling a biographer later that he thought the arrogant Germans had learned nothing from the war.[31]

Best Years had been playing overseas since March, when the film had its British premiere in London. The English film critic C. A. Lejeune, who wrote for the *Observer*, praised *Best Years* in her inimitably withering manner. "The film is primarily designed for American audiences, speaking to them in a language they appreciate and understand," she wrote a week after the film had swept the Academy Awards in the United States. "That is to say, it is smartly appointed, frankly sentimental, inclined towards facile political discussions, but it has guts." She noted that *Best Years* was the type of film that would never get made in England, "where we incline to keep our emotions stopped down."[32] Her fellow Londoners were somewhat more enthusiastic, standing in record-setting queues to see the film at theaters around the city. At the Odeon in the Richmond neighborhood, for instance, lines were so long that the theater manager took to running the first reel a second time *after* the end of the film so that those who might have missed it had the opportunity to watch the entire movie.[33]

Most of *Best Years'* international reviews took issue with its lengthy running time. Given that the film had been honored by members of the foreign press with a Golden Globe earlier that year, however, it came as little surprise that most international reviewers liked the film. The critic for the *Glasgow Herald* called it a "rare" Hollywood film that, despite "too much advance trumpeting," was still a "good" film. The French critic Jean Morienval wrote that the film's treatment of its postwar subject "is worth all the praise." And at the film's premiere in Berlin, the German audience applauded *Best Years*, with one attendee getting word back to Wyler that the film "was one of the very few American pictures released since V-E Day" to receive such a warm reception in Germany.[34]

The Wylers' return to the States coincided with the release, at long last, of Willy's wartime documentary *Thunderbolt*. Jimmy Stewart's prologue, with Stewart dressed in civilian clothes and seated in a leather armchair, offers a bit of Hollywood glamour and necessary context for the film, whose images had been shot and edited nearly three years earlier. Stewart reads from a telegram sent by General Carl Spaatz, the general who had approved Wyler's commission when they met at a Washington cocktail party in the summer of 1942. Spotlighting the role of the P-47 Liberators in Operation Strangle, a mission of the Fifty-Seventh Fighter group, the documentary was shot in Technicolor and narrated by the actor Lloyd Bridges and the Broadway star Eugene Kern, the uncredited narrator of *The Memphis Belle*. (It was the military's custom during the war to dispense with most film credits.) *Thunderbolt* recounts the bombers' efforts to weaken the German front along Italy's southern coast by destroying bridges, train tracks, and other infrastructure. "The film has the courage to label the bombing of Cassino, the wasteful, pointless maneuver it turned out to be," wrote Arthur Spaeth in the *Cleveland News*. "It did, however, underscore the need for Operation Strangle." A reviewer for the *Chicago Tribune* called it "memorable and grafic [*sic*]," and another critic described it as "completely engrossing" in its sympathetic portrait of the fighter pilots. In general *Thunderbolt* received positive notices, but as Wyler feared, its delayed release made its subject matter seem severely out of date.[35]

Since Liberty had been acquired by Paramount the previous spring, Willy had been working out of an office on the studio's lot off Melrose Avenue. It was there in September, across the street at Lucey's restaurant, that he met up with his friends Philip Dunne and John Huston to discuss mounting concerns about the House Un-American Activities Committee. Formed in the US House of Representatives in the late 1930s, the investigative committee went more or less dormant at the start of World War II but had quietly resumed its mission to ferret out suspected communists in Hollywood. Some in the film industry had already experienced its dangerous reach. Over two days in August 1940, Dunne, a screenwriter of films such as *How Green Was My Valley* (Ford, 1941) and *Forever Amber* (Preminger, 1947), had been summoned to Los Angeles's Biltmore Hotel by the committee's chairman, Martin Dies (R-Texas), to give testimony about his connection with the Communist Party. *Best Years'* Fredric March also gave testimony at that time. The next day, a former communist organizer named John L. Leech identified March and Dunne, among others, as having been members of the party during the 1930s. While nothing much came of the charge for Dunne, March had to clear his name in 1949 when the Hollywood blacklist—a roster of those ineligible to work in the industry because of suspected communist or other "subversive" ties—was in full force. According to a "secret FBI report," March and his wife, Florence Eldridge, were mixed up in an espionage trial involving the suspected Soviet spy Judith Coplon.[36]

During the summer of 1947, Representative J. Parnell Thomas (D-NJ) arrived in Hollywood to meet with several industry insiders who were concerned about potential "reds" in the filmmaking community. Thomas had replaced Martin Dies, who retired from the House in 1944. The Hollywood insiders with whom Thomas met were cooperative, or "friendly," witnesses, a group that included the actor Robert Taylor and Ginger Rogers's "mom-ager," Lela. Together, they provided the names of industry players whom they suspected of having communist leanings. Their list of names encompassed the "Unfriendlies" (as they were collectively known), a group of writers and directors who would be called to testify in front of the committee the following month in Washington. The original, longer list was whittled down to what would become known as the "Hollywood Ten."[37]

Over lunch that September day at Lucey's, Wyler, Huston, and Dunne began to sketch out a mission statement for a political action group that came to be known as the Committee for the First Amendment (CFA). As Wyler later explained to Lillian Hellman, the committee came together quickly ("spontaneously, almost overnight") a couple of weeks before the first hearings began in

Washington. "There is an atmosphere of fear in Hollywood which makes it difficult to work," Wyler wrote to Hellman. Unbeknownst to him at the time, the Los Angeles field office of the Federal Bureau of Investigation had included *The Best Years of Our Lives* on a list of films that was being forwarded to the FBI's Washington headquarters. The eight films, including *It's A Wonderful Life*, had been categorized by the bureau as containing "Communist propaganda."[38]

At first, meetings among like-minded people in Hollywood took place in private residences such as Ira Gershwin's mansion on North Roxbury Drive in Beverly Hills. Organizers were soon gathering almost daily at the popular restaurant Chasen's, whose owner, Dave Chasen, was sympathetic to the CFA's cause. The group included stars (Lauren Bacall and her husband, Humphrey Bogart, Paulette Goddard, Eddie Cantor, and Vincent Price), filmmakers (George Stevens, Edward Dmytryk, and John Houseman), and producers (David O. Selznick and Jerry Wald), who met to discuss how they might fight back against the committee. Norman Corwin, a well-known and politically connected writer for radio, was in on the earliest conversations with Dunne, Wyler, and Huston. It was Corwin who spearheaded the plan to produce two star-studded radio broadcasts to publicize the CFA's call to action.[39]

By mid-October, 35 people representing the CFA had signed a letter of protest against the hearings that were scheduled to begin in Washington on October 20. The hearings would focus specifically on the ten "unfriendly" witnesses who had been called to testify. Supporters of the CFA, whose membership would grow to around 135 people, included writers as well as actors, directors, and producers concerned about what they believed was an attack on civil liberties. "Those were wild days," recalled Myrna Loy, who had signed the protest. Loy had always been politically active, and her wartime work with the Red Cross had made her even more so. Her relationship with Eleanor Roosevelt, with whom she would work to help create the United Nations after working on *Best Years*, led to her being labeled "pink" (not quite "red," but still suspect) at the height of the Hollywood blacklist era in the 1950s.[40]

The CFA planned to use the star power of its most celebrated members to call attention to HUAC's bullying and dangerous tactics. The CFA spent $13,000 to charter a plane from Howard Hughes's airline, TWA. Hughes had dealt with Thomas that summer, so he was willing to support the CFA in its efforts. He offered the use of a plane free of charge, but Wyler and the others orchestrating the event wanted to keep everything aboveboard. Instead, CFA members donated funds to cover the flight. About two dozen of them agreed to fly to Washington, where they would take a stand against HUAC on October 27, the day that Eric Johnston, the head of the industry's largest trade organization, was scheduled to appear in front of the committee.

On the morning of Sunday, October 26, celebrities including Bacall, Bogart,

Gene Kelly, Marsha Hunt, and Danny Kaye boarded the chartered flight, which made stops along the way to raise awareness of their cause. In Kansas City, Kaye spoke to reporters about a heightened level of anxiety that had taken hold in Hollywood. No genre of moviemaking was safe, he said: "It's reached the place where you have to be careful even shooting a Wild West picture." Using a scene of a bank holdup as an example, the performer described how even the most innocent exchange between a sheriff and an onlooker about the bad guys could be misconstrued. "If you say 'they went left,' the first thing you know you're up before the House Un-American Activities Committee."[41]

Still forbidden to fly by his doctors, Wyler remained in Los Angeles as Dunne and Huston accompanied the stars to Washington. Before their departure, Wyler had counseled the group on their politics, their clothes, and other matters. If any member of the group hadn't been forthcoming about past communist activity or affiliations, Wyler said, don't show up at the airport. But if they chose to go, "We must not look like slobs," Wyler told them.[42]

As the Hollywood contingent touched down in Washington that Sunday evening, the local radio station WMAL began its broadcast of *Hollywood Fights Back!*, the first of the two radio programs produced by Norman Corwin. The program was a mix of live and prerecorded statements read by forty-five members of the CFA and four US senators, all Democrats. Gene Kelly, Lauren Bacall, Danny Kaye, and other members of the "Airborne 22" had recorded their statements in advance. In Los Angeles, another twenty or so stars broadcast their statements live from a local radio station. Fredric March, still wearing period sideburns and a bushier-than-normal mustache from his most recent role, took part, as did his wife, Florence Eldridge. Myrna Loy read her statement after Eldridge, and March read his after Wyler. In essence, everyone echoed the comments by Judy Garland, who was the first to speak. Asking listeners whether they had been to any movies that week or read any newspapers or magazines, Garland said, "It's always been your right to read or see anything you wanted to—but now it seems to be getting kinda complicated. For the past week in Washington, the House Committee on Un-American Activities has been investigating the film industry. . . . I've been following this investigation and I don't like it!"[43]

The hearings, which had begun a week earlier, on October 20, were held on the third floor of the stately Old House Office Building, whose Caucus Room was filled to overflowing with approximately four hundred people in attendance. As the historian Thomas Doherty observes, "It was the first full-on media-political spectacle of the postwar era."[44] The hearings were accessible via print, radio, or newsreel, with NBC offering a highlight reel on television every evening. Televised coverage would have been more extensive, but the electrical outlets in the forty-year-old structure couldn't power the transmission, as engineers realized in the days before the hearings started. By 1947, just under forty-five thousand television sets were in operation in the United States, most of them in taverns and other public spaces. Like many others, Talli and Willy followed the hearings in the newspaper and on the radio.[45]

Dressed in a pinstriped suit, J. Parnell Thomas presided over the proceedings from atop a pillow and a telephone book that had been added to his chair to enhance the diminutive senator's sight line. He opened the proceedings that Monday morning by reading from a prepared statement. His brown eyes blinked from behind wire-rimmed glasses, and his moon-shaped face hovered above a fat radio microphone. Describing the film business as an industry that "offers a tremendous weapon for education and propaganda," Thomas justified the committee's investigation by identifying certain Hollywood entities such as the Screen Writers Guild, of which all but one of the Hollywood Ten were members, as "lousy" with communists.[46]

The Friendlies appeared throughout that first week. Walt Disney talked about "smoking out" communists within the industry, while Gary Cooper struck an "aw-shucks" attitude in front of the committee. Robert Taylor was all business, naming the actor Howard Da Silva and the writer Lester Cole as communists.[47]

Having arrived in Washington on the Sunday evening before the hearing entered its second week, the Hollywood supporters showed up en masse the next morning, October 27. Eric Johnston, president of the MPAA, was scheduled to speak on behalf of the film industry. Weary from their cross-country travel and late arrival the previous night, Bacall, Bogart, Kaye, and their colleagues met with the press before entering the building. The Hollywood contingent had been joined the night before by New York counterparts from the theater, a group led by the actor John Garfield.

Eric Johnston was one of the first to speak that Monday morning. He read from a prepared statement that took Thomas's committee to task for the previous week's spectacle. "You have a lot of sensational testimony about Hollywood. From some of it the public will get the idea that Hollywood is running over with Communists and communism," Johnston said. He requested that HUAC make public its list of films that purportedly promoted communism. "Expose communism, but don't put any American who isn't a Communist in a concentration camp of suspicion," said Johnston, invoking perhaps the most haunting specter from the war. Johnston finished his statement by reminding the committee, "We are not willing to give up our freedoms to save our freedoms."[48]

Then it was time for the Unfriendlies to testify. Although nineteen witnesses had been subpoenaed, only eleven would take the stand that week. In response to such questions as "Are you a member of the Screen Writers Guild?" and "Are you a member of the Communist Party or have you ever been a member?," the producer Adrian Scott, as well as the writers John Howard Lawson and Dalton

Trumbo, chose instead to discuss their reasons for not answering such questions. The soft-spoken Scott, who had recently produced *Crossfire* for RKO, began his statement by saying, "I don't think it's a proper question . . . It invades my right as a citizen and invades the First Amendment." Trumbo and Lawson were more confrontational. Trumbo asked to see the committee's reported "evidence" of his being a communist, and Lawson began to read from a prepared statement, becoming increasingly agitated as Thomas repeatedly pounded his gavel and harassed the writer for not answering the committee's questions.[49]

Meanwhile, Sam Goldwyn was killing time in New York in a suite on the tenth floor of the Sherry-Netherland Hotel, waiting to be called as a witness. Goldwyn had been subpoenaed in late September, along with his fellow studio heads Jack Warner and Louis B. Mayer, but unlike his colleagues, he had not been summoned to testify. Warner and Mayer had opened the hearings on October 20, but by the second week, Goldwyn still hadn't been called. By three in the afternoon on October 30, it became clear that Goldwyn wouldn't be traveling to Washington: Representative Thomas abruptly announced the conclusion of the "first phase" of the committee's investigation.[50]

When Goldwyn learned, along with the rest of the country, that the hearings had come to a sudden end, he arranged to give a press conference the following day. "I had an idea it would be a flop," the producer boasted to reporters. Goldwyn and Wyler may not have been on speaking terms that fall, but they shared a similar sense of outrage that *Best Years*, of all films, had made the short list of pictures reportedly containing communist propaganda. "The most un-American activity which I have observed has been the activity of the committee itself," said a defiant Goldwyn.[51]

That Sunday, the *New York Times* ran an editorial by the film critic Bosley Crowther, a fan of Wyler's and of *Best Years*. Subtitled "Will Filmmaking Be Complicated by the 'Un-American' Probers?," the article expressed concern about the impact that HUAC's two weeks of hearings might have on movie screens: "This much is clearly evident to an observer of American films—and indeed, it was frankly acknowledged by Mr. Johnston in his statement last week: so long as this House committee can ride herd on the movie industry as it has, the freedom of film producers will be intimidated and coerced." An appreciative Wyler wrote to Crowther a few days later. "You must be as outraged as I am by these vicious attacks on the film industry," he began. Wyler expressed his concern that a loss of authenticity onscreen would compromise audiences' acceptance ("both here and abroad") of American films. "In going over in my mind the great films of the past twenty years, it shocks me to realize how many of them couldn't be made today in the same way."[52]

Wyler was upset by the hearings, but he was also frustrated by the behavior on the stand of the Hollywood Ten. Before the Airborne 22 had left for Washington, he reminded the group that they were going to support the MPAA's Johnston, who in turn was defending the film industry to HUAC. Stay away from the Unfriendlies, Wyler said of Lawson, Trumbo, and the others. "I told them the newspapers would say that they were there to defend the Communists, but they were going to Washington to attack HUAC and not defend any Communists," he recalled nearly a decade later.[53]

Despite his frustration, Wyler continued to be a part of the CFA's steering committee, writing to Hellman in mid-November about plans to expand the CFA's reach. The second broadcast of *Hollywood Fights Back!* had aired on Sunday, November 2, and the CFA had received nearly one thousand letters ("only 10% unfavorable"). Wyler and the others wanted to capitalize on the momentum. Plans were in the works to print additional pamphlets and to release the two CFA radio broadcasts as record albums, in part to reach industry people who, while not usually politically active, might be moved by the "atmosphere of fear" to get involved. "I hope you can help us in New York by joining with us, raising money and ideas and in general to give us what support you can," Wyler wrote to Hellman. "It's all the same fight." Indeed, Hellman's own battle with HUAC was just beginning. Within a couple of years, she found herself blacklisted in Hollywood after appearing in front of the committee to defend her political activism and to deny being a member of the Communist Party. She struggled to find work, getting by with financial help from Willy and Talli.[54]

In the end, Johnston and his seemingly hard-line stance in front of HUAC underwent a profound shift. Over two days in late November, Johnston convened approximately fifty members of the film industry at the Waldorf Astoria on Park Avenue in New York City.[55] Studio heads, top producers, key executives, and attorneys began gathering on the hotel's fourth floor around noon on November 24, making their way into the lavish two-room Le Perroquet Suite, named for the wild parrots cavorting in the murals that decorated its walls. The reception area and adjoining small banquet room, with its cloth-covered tables, provided an elegant backdrop for a series of tense and occasionally contentious meetings. More than two hundred miles away in Washington, members of the House of Representatives were casting their votes to uphold the HUAC contempt citations issued for the Hollywood Ten.

What a difference a year made. Almost to the day a year earlier, Samuel Goldwyn had been in New York for *Best Years'* triumphant premiere at the Astor Theatre. Now he and his fellow independent producers David O. Selznick and Walter Wanger were in closed-door meetings to discuss with their colleagues what seemed like the fate of the industry. Goldwyn was among a minority group of liberals who opposed Johnston's recommendation to purge the industry of the Hollywood Ten and any known communists. Before the meeting, Goldwyn had prepared a statement saying, in effect, that industry leaders would withhold judgment and suspend action until the US Supreme Court had weighed in on the fate of the ten. Johnston and the others vehemently opposed such a delay.[56]

Discussion and debate continued into the evening. By two o'clock on the following afternoon, a two-page statement had been written. It was printed, mimeographed, and distributed to members of the press, and Johnston was filmed reading the declaration before a newsreel camera, a segment that would be screened for motion picture audiences in theaters around the country. Sitting to the left of an appropriately funereal spray of flowers, Johnston addressed the camera: "We will forthwith discharge or suspend without compensation those [on the blacklist] in our employ, and we will not reemploy any of the 10 until such time as he is acquitted or has purged himself of contempt and declares under oath that he is not a Communist," he read in part. Further, he stated that members of the MPAA would not "knowingly employ a Communist" or any other member of a group that supports the overthrow of the US government.[57]

Goldwyn wasn't happy to have been on the losing end of the Waldorf meetings, but once the declaration was adopted, he went along with it. Although the CFA didn't officially disband until February 1948, the abrupt end to the chaotic hearings on October 30, and Hollywood's Waldorf statement three weeks later, took much of the wind out of the group's sails. In later years, Wyler acknowledged that mistakes were made in developing the CFA's strategy. "We attacked the hearings, when the HUAC legally had the right to investigate. We should have attacked the Committee's methods rather than the Committee itself," he said.[58]

Wyler was never called before the committee in 1947, nor was he summoned in later years, as his good friend Lillian Hellman was. Heavily redacted FBI documents from the time show quite clearly that Wyler was under regular surveillance in September and October 1947. Philip Dunne, for one, thought that Paramount might have protected Wyler from being called to testify and defend his involvement in organizing the CFA. "He was a bankable director, a major figure," Dunne explained to Wyler's biographer. "He made them money."[59] And while Wyler made *Best Years* for a studio other than Paramount, the film had earned more than $11 million by the end of 1947 and continued to receive high praise wherever it played, which only enhanced Wyler's bankability.

CHAPTER 8

A Training Film for All of Us

As long as we have wars and returning veterans, some of them wounded, The Best Years of Our Lives will not be dated.
ROGER EBERT

Throughout the fall of 1947, during the HUAC hearings and the subsequent Waldorf meeting, *Best Years* continued to play in theaters around the world. Harold Russell's speaking engagements in the spring of 1947 had proved very successful. While not directly tied to the film, his appearances in cities throughout the country no doubt helped maintain interest in the movie. He spoke to high school and college students, fellow veterans, GIs, and civic groups. "It was tiring, exhausting work," Russell said of the relentless schedule, which had him moving from town to town almost daily. "But it was deeply satisfying, too."[1]

Russell proved so popular that he acquired a manager and an offer from the William Morris Agency to put together a kind of live variety act that would open that summer. For $1,750 a week, Russell would share behind-the-scenes Hollywood stories, play "Tea for Two" on the piano, and mix in a bit of discussion about democracy and racial unity. "I knew that a lot of people wanted to see the fellow without hands who had won two Oscars in Hollywood," said Russell of the audiences who came to his "performance." But within minutes of taking the stage for his first appearance, he knew he had been miscast. "In a sense I was merely a glorified freak being exhibited in a high-class sideshow."[2]

Russell honored his contract with William Morris despite the bad fit and appreciated that the audiences that came to the show were mostly sympathetic and polite. One attendee in particular sought out Russell after one of his performances. Lou Sidman headed up the Denver branch of the Anti-Defamation League (ADL), a Jewish organization that since 1913 had worked to combat anti-Semitism. Since the end of the war, the ADL had sought to broaden its message to promote civil liberties for all. Sidman was especially impressed by Russell's comments about tolerance, and he thought Russell could do good work for the ADL by visiting high schools around the country. Taking a sizable pay cut, Russell signed on with the organization for $250 a week. Thanks to having worked with kids at the YMCA in Cambridge, Russell knew how to relate to teenagers. By sharing the story of his accident and his subsequent rehabilitation at Walter Reed with other veterans from different backgrounds, he drew connections between physical and mental handicaps and encouraged his young audiences to think for themselves.[3]

One of Russell's most meaningful appearances occurred in Chicago on October 19, 1947, on the eve of the HUAC hearings in Washington. Russell had been invited to speak in honor of the first war dead sent home from the Pacific. The ceremony took place at Soldier Field, the football stadium that overlooked Lake Michigan. Tens of thousands of people filled the historic arena to pay tribute to the fallen men. The stadium's blazing lights went dark as an honor guard made its way onto the field. Candlelight rippled across the stadium as attendees lit tapers. Soldiers, sailors, and marines accompanied the procession of funeral caissons bearing ten caskets draped in American flags. Russell joined other notables on the stage, including the opera singer James Melton, the governor of Illinois, and Admiral James Foskett, who attended on behalf of President Truman.[4]

Russell's presence at the ceremony was doubly poignant. Most of those in attendance probably recognized him as Homer, the disabled sailor in *Best Years*. They also likely knew Russell's story of sacrifice as a soldier wounded while on duty at Camp Mackall. Of the notables on stage, Russell was the last to speak. His brief remarks focused on what he imagined the war dead might say if they could speak to those gathered in Soldier Field that evening. "Keep faith with us! Make sure that we have not died for nothing. Make sure that the work we began is finished. Pray—work—fight—to build a nation that will stand, united and strong and beautiful, that will work for peace always, that will give the world that faith, that hope and leadership it so desperately needs," Russell told the hushed crowd. The next morning in Washington, J. Parnell Thomas convened the hearings of the House Un-American Activities Committee.[5]

In early 1948, William Wyler shifted his focus back to filmmaking. Although he and Lillian Hellman had made a deal to collaborate on *Sister Carrie*, that project was put off, in part because of Hellman's presence on the Hollywood blacklist, which prevented Wyler from hiring her. At the start of the new year, Wyler had received a call from Olivia de Havilland about developing a film for her based on Ruth and Augustus Goetz's play *The Heiress*, itself an adaptation of the Henry James novel *Washington Square*. De Havilland was in the news as much for her acting accomplishments as for her ongoing rift with the actress

Joan Fontaine, her sister, but it was her successful suit against Warner Bros. during the war that earned her renewed respect among her peers. Her challenge of the studio's notoriously binding seven-year contract, which had been extended in her case to account for multiple suspensions, led to a period without work. Despite de Havilland's triumph in court, Warner Bros. had effectively black-balled her in the industry.

After three years of inactivity, de Havilland began working again shortly after the end of the war. By early 1948, she had wrapped *The Snake Pit* at Twentieth Century–Fox with Anatole Litvak, a gripping drama about mental illness that, like *Best Years*, would influence mainstream attitudes, in this case leading to real change in the country's mental health system. De Havilland's role as a woman grappling with schizophrenia was a demanding one, and she was eager to follow it with something completely different. In January, Wyler traveled to New York to see *The Heiress*, which had been running at the Biltmore Theatre since the previous fall with Wendy Hiller in the lead role as Catherine Sloper, a wealthy plain Jane being romanced by a young suitor with presumably dishonorable intentions. After some back-and-forth with Paramount, Wyler acquired the screen rights to the period piece, hired the husband-and-wife playwrights to adapt the script, and set about casting an ensemble of actors to support de Havilland in the starring role.[6]

Unlike Wyler and the others who had worked on *Best Years*, Samuel Goldwyn had yet to move on to a new project. It was unusual for Goldwyn not to have a new film in production or development while his current picture was playing in theaters. But by early 1948, nearly a year after winning the Academy Award, he had nothing in the pipeline. As the months wore on, Goldwyn grew anxious. He wasn't sleeping well, and his moodiness and distraction were affecting his home life. His wife, Frances, must have felt a little like Wyler did on the release of *Best Years*. In the many interviews Goldwyn gave and the comments he made to the media, he never acknowledged his wife's role in spotting the original *Time* magazine article. Frances had been moved to read the article in part because of their son Sammy's involvement in the war. By 1948, Sam Jr. was living in London and beginning his own career in the film business, and their daughter, Ruth, was married and raising her family. Frances had always been Sam's trusted adviser, but his preoccupation with his own problems created distance between them.[7]

As the producer of *Best Years*, Goldwyn had the responsibility of keeping tabs on its ongoing distribution, which by 1948 included screenings in more than a dozen countries. *Best Years* had been such a hit in London and other parts of England that it became the highest-grossing film ever released in the country. By 1949, *Best Years* had received multiple awards overseas, including the Victoire du cinema français in France (Wyler had previously won for

Mrs. Miniver); the Best Director award for Wyler at the Karlovy Vary Film Festival in Czechoslovakia; and a Hannya from the Japanese in acknowledgment of the film's role in honoring the revival of importation of US motion pictures. In recognition of the Hannya award, the Japanese government sent two masks and a painting of Mount Fuji to Goldwyn's office. The studio engaged in a series of comical memorandums with the Japanese in an effort to determine which mask was intended for Goldwyn and which for Wyler. In the end, Goldwyn received the Hannya (female demon) and Wyler, the Okina, or "benevolent old man," mask. The painting, noted the Japanese, was meant for Harold Russell. Closer to home, a trade group of US exhibitors crowned *Best Years* the "Top Money Picture of the Year" at the end of 1948. Goldwyn's arrangement to keep the film in limited release at advance-admission prices for a year after its premiere undoubtedly helped it earn this particular recognition.[8]

Two years after its initial release, *The Best Years of Our Lives* had begun to take on a life of its own. Goldwyn was pleased to assist the War Department when General Robert McLure requested a print of the film to use in "re-educating the Germans." McLure was a psychological-warfare specialist stationed in Germany during the Occupation, and he told Goldwyn the army also planned to distribute *Best Years* in Austria, Japan, and Korea.[9] In the United States, William Paley, the president of CBS, chose the film as the subject of *The Hollywood Story*, a radio program about the film industry and the "social implications of picture making." In March 1948, a CBS reporter named Peter Lynn visited the Goldwyn lot to meet with Sam and tour the facilities where *Best Years* was made. The project required months of preparation as Goldwyn, Wyler, and others connected with the film sat for interviews. The producer opened his files for Lynn and others working on the broadcast, and authorized the use of audio clips from the film. But when the producer read a copy of the final script for the program in the summer of 1948, he was livid. He wrote to Paley, whom he and Frances had known since the late 1920s, claiming to be "shocked and surprised" at how he was portrayed. For starters, Goldwyn took issue with how the script characterized his handling of the Breen Office's objections to the *Best Years* screenplay. "I didn't treat the matters raised in the cavalier manner the script sets out," Goldwyn wrote.[10]

The producer's objections delayed the project by a few months, and it was finally broadcast in November, two years after *Best Years'* initial release. John Hansen, reviewing the CBS broadcast for *PM* magazine, was most impressed by the program's handling of Breen's objections to the screenplay. Quoting Breen's warning about the script's depiction of the breakup of Fred and Marie's marriage ("The several scenes . . . should be re-examined, and, possibly rewritten. . . . This is important."), Hansen wrote that upon hearing the "voice" of the Breen Office through its letters to Goldwyn, "the broadcast took on, for one listener at least, the spine-chilling tones of harsh reality. . . . Would that the rest of the show had been as real." For his part, Goldwyn seemed pleased with the entire production in its final form. Writing to Paley the morning after *The Hollywood Story* aired, Goldwyn declared, "To my mind it is one of the best jobs to date on any network."[11]

Goldwyn was more guarded in his response to the cartoonist Milton Caniff, who wrote to the studio to request permission to reproduce scenes from the film in his newest comic strip. Caniff's popular adventure strip *Terry and the Pirates* had run in syndication for a dozen years, and during the war he had drawn *Male Call* for military newspapers. His newest strip, *Steve Canyon*, chronicled the exploits of a former air force pilot operating his own air-transport business. In one story line, the character Reed Kimberly screens an American film for a foreign princess in order to show her what American life is really like. The cartoonist appealed to his readers, organizing a contest to determine which film he should use. *Best Years*, he told Goldwyn, was hands down his readers' top pick.[12]

As always, Goldwyn was mindful of his reputation, which now had the additional "burden" of an Academy Award. At seventy, the producer was highly suspicious of the Best Picture winner being visually interpreted by a cartoonist and reduced to scenes within the panels of a comic strip. Bill Hebert, Goldwyn's head of publicity, stepped in and assured his boss that having *Best Years* featured in a series of *Steve Canyon* strips was a "unique and exceptional" opportunity. In the strip's multiweek story, Kimberly's international audience is prepared to criticize the film's message. As Canyon begins the "Yankee" film, a skeptical viewer remarks, "Now we shall see the sort of propaganda they use to take their own people's minds off their miserable conditions." Another character dismisses Harold Russell as an "actor made up as if he has no hands," but they all marvel at the size of the Stephensons' apartment, given Al's rank as a "mere" sergeant. In the final panel of the story, one of Princess Snowflower's lackeys, agitated by the film's emotional power, shoots the projector.[13]

Clearly the times were changing, but could Goldwyn change with them? His son, Sam Jr., had returned to the United States and was now working alongside his father at the studio. Sam Jr. was also an army reservist, and when North Korea's tanks rolled across the border into South Korea in the summer of 1950, Sam Jr. received a letter informing him that he was being called back into duty. As with *Best Years*, Samuel Goldwyn's personal situation inspired his next project. He channeled his anxiety about his son's welfare into a new picture about "the effect of America's rearming on the lives of the American family today." It would be called *I Want You*, a reference to the iconic World War I recruiting poster of a finger-pointing Uncle Sam, illustrated by James Montgomery Flagg. Like *Best Years*, it would focus on three men, but *I Want You*'s characters would all be part of the same family; they would represent different generations and conflicting ideologies about the war. Making comparisons with *Best Years* almost inevitable, Goldwyn cast Dana Andrews, now his top contract player, in one of the film's lead roles as Martin Greer. At one time, Goldwyn had considered Farley Granger for the part of Homer Parrish in *Best Years*. Now Goldwyn cast the twenty-five-year-old Granger as Martin's teenage brother.[14]

Goldwyn had even approached Robert Sherwood about writing the screenplay for *I Want You*. Sherwood begged off, but not before encouraging Goldwyn to act quickly on the timely story. The producer hired Irwin Shaw to write the script and Mark Robson to direct. Robson, who had directed the provocative *Home of the Brave* (1949) for Stanley Kramer's independent company, had also done *Edge of Doom* (1950) for Goldwyn, considered one of the producer's biggest flops at the box office. Goldwyn released *I Want You* just before Christmas 1950, with distinctive red posters that were reminiscent of those designed to promote *Best Years*.

Critics couldn't help comparing Goldwyn's latest to his Oscar winner from 1946. One reviewer noted that while Goldwyn's "average for producing superior pictures is far better than average," his current production didn't fit the Goldwyn mold. "Unfortunately he did not re-engage Robert E. Sherwood . . . nor William Wyler," wrote Wood Soanes, who concluded, "The results are not happy." The *New York Times*' Bosley Crowther was more direct: "A straight recruiting poster would be more convincing and pack more dramatic appeal." Even the most positive reviews of *I Want You* were qualified in their praise, acknowledging the motion picture's "provocative" story line while admitting that it was a flawed film.[15]

Unlike his former producer, William Wyler seemed to be moving forward with ease. *The Heiress* had done well at the box office upon its release in 1949, and the film received eight Academy Award nominations in early 1950, including nods for best picture and best director. Although Wyler did not win, the academy awarded statuettes to de Havilland and to the film's crew heads for art direction and set decoration (John Meehan, Harry Horner, and Emile Kuri), costume design (Edith Head and Gile Steele), and original score (Aaron Copland).

Wyler couldn't completely move on from *Best Years*, however. His stake in the film entitled him to 20 percent of its net profits, and in the summer of 1948, he retained an accountant to begin looking over the receipts. A year later, Wyler officially sued Goldwyn for underreporting *Best Years*' net profits by approximately $200,000. Included in the suit was Wyler's claim that Goldwyn had given a 5 percent stake in the film's net profits to Sherwood "as a gratuity," without Wyler's approval. Additionally, this amount had been subtracted as a production cost when calculating Wyler's "additional compensation," reducing the overall amount he had received to date. The lawsuit made the trade papers, and while Wyler was committed to earning his fair share of *Best Years'* profits, he was wary of the "ordeal and publicity" that a trial might bring. The suit became even more complicated in the mid-1950s when Goldwyn stopped trying to duplicate his success with *Best Years* and simply reissued the film.[16]

"I am bringing the picture back," Goldwyn told the press in early 1954, several months after the armistice marked the end (on paper, at least) of the hostilities between North and South Korea. But what really convinced him, he said, was the "avalanche" of requests to rerelease the film after a three-minute clip from *Best Years* aired on Ed Sullivan's television variety show *The Toast of the Town*. "As a matter of imagination, Goldwyn may have planned the whole thing himself," remarked one skeptical journalist on hearing about the public clamor for the film's rerelease. Whatever the impetus, Goldwyn planned a gala premiere in the nation's capital to mark the event. Myrna Loy, who had recently married her fourth husband, Howland H. Sargeant, was in attendance at the premiere. Sargeant's position as assistant secretary of state for public affairs and Loy's ongoing work with UNESCO had required a move to Georgetown, although she continued to appear in movies. Interviewed during *Best Years'* 1954 run, Loy observed, "I still think it is my best piece of work."[17]

Refusing to call the film's second release a "reissue," Goldwyn spent $250,000 to advertise it as "The Most Honored Picture of All Time." In addition, he made the point in several interviews that *Best Years'* rerelease used widescreen technology, which set it apart from the current television fare. The increased popularity of TV was partly responsible for the more than 30 percent drop in weekly attendance at the movies since 1946, when approximately 90 million Americans went to the movies weekly. But neither the widescreen novelty of the rerelease nor Goldwyn's ballyhoo had much effect on dwindling movie audiences in 1954. The film earned less than $300,000 during its limited run. While that was a paltry amount compared with *Best Years'*s $11.3 million box-office gross during its initial release, the figure was fairly typical for a reissue at the time.[18]

In contrast, William Wyler's latest film, *Roman Holiday*, was doing quite well in theaters. Having premiered the previous summer, the romantic comedy starring Audrey Hepburn and Gregory Peck was by 1954 making its debut overseas. During *Best Years'* rerelease, in fact, *Roman Holiday* began to set box-office records and turn Hepburn into a worldwide sensation. William Holden, who had recently wrapped *Sabrina* with Hepburn for Billy Wilder and Paramount, returned in September from a press tour in Europe. In an interview with the *Hollywood Reporter*, he remarked that two films in particular seemed to be instrumental "in building American prestige abroad." One was *Roman Holiday*, and the other, *The Best Years of Our Lives*. "All we need is more directors like

Wyler," said Holden, "who realize you don't have to sacrifice honesty to make great films."[19]

The reissue of *The Best Years of Our Lives* coincided with Harold Russell's rising profile as a national advocate for veterans and disabled citizens. After the initial success of *Best Years*, President Truman had appointed Russell to the newly formed President's Committee on the Employment of People with Disabilities. In 1949, Russell was elected by his peers to head AMVETS. Chartered by Congress in 1944, AMVETS was created to assist World War II veterans in receiving federal benefits at a time when most veterans' groups were focused on those who had served in World War I. Russell's role in *Best Years* gave him a certain amount of celebrity, but it was his own experience as a disabled veteran that ensured his credibility. One of his goals as head of AMVETS was to help reform the Veterans Administration, which by the 1950s was struggling to accommodate not only those who had fought in World War II but also those veterans who had participated in the Korean War. Giving testimony on Capitol Hill in 1950, Russell observed, "Neither the public nor the veteran wants to see the VA's precious skills and experience in treating war injuries lost in a shuffle of confusion."[20]

Russell and Wyler kept in touch over the years, and if Russell found himself heading to Los Angeles, he would reach out to the filmmaker. They would have dinner together at a Chinese restaurant in Beverly Hills, where they caught up on news about their work and their families. By the 1960s, Harold and Rita's two children, Gerald and Adele, were in their teens. Willy and Talli's family now included two more children, David and Melanie. Tragically, their toddler son Billy had died during the Thanksgiving holiday in 1949. Vacationing with the family in Palm Springs, the couple had rushed the three-year-old to the hospital after he became seriously ill. It seemed to be a violent allergic reaction, but the doctors weren't certain. At one point they did a spinal tap, testing for polio. Later, even an autopsy couldn't confirm the cause of death. Willy, Talli, Cathy, and Judy: all were inconsolable. Willy blamed himself for not trying harder to get Billy back to Los Angeles, which at the time had more sophisticated medical care than the desert resort town. Talli later admitted that she wasn't just grief stricken. "I was furious angry," she told Willy's biographer. "I thought, I'm going to have another child." Nearly a year to the day that Billy died, Talli gave birth to her third daughter, Melanie, whom they named for Willy's mother.[21]

One topic Russell and Wyler rarely discussed was their disabilities. Occasionally, though, they would share humorous stories that resulted from the public's misunderstanding of their handicaps, like the fact that Russell's driver license read, "Must wear hooks while driving." By the 1960s, Wyler was using hearing aids regularly, and he sometimes complained about them to Russell. "It makes so much goddamned noise I can't hear anything else," Wyler groused. "I hope you don't have as much trouble with those hooks as I do with the goddamned hearing aid."[22]

In 1960, the Hollywood Walk of Fame Committee voted to give Wyler a star, and he may have been instrumental in Russell's nomination the same year. Each man received a five-pointed brass star embedded in the terrazzo tile that makes up the Walk on Hollywood Boulevard and Vine Street. The recognition was a fun distraction for Russell, but his life was focused elsewhere. In 1961, Russell became vice chairman of the President's Committee on the Employment of People with Disabilities under President John F. Kennedy. When Kennedy pushed to expand the committee to include people with mental illnesses and mental retardation, Russell was one of only a handful of committee members who supported what was then a controversial change.

At the time, many members of Congress were veterans of World War II, and they saw Russell as both a peer and a hero. He used his celebrity in that world to build bridges between lawmakers and disability advocates who might not otherwise have an entrée with legislators in Washington. Whether Russell was focusing on access, transportation, or integration, he understood that one of his goals—perhaps the most important one—was to change the way that the nation thought about disability. Thanks to the lessons he learned from Charlie McGonegal soon after his own accident, Russell understood he first needed to connect with people and put them at ease. His ability to do this, and do it well, made him a powerful advocate for the rights of the disabled. His behind-the-scenes organizing of key lobbying groups led to the passage of the Rehabilitation Act of 1973, a federal law that prohibited discrimination against disabled persons by federal agencies and by programs that received governmental funding.[23]

By the early 1970s, Samuel Goldwyn was fading. His memory was cloudy, his moods were unpredictable, and he rarely left his and Frances's home on Laurel Lane. Sam Jr. was in charge of the company. One day in the spring of 1971, the White House called and informed Frances that President Nixon would be paying a visit to her husband the following morning. By the time Richard Nixon arrived, at eleven, Goldwyn was waiting for him, dressed impeccably in a dark suit and looking like his old self except for the wheelchair in which he was sitting. The president honored Goldwyn with the Medal of Freedom, but within hours, the former producer who had once reduced stars to tears was back in his bedroom. Goldwyn passed away three years later, on the last day of January 1974.[24]

A decade before Goldwyn's death, he and Wyler finally settled the lawsuit over *Best Years*. Wyler's suit had grown more complicated as both men dug in their heels. In addition to the money that Wyler felt he was owed from the 1954 rerelease of the film, he was also suing for funds from the overseas exhibition of the movie and general "under-reporting" of its box office. By 1958, the amount at stake was more than $400,000, one-third of which represented Wyler's earnings from the reissue. By that time, a dozen years after its initial release, *The Best Years of Our Lives* had earned approximately $15 million.[25] Wyler was in Rome directing *Ben-Hur* when he wrote to his attorney, Leon Kaplan, after an article about the suit ran in the *Hollywood Reporter*. Wyler reminded the attorney of his preference for a settlement over a trial, and in the process he revealed his conflicted feelings about the suit in general. "I don't much like the use of words like 'fraudulent' but I assume they are necessary in an action of this kind," he wrote. "Whenever possible in the future, please avoid saying anything that sounds insulting to Goldwyn." Then, in a postscript, Wyler wrote, "But since we *are* suing—let's WIN!"[26]

Four years later, in 1962, a trial seemed inevitable. Goldwyn was standing firm, as was Wyler. Kaplan was urging his client to settle, emphasizing that the money from the film's rerelease wouldn't increase substantially in the future. Robert Sherwood had passed away in 1955 at the age of fifty-nine, and Kaplan reminded Wyler that because Goldwyn had given the playwright an additional 5 percent bonus on future profits, Sherwood's estate would receive a share of any future monies as well. In September, days before a trial was scheduled to take place, Goldwyn and Wyler settled the suit. Wyler would receive approximately $80,000 and prints of seven of the eight films he made for Goldwyn Studios. Wyler reached out to Goldwyn a few weeks after the settlement was finalized. "Just a word to tell you how pleased I am that our small financial differences have been amicably settled and that they never had any effect on our regard and friendship for each other," he wrote. A few years later, an amended agreement adjusted the settlement to include television revenues from the airing of *The Westerner*, *The Little Foxes*, and *Best Years*.[27]

Another decade would pass, however, before Wyler's films for Goldwyn made it to the small screen. And even before *Best Years* was broadcast on television for the first time, it was reimagined as a made-for-TV movie in 1975, a year after Goldwyn's death. Lorimar Productions partnered with Sam Jr.'s production company on *Returning Home*, an updated version of the *Best Years* story about three returning veterans. Its most intriguing element was the casting of James R. Miller, a former marine and Vietnam veteran who lost his hands in an accident similar to Russell's. Calling *Best Years* "a minor classic" that "carefully treads the thin line between realism and sentimentality," the *New York Times* television critic John J. O'Connor described its remake as an "opportunistic project" that still managed to be "above-average TV fare."[28]

At the time, Harold Russell was still serving on the President's Committee on the Employment of People with Disabilities. In the mid-1960s, Lyndon B. Johnson had promoted Russell to chairman of the committee. In the 1970s, Russell's son Gerald went off to Vietnam, a war that Russell struggled to understand. "To this day, I am unable to figure out why we were fighting there," he said. "It was a wrong war in a wrong place."[29] Perhaps because of this, Russell made Vietnam veterans' issues, particularly homelessness, his focus after he stepped down from the committee in 1989, a year before the passage of the Americans with Disabilities Act. According to Ken Smith, an activist and Vietnam veteran, "If you look carefully, you will see Harold's DNA stamped all over that legislation."[30]

Russell's second memoir came out several years before his retirement. *The Best Years of My Life* was a recap of the material in *Victory in My Hands* (1949)—his accident, being discovered in *Diary of a Sergeant* by Wyler, making *Best Years*, and his early advocacy—as well as a chronicle of his family life with Rita and their kids and his later work as a motivational speaker and advocate on behalf of disabled veterans. In a chapter entitled "Goldwyn Uses Me," Russell is candid about his growing bitterness toward the producer for being paid a fraction of what his costars made for appearing in the film. Even with a postproduction bonus, Russell made less than $8,000 for *Best Years*, a film that grossed just over $11 million in its first year of release. Russell considered suing Goldwyn at one time, but he decided against it, in part because he truly felt affection for the "old man," with whom he reconciled not long before Goldwyn's death in 1974. "Goldwyn took a helluva chance," Russell later admitted. "Here I was an amateur guy who'd never been in a picture before."[31]

Two years after Goldwyn's death, William Wyler reached out to Sam Jr. after one of his occasional visits with Russell. "In view of the fact that we've all made a considerable amount of money on *Best Years* would it not be a happy thought if Harold Russell were to receive say another $10,000," wrote Wyler, "as a belated bonus for the picture to which he contributed so much?" Wyler offered to chip in 20 percent of that amount from his earnings on the film and suggested the overall amount be treated as a "distribution expense." Russell received the money.[32]

Wyler's affection and respect for Russell never waned. He even wrote the introduction to Russell's second book, which was released in June 1981. A month later, Willy and Talli returned to the States from London, where the seventy-nine-year-old Willy had been honored by the British Film Institute with a series of screenings. The Wylers arrived back home on a Sunday evening, dropping their bags in the entryway of their house on Summit Drive. Willy walked into the living room, looked around and said, half to himself, "Now what are we going to do." The next afternoon, Monday, July 27, he suffered a fatal heart attack.[33]

Harold Russell often said that while he had met many fine people in Hollywood, William Wyler was the most impressive, a deep and sensitive artist:

"In an opium dreamland crawling with 'geniuses' of all sizes, shapes, and colors, Willy Wyler was one of the few men of shining talent, one of the very few who possessed a profound understanding of his art."[34]

Russell created a bit of controversy in the early 1990s when he decided to put his Best Supporting Actor Oscar up for auction. By 1992, Rita had passed away and Harold had remarried. His second wife, Betty, needed routine eye surgery, although that wasn't quite the reason for putting his statuette on the auction block. He wanted a "cushion," he said later. The Academy of Motion Picture Arts and Sciences (AMPAS) was less than thrilled. The actor Karl Malden, who was the AMPAS president at the time, pleaded with Russell to reconsider, offering him an interest-free loan of $20,000 from the academy if he were to return the statuette to AMPAS. Russell declined. The nine-and-a-half-inch gold statuette sold for $60,500 to an anonymous buyer said to be a movie buff.[35]

Anniversaries marking the release of *The Best Years of Our Lives* came and went with little fanfare. In 1989, the Library of Congress included *Best Years* in its inaugural list of 25 films for the National Film Registry, a collection of motion pictures considered "culturally, historically, or aesthetically significant enough" to preserve. (Wyler's wartime documentary *The Memphis Belle: A Story of a Flying Fortress* was added in 2001.) In 1997, shortly after *Best Year*'s fiftieth year in release, the American Film Institute in Los Angeles chose 100 American films to mark the movie industry's centennial. A jury of 1,500 artists, producers, and other creative types initially selected 400 feature-length fictional films, made between 1912 and 1996, that best represented a "capsule of the first 100 years of American cinema, across decades and across genres." This pool of 400 was then narrowed to 100 for the final selections. On the list, which began with *Citizen Kane* (1941), *Casablanca* (1942), and *The Godfather* (1972), *The Best Years of Our Lives* was chosen as number thirty-seven. When the AFI list was revisited in 2007, on its tenth anniversary, *Best Years* was one of only three films whose position on the list remained unchanged.[36]

If one were to evaluate the legacy of *The Best Years of Our Lives* based solely on its number of appearances on the cable movie channel Turner Classic Movies (TCM), the film's reputation as a Hollywood classic would seem assured. TCM airs *Best Years* at least a few times a year, most notably on Veterans Day. Among film historians and movie buffs, the film is still celebrated. But as Francis Davis observed in the *Atlantic*, when *Best Years* screened at Film Forum shortly after the first anniversary of the 9/11 attacks, just a few subway stops from Ground Zero, the film that one admirer had called "a training film for all of us" seemed to be only "dimly" remembered among the general public.[37]

Still, fans from a new generation continue to discover and appreciate *Best Years*. The comedian John Mulaney mentioned the film as one of the "cultural essentials" that shaped his worldview. In a 2019 interview, the thirty-seven-year-old Mulaney described watching the film on television when he was younger. "This was the first time I thought about people coming back from the Second World War, and it not having been simply a heroic, great time," he said. And although the black-and-white movie was made during another era, Mulaney thought its authenticity has stood the test of time. "It's scored and presented in what I bet some people would find a saccharine way, but I find it a pretty stark movie."[38]

Harold Russell made his last trip west in 1999, a few years before his death, at age eighty-eight. He was invited to appear on *Hollywood Salutes Easter Seals*, a television special showcasing the disabled community in the entertainment industry. Mark Montgomery, the program's producer, was Russell's tour guide for his weeklong stay in Los Angeles. William Wyler's star on the Hollywood Walk of Fame took precedence among the sights that Russell told Montgomery he wanted to see. Throughout the trip, Russell talked at length about Wyler's influence on his life. He also insisted that Montgomery rewatch *Best Years* even though the younger man was very familiar with the film.

As Montgomery watched *Best Years* again, he realized that the complexity of the film's familiar images had deepened over time: Mrs. Parrish's strangled cry when Homer raises his hook to say good-bye to Al and Fred as their taxi pulls away from the curb; Al and Milly's passionate hallway reunion; Fred's haunting catharsis in the bomber graveyard; Homer and Wilma ascending the stairs to his bedroom as he prepares to show her his nightly routine; the anticipation of the wedding guests as Homer's hook nudges Wilma's wedding band onto her finger. "Harold realized another glimpse would give me a new sense of appreciation for the film's contemporary themes," Montgomery said. "The drama continues to strike a familiar chord."[39]

Russell was always surprised that most people couldn't get past the flash of his prosthetics. "People frequently marvel at the things I can do with my hooks," he wrote in his first memoir. But as William Wyler recognized early on, the veteran's "incredible prowess" with his "miraculous hooks" was merely the "icing on the cake." It was Russell's innate warmth and hard-won optimism that deserved the most attention. As Wyler once wrote, "He had a wonderful face which expressed strength, courage and great faith in the future."[40]

Russell himself marveled at his ability not just to overcome "utter disaster," but also to "master" it. "For me, that was and is the all-important fact—that the human soul, beaten down, overwhelmed, faced by complete failure and ruin, can still rise up against unbearable odds and triumph."[41]

Seventy-five years after its initial release, *The Best Years of Our Lives* still has the power to remind us of this—and much more.

Acknowledgments

I have been a fan of *The Best Years of Our Lives* for more than three decades. During my first viewing, it seemed unfathomable to me, a twenty-three-year-old film history graduate student, that a movie made just after World War II could still feel modern. I continue to feel that way. For that reason alone, perhaps, this project feels more personal than my previous books.

The fact that I lost both my parents during the four years I worked on this book marks it as a deeply personal experience. Hatching the idea for the book and working on a proposal provided a welcome distraction during my father's yearlong final illness, when I would fly back and forth from Austin to my childhood home in New Jersey to spend time with him. I am grateful for our discussions about the project and about classic movies in general, even though I suspect my father went to his grave believing that my PhD in film history means that I should be able to name every actor in every movie on Turner Classic Movies.

I am also fairly certain my mother never read my books, but I know she took great pride in me and in their existence. Especially during the last two years of her life, she enjoyed introducing me to doctors and caretakers as "my daughter, the author." She seemed to take a real interest in this book, however, and she was almost as thrilled as I was when I learned, two months before she died, that I had received a Public Scholars grant from the National Endowment for the Humanities (NEH) to complete the project.

The six-month grant enabled me to make a final research trip to Los Angeles and to complete a first draft of the manuscript. Receiving the grant gave the project a much-needed boost, and I will always be grateful for the support. And while the NEH's award recognizes the potential relevance and reach of this project, any views, findings, conclusions, or recommendations expressed in this book do not necessarily reflect those of the National Endowment for the Humanities.

Researching and writing about *Best Years* forced me out of my comfort zone in the best way possible. While I was able to conduct a small amount of archival research in Texas, I had to do the bulk of my sleuthing in Los Angeles. I am especially grateful to the Samuel Goldwyn Estate for allowing me access to the Samuel Goldwyn Papers, a treasure trove of primary materials related to the production, distribution, and reception of the film. The Goldwyn collection is housed at the Margaret Herrick Library of the Academy of Motion Picture Arts and Sciences, the beautifully refurbished former water-treatment facility in Beverly Hills that is also home to two of the William Wyler collections I consulted. Thanks to Louise Hilton, who served as my first point of contact at the Herrick, for facilitating my access to the Goldwyn papers and making sure I had what I needed. Marisa Duron handled the day-to-day needs of my research visits with efficiency and good humor. Everyone at the Herrick, including the experts who staffed the Special Collections room and one of the friendliest security guards I have ever met, made each visit a pleasure.

I also spent time at the University of California, Los Angeles, where I sifted through the William Wyler Papers at the Charles E. Young Research Library Special Collections. I appreciated the help and guidance I received from Peggy Alexander and the capable staff of student assistants in the library's Special Collections department.

I am grateful to the staff of the DeGolyer Library at Southern Methodist University, in Dallas, who assisted me with materials in the Ronald L. Davis Oral History Collection; to the archivist David Olson and the Columbia Center for Oral History, Rare Book and Manuscript Library, Columbia University, for mailing me a copy of a transcribed interview with Myrna Loy (literally, wrapped up with a bow); and to the archivists at the Howard Gotlieb Archival Research Center at Boston University, who offered long-distance advice and assistance relating to the Harold Russell collection housed there.

I am indebted to the filmmaker Juan Gerard, who provided an unexpected introduction to Catherine Wyler, William and Talli Wyler's oldest child. After an entertaining telephone interview, Catherine offered to put me in touch with her sister Melanie, who shared family photos. Catherine, Judy, Melanie, and David Wyler generously allowed me to include four of their personal photos in this book. They have been nothing but supportive of this project, but any errors or misstatements of facts are strictly my own.

This is my third book for the University of Texas Press. Given the tumultuous personal circumstances surrounding this project, which was completed during the COVID-19 global pandemic, I relied more than ever on the steadying presence of my sponsoring editor, Jim Burr. Jim's thoughtful advice was always on-target, and his ability to keep the big picture in mind steered me through some of this project's bumpier moments. I appreciate the anonymous readers who weighed in on an early draft of the manuscript, and I am especially indebted to the suggestions, insights, and corrections from my final reader, the former archivist and current author Barbara Hall, herself a *Best Years* superfan. I am grateful to Kip Keller, a freelancer, for his careful reading and polishing of the final draft.

My friends and family offered unconditional support. Thank you to my BIO writing group, who were this project's first outside readers: Laura Castro, Laura Cottam Sajbel, Susan Morrison, P. J. Pierce, and Ann Seaman. Their early advice and enthusiasm were invaluable. Chale Nafus is a dear friend who read multiple chapters and offered unwavering enthusiasm from the start. Kathryn Burger and I reconnected just in time for her to remind me about *Courage of Lassie*. My Los Angeles friends made me laugh and kept me fed during my research trips: thank you, Brian Flaherty, Kevin Shivers, and Jason White. Equally supportive friends closer to home include Amy Lowrey, Sue Murray, Joellen Peters, Kim Smith, and Leslie Wolke. Love and thanks to my Mitchell family: Joyce and Harvey, and Linda and Harvey (especially for the ongoing conversations about movies). And to my sisters, Ellen Reilly and Elizabeth Groupp: I would be lost without you.

As always, my husband, Paul Mitchell, heard about the idea for this book long before anyone else. He understands the unique rhythms of long-term projects, and I am lucky to have his love and support. One of the joys of my life is sharing Friday movie nights with him and our son, Truman, who is now old enough to have actual (and interesting) opinions about the films we watch together.

Once I began teaching undergraduate film courses, I tried to include *Best Years* on as many syllabi as possible: "Film History," "American Independent Cinema," "Films of the 1940s," "Hollywood Film Noir." Its postwar subject, independent production history, timeless themes, and documentary-style realism give the movie immense versatility and crossover potential. I am especially grateful to the many students who shared their enthusiasm for the film and encouraged me to continue thinking about it long after I stopped teaching. It is my hope that this book will introduce *Best Years* to a new generation of fans.

Note on Sources

This book draws extensively from a range of primary materials and secondary sources, including archives, scholarly works, newspaper and magazine articles, and biographies, memoirs, and autobiographies. Biographical details and other background information come from primary materials (and, when necessary, are verified with other sources) unless otherwise noted. When thoughts are attributed to someone, they are drawn from primary materials or interviews.

I spent several weeks at the Margaret Herrick Library at the Academy of Motion Picture Arts and Sciences in Los Angeles. I am very grateful to the Samuel Goldwyn Estate for granting me access to the Samuel Goldwyn Papers, an extensive special collection that holds the core production materials related to *The Best Years of Our Lives*. These include files about the project's development and preproduction, its shooting and postproduction, as well as the film's distribution and reception (domestic and international). The Herrick is also home to two collections of William Wyler materials. I am deeply indebted to Jan Herman, whose research materials for the invaluable Wyler biography *A Talent for Trouble* were used to establish the William Wyler Collection at the Herrick. My book benefited from other collections there as well, such as the papers of George Jenkins (art director) and the Production Code Administration files.

I also made several visits to the University of California, Los Angeles, where I worked in the Charles E. Young Research Library Special Collections. There I relied on materials from the William Wyler Papers, including annotated scripts for *Mrs. Miniver* and *The Best Years of Our Lives* and files related to *The Memphis Belle* and *Thunderbolt*. UCLA's Wyler collection also includes several files of photographs, which were quite useful in providing visual details to supplement descriptions of specific figures, situations, and events.

The Ronald L. Davis Oral History Collection, located in Southern Methodist University's DeGolyer Library, was a terrific resource closer to home. I made use of several oral histories housed there, including interviews with Virginia

Mayo, the producer Hal Wallis, William Wyler, and Talli Wyler, a Dallas native. An oral history of Myrna Loy conducted by Mr. and Mrs. Robert C. Franklin is part of the Popular Arts Project housed in the Oral History Archives at Columbia University.

For information about Harold Russell, particularly his wartime accident and his experiences while making *Best Years*, I relied on his memoirs, both written with collaborators. Whenever possible, I cross-checked this information with other sources and public accounts of the same events, such as the 1947 Academy Awards ceremony and his speaking engagements related to *Best Years*, which were often covered in local newspapers around the country. Russell's personal papers are housed in the Howard Gotlieb Archival Research Center located at Russell's alma mater, Boston University. These files focus for the most part on Russell's life after *Best Years* and document his extensive involvement with presidential committees on veterans' affairs and with disability rights organizations.

Ben Shephard's *A War of Nerves* brings together a great deal of research about war-related psychological trauma, and I returned to it again and again for assistance in tracing the evolution of the condition that has come to be known as post-traumatic stress disorder. I also consulted several primary sources on the subject, such as military pamphlets and Charles Myers's 1915 article in the *Lancet*, one of the earliest published accounts of war trauma.

For a film as beloved as *Best Years*, there are surprisingly few resources dedicated to its production history. The only book that I am aware of is Sarah Kozloff's excellent introduction to the film, part of the British Film Institute's well-regarded monograph series. Kozloff's book offers a close reading of *Best Years* and a brief discussion of its production, distribution, and reception. Similar accounts of the making of *Best Years* appear in biographies of Wyler. Of these, I found Jan Herman's *A Talent for Trouble* to be the most reliable and detailed. Condensed discussions of *Best Year*'s production and reception also appear in books such as A. Scott Berg's seminal biography of Samuel Goldwyn (*Goldwyn*) and Mark Harris's chronicle of the World War II experiences of Wyler and four other directors and the way the war influenced their subsequent films (*Five Came Back*).

Notes

List of Abbreviations

DOHC   Ronald L. Davis Oral History Collection, DeGolyer Library, Southern Methodist University, Dallas

MPAA   MPAA Production Code Administration Records, Margaret Herrick Library, Academy of Motion Picture Arts and Sciences, Los Angeles

SGP   Samuel Goldwyn Papers, Special Collections, Margaret Herrick Library, Academy of Motion Picture Arts and Sciences, Los Angeles

UCLA   William Wyler Papers, 1925–1975, Arts Library Special Collections, Charles E. Young Research Library, University of California, Los Angeles

WWC   William Wyler Collection compiled by Jan Herman, Margaret Herrick Library, Academy of Motion Picture Arts and Sciences, Los Angeles

WWP   William Wyler Papers, Special Collections, Margaret Herrick Library, Academy of Motion Picture Arts and Sciences, Los Angeles

Introduction

1. For discussions of Wyler's tendency to film multiple takes of the same scene, see, for example, Jan Herman, *A Talent for Trouble: The Life of Hollywood's Most Acclaimed Director, William Wyler* (New York: Da Capo, 1997); A. Scott Berg, *Goldwyn: A Biography* (New York: Knopf, 1989); and Sarah Kozloff, *The Best Years of Our Lives* (London: Palgrave Macmillan, 2011).

2. Jack Warner to William Wyler, June 27, 1940, and Wyler's undated response (possibly not sent), file 86, WWC.

3. Harold Russell, *Victory in My Hands*, with Victor Rosen (New York: Creative Age, 1949), 208.

4. Herman, *A Talent for Trouble*, 284.

5. Robert Sherwood to Samuel Goldwyn, August 27, 1945, *Best Years* Production Correspondence, File 177, Samuel Goldwyn Papers (hereafter cited as SGP).

6. David Gerber, "Heroes and Misfits: The Troubled Social Reintegration of Disabled Veterans in *The Best Years of Our Lives*," *American Quarterly* 46, no. 4 (Dec. 1994): 557.

7. Kozloff, *Best Years of Our Lives*, 30–31.

8. "The Way Home," *Time*, August 7, 1944, 15, 16.

9. For a social history of the "veterans problem," see Gerber, "Heroes and Misfits," 545–574.

10. Ibid., 545.

11. Ibid., 549.

12. Matthew J. Friedman, "History of PTSD in Veterans: Civil War to DSM-5," US Department of Veterans Affairs, National Center for PTSD, www.ptsd.va.gov/understand/what/history_ptsd.asp.

13. Charles S. Myers, "A Contribution to the Study of Shell Shock," *Lancet*, February 13, 1915, 316–320.

14. Ben Shephard, *A War of Nerves: Soldiers and Psychiatrists in the Twentieth Century* (Cambridge, MA: Harvard University Press, 2001), 41.

15. Berg, *Goldwyn*, 393.

16. MacKinlay Kantor, *Glory for Me* (New York: Coward-McCann, 1945), 13–14.

17. Russell, *Victory in My Hands*, 187.

18. Gerber, "Heroes and Misfits," 546.

19. Review in *Life*, December 16, 1946, 71, quoted in Charles Affron and Mirella Jones Affron, *Best Years: Going to the Movies, 1945–1946* (New Brunswick, NJ: Rutgers University Press, 2009), 231.

20. Anonymous RAF pilot to Samuel Goldwyn, May 4, 1948, *Best Years* Correspondence File, SGP.

21. Bill Mauldin to Samuel Goldwyn, January 3, 1947, in ibid.

22. Omar Bradley to Samuel Goldwyn, December 12, 1946, in ibid.

23. Numerous "favorite movie" lists overlook *Best Years*, while *It's a Wonderful Life* often makes an appearance. For example, in a 2014 poll of industry insiders about their favorite 100 films, conducted by the *Hollywood Reporter*, *Best Years* didn't make the cut, while *It's a Wonderful Life* placed twentieth; see "Hollywood's 100 Favorite Films," *Hollywood Reporter*, June 25, 2014, hollywoodreporter.com/lists/100-best-films-ever-hollywood-favorites-818512.

24. Jonathan Rosenbaum, "The Best Years of Our Lives: Half a Dozen Responses," July 16, 2017, jonathanrosenbaum.net/2017/07/the-best-years-of-our-lives.

25. Frances Ford Coppola, "The Greatest Films of All Time," *Sight & Sound*, 2012, https://www2.bfi.org.uk/films-tv-people/sightandsoundpoll2012/voter/948; Steven Spielberg, on-camera interview, 2017, in Laurent Bouzereau, dir., *Five Came Back*, episode 3: "The Price of Victory." Los Gatos, CA: Netflix, 2017.

26. "Martin Scorsese's Top Ten," Criterion Collection, January 29, 2014, criterion.com/current/top-10-lists/214-martin-scorsese-s-top-10.

27. Thomas Pryor, "William Wyler and His Screen Philosophy," *New York Times*, November 17, 1946, 77.

Chapter 1: Warstruck

1. Sara Hamilton, "Important Import," *Photoplay*, November 1943, 59, 108.

2. Ibid., 59.

3. Axel Madsen, *William Wyler: The Authorized Biography* (New York: Crowell, 1973), 214.

4. Sarah Kozloff, "Wyler's Wars," *Film History* 20, no. 4 (2008): 457.

5. Donald Spoto, *A Girl's Got to Breathe: The Life of Teresa Wright* (Jackson: University Press of Mississippi, 2016), 51–52.

6. "Roosevelt Sends Note to Mikado," *Los Angeles Times*, December 7, 1941, A1, and S. Fraser Langford, "Chance to End Sewage Peril," *Los Angeles Times*, December 7, 1931, A4.

7. Multiple versions of how the Wylers heard about Pearl Harbor have been written over the years, but nearly all mention the tennis game and Talli's conveying the news to her husband and John Huston. For one account of the Wylers' experiences, see Jan Herman, *A Talent for Trouble: The Life of Hollywood's Most Acclaimed Director, William Wyler* (New York: Da Capo, 1997), 233. For the general context of how the day unfolded in Los Angeles, see Otto Friedrich, *City of Nets: A Portrait of Hollywood in the 1940's* (New York: Harper and Row, 1986), 99.

8. Mary Pickford to William Wyler, July 8, 1942, file 359, WWC.

9. Quoted in Roy Hoopes, *When the Stars Went to War: Hollywood and World War II* (New York: Random House, 1995), 23.

10. Herman, *Talent for Trouble*, 238.

11. Hoopes, *When the Stars Went to War*, 80.

12. *Los Angeles Times*, December 9, 1941, 1.

13. *Mrs. Miniver*, dir. William Wyler, 1942 (Burbank, CA: Warner Home Video, 2004), DVD.

14. See Greer Garson's interview in *Directed by William Wyler*, dir. Aviva Slesin (New York: Kino Lorber, 2002), DVD.

15. Spoto, *Girl's Got to Breathe*, 54.

16. Bosley Crowther, "'Mrs. Miniver,' Excellent Picture of England at War, Opens at the Music Hall," *New York Times*, June 5, 1942, 23.

17. Herb Golden, "Mrs. Miniver," *Variety*, May 13, 1942.

18. Hellman, interviewed in *Directed by William Wyler*; see also Hellman, interview by A. Scott Berg for *Directed by William Wyler*, transcript, 2, file 166, WWC.

19. This account of Wyler's encounter with Bartlett and his subsequent interaction with General Spaatz comes from Madsen, *William Wyler*, 227, and Herman, *Talent for Trouble*, 243. Wyler's statement to Spaatz is from Wyler's own account in *Directed by William Wyler* and is reprinted in Catherine Wyler's edited transcript, "William Wyler, Director" (1981), in Gabriel Miller, ed., *William Wyler: Interviews* (Jackson: University Press of Mississippi, 2010), 131.

20. William Wyler, physical exam, June 10, 1942, file 373, WWC.

21. Talli Wyler, interview by Jan Herman, January 25, 1990, file 348, WWC.

22. Herman, *Talent for Trouble*, 249.

23. The training course is described by Wyler in *Directed by William Wyler*; Jerome Chodorov, request for reassignment, October 6, 1942, file 361, WWC.

24. Detail from footage featured in *The Cold Blue*, dir. Erik Nelson, 2018; broadcast on HBO, June 6, 2019.

25. Vincent Evans quoted in David Chandler, "Willy Makes the Stars Tremble," *Collier's*, February 4, 1950, file 382, WWC.

26. Herman, *Talent for Trouble*, 252.

27. Ken Doeckel, "William Wyler: A Great Director Has Been Reduced to Exploiting His Virtuosity," *Films in Review*, October 1971: 476.

28. Quoted in the Academy Awards Acceptance Speech Database, Academy of Motion Picture Arts and Sciences, http://aaspeechesdb.oscars.org/link/015-9.

29. William Wyler to Talli Wyler, ca. March 1943, file 353, WWC.

30. Wyler quoted in Hermine Rich Isaacs, "William Wyler: Director with a Passion and a Craft," *Theatre Arts* 31, no. 2 (February) 1947: 21–24, reprinted in Miller, *William Wyler: Interviews*, 14.

31. William Wyler, military report, June 8, 1943, file 361, WWC.

32. Wyler's account of his conversation with Queen Elizabeth appears in C. Wyler, "William Wyler, Director," in Miller, *William Wyler: Interviews*, 113.

33. Herman, *Talent for Trouble*, 259.

34. Robert Morgan, interview by Jan Herman, February 11, 1990, file 100, WWC.

35. Wyler telegrams dated June 4, 1943, and June 17, 1943, file 353, WWC; T. Wyler interview by Herman.

36. "Culver City Army Air Forces Motion Picture Unit," Historic California Posts, Camps, Stations, and Airfields, militarymuseum.org/HalRoachStudio.html.

37. Videos of stops along the *Memphis Belle*'s 1944 tour can be viewed at Critical Past; see, for example, https://www.criticalpast.com/video/65675046274_Memphis-Belle-crew_B-17F-Flying-Fortress_pilot-addressing-crowd_cocker-spaniel.

38. Notes on the *Memphis Belle*'s visit to Los Angeles, August 1943, file 99, WWC.

39. Beirne Lay to William Wyler, n.d., file 361, WWC.

40. Documents detailing Wyler's request and the granting of an extension until January 4, 1943, file 361, WWC.

41. Drafts of narration for *25 Missions*, n.d., file 96, WWC.

42. The description of Wyler's meeting with the president, in this paragraph and the following one, comes from William Wyler to Jock Whitney, March 1, 1944, file 363, WWC.

43. Bosley Crowther, "Vivid Film of Daylight Bomb Raid Depicts Daring of Our Air Forces," *New York Times*, April 14, 1944, 1. See also Crowther to Wyler, March 19, 1979, confirming the historic precedent of the film review's placement, file 99, WWC.

44. Goldwyn to Wyler, telegram, ca. February 1944, file 362, WWC.

45. Wyler quoted in a transcript of his interview with *The Army Hour* radio program, 1943, reprinted in Miller, *William Wyler: Interviews*, 6.

Chapter 2: Every Veteran a Potential Mental Case

1. Harold Russell, *Victory in My Hands*, with Victor Rosen (New York: Creative Age, 1949), 8.

2. Harold Russell, *The Best Years of My Life*, with Dan Ferullo (Middlebury, VT: Eriksson, 1981), 8–9.

3. Ibid., 9–10.

4. Ibid.; see also Harold Russell, "I'm a Lucky Guy," *Photoplay*, March 1947, 54–55, *Best Years* Publicity, box 25, file 180, SGP.

5. Russell, *Victory in My Hands*, 3–4, 8, 33.

6. Ibid., 7.

7. For a history of Walter Reed, see the army medical center's website, walterreedlra.com/background/history.

8. Russell, *Victory in My Hands*, 92–93; Russell, *Best Years of My Life*, 19–20.

9. Russell, *Victory in My Hands*, 42.

10. Ibid., 104.

11. *Meet McGonegal*, 16 mm, Army Service Forces, Signal Corps Production

(Washington, DC: US War Department, 1944), available on C-SPAN, www.c-span.org /video/?322505-1/1944-film-meet-mcgonegal.

12. Russell, *Victory in My Hands*, 105–106.

13. Ibid., 17–18.

14. Ibid., 134.

15. Ibid., 135.

16. Ibid., 121.

17. Ibid., 119.

18. Ben Shephard, *A War of Nerves: Soldiers and Psychiatrists in the Twentieth Century* (Cambridge, MA: Harvard University Press, 2001), 242.

19. Matthew J. Friedman, "History of PTSD in Veterans: Civil War to DSM-5," US Department of Veterans Affairs, National Center for PTSD, www.ptsd.va.gov /understand/what/history_ptsd.asp.

20. Auenbrugger did not coin the term "nostalgia." In a dissertation in 1688, the Swiss physician Johannes Hofer combined the Greek words *nostos* (return home) and *algos* (pain) to describe a pathological type of homesickness.

21. Friedman, "History of PTSD in Veterans."

22. Caroline Alexander, "The Shock of War," *Smithsonian*, September 2010, smithsonianmag.com/history/the-shock-of-war-55376701.

23. Shephard, *War of Nerves*, 2, 33.

24. Charles S. Myers, "A Contribution to the Study of Shell Shock," *Lancet*, February 13, 1915, 316–320.

25. Shephard, *War of Nerves*, 28, 75.

26. "The Legacy of General John J. Pershing," *Nebraska Stories*, PBS, pbs.org/video /nebraska-stories-legacy-general-john-j-pershing.

27. Shephard, *War of Nerves*, 126.

28. Ibid., xviii.

29. Ibid., 110, 31.

30. Charles S. Myers, *Shell Shock in France, 1914–1918: Based on a War Diary* (1940; Cambridge: Cambridge University Press, 2012), 25–29; quoted in Shephard, *War of Nerves*, 31.

31. Shephard, *War of Nerves*, 123.

32. Ibid., 198; see also Otto Friedrich, *City of Nets: A Portrait of Hollywood in the 1940's* (New York: Harper and Row, 1986), 222.

33. W. C. Menninger, *Psychiatry in a Troubled World: Yesterday's War and Today's Challenge* (New York: Macmillan, 1948), 267.

34. Mental Health America, "Our History," mentalhealthamerica.net/our-history.

35. Shephard, *War of Nerves*, 129.

36. Shephard, *War of Nerves*, 217; see also "Omar N. Bradley," History, A&E Television Networks, October 27, 2009, updated August 21, 2018, history.com/topics//world -war-ii/omar-bradley.

37. "General Patton Rebuked by Eisenhower for Flareup," *Elmira (NY) Star-Gazette*, November 23, 1932, 1.

38. Shephard, *War of Nerves*, 201–202.

39. Ibid., 226.

40. Ibid., 223, 244.

41. Wyler, interview by *The Army Hour* radio show, 1943, reprinted in Gabriel Miller, ed., *William Wyler: Interviews* (Jackson: University Press of Mississippi, 2010), 7.

42. Shephard, *War of Nerves*, 281–283, 291.

43. Gabriel Miller, *William Wyler: The Life and Films of Hollywood's Most Celebrated Director* (Lexington: University Press of Kentucky, 2013), 234; see also Mark Harris, *Five Came Back: A Story of Hollywood and the Second World War* (New York: Penguin, 2014), 348.

44. William Wyler to Colonel William Keighley, November 22, 1944, file 418, WWP.

45. Handwritten note attached to "revised rough draft" of *Thunderbolt*, February 14, 1945, file 414, WWP. As Mark Harris argues, the unsigned note appears to be in Wyler's hand (*Five Came Back*, 479).

46. The details about *Thunderbolt*, Wyler's final flight to film additional footage, and Wyler's resulting injury are summarized from Wyler's account to Axel Madsen in *William Wyler: The Authorized Biography* (New York: Crowell, 1973), 254–256.

47. Talli Wyler, interview by Jan Herman, January 25, 1990, file 348, WWC. This account of the Wylers' first phone call after the accident also relies on Madsen, *William Wyler*, 255.

48. Lillian Hellman, interviewed in *Directed by William Wyler*, dir. Aviva Slesin (New York: Kino Lorber, 2002), DVD.

49. Harris, *Five Came Back*, 364; Madsen, *William Wyler*, 255.

50. Jan Herman, *A Talent for Trouble: The Life of Hollywood's Most Acclaimed Director, William Wyler* (New York: Da Capo, 1997), 276.

51. Wyler tears up recalling his wartime injury and recovery in *Directed by William Wyler*. Wyler's comment about his readjustment can be found in Madsen, *William Wyler*, 255.

52. Talli Wyler quoted in Herman, *Talent for Trouble*, 276; see also Madsen, *William Wyler*, 256.

53. Susan M. Hartmann, "Prescriptions for Penelope: Literature on Women's Obligations to Returning World War II Veterans," *Women's Studies* 5 (1978): 224, 225.

54. Ibid., 236, 228.

55. See Diane J. Keranen's discussion of PTSD in "Veteranness: Representations of Combat-Related PTSD in U.S. Popular Visual Media" (PhD diss., Michigan Technological University, 2014), 45.

56. Russell, *Victory in My Hands*, 122–124.

57. Ibid., 150.

58. Paul J. Dougherty and Marlene DeMaio, "Major General Norman T. Kirk and Amputee Care during World War II," *Clinical Orthopaedics and Related Research* 472, no. 10 (October 2014): 3107–3113, https://journals.lww.com/clinorthop/Fulltext/2014/10000/Major_General_Norman_T_Kirk_and_Amputee_Care.28.aspx.

59. Russell, *Victory in My Hands*, 153–155, 160.

60. Myrna Oliver, "Julian Blaustein; Veteran Movie Producer," *Los Angeles Times*, June 21, 1995; "Julian Blaustein, 82, Film Producer, Dies," *New York Times*, June 22, 1995, B6.

61. Russell, *Victory in My Hands*, 156–159; see also Russell, *Best Years of My Life*, 28.

62. Russell, *Victory in My Hands*, 163.

63. Russell's account of his first semester at Boston University and his visit to Washington is taken from his two autobiographies: *Victory in My Hands*, 165, and *Best Years of My Life*, 29.

64. Russell, *Victory in My Hands*, 166.

Chapter 3: The Way Home

1. Otto Friedrich, *City of Nets: A Portrait of Hollywood in the 1940's* (New York: Harper and Row, 1986), 179.

2. Samuel Goldwyn to K. Brown, interoffice correspondence, August 5, 1944, *Best Years* Production Correspondence, file 177, SGP; see also A. Scott Berg's version in *Goldwyn: A Biography* (New York: Knopf, 1989).

3. Lillian Hellman, interview by A. Scott Berg (transcript), n.d., for *Directed by William Wyler*, dir. Aviva Slesin (New York: Kino Lorber, 2002), file 166, WWC.

4. Talli Wyler, interview by Jan Herman, January 10, 1990, file 348, WWC.

5. Talli Wyler, interview by Jan Herman, January 25, 1990, ibid.

6. Lester Koenig to William Wyler, September 13, 1945, file 362, WWC.

7. William Wyler to Major Monroe Greenthal, Bureau of Public Relations, July 11, 1945, box 23, folder 3, UCLA.

8. William Wyler to Charles Regan, August 8, 1945, file 99, WWC.

9. William Wyler to General Eaker, October 17, 1945, and Wyler to General Arnold, telegram, ca. October 1945, both in box 23, folder 3, UCLA.

10. "AAF's 'Thunderbolt' Crashing Epic of Italy Air War," *Variety*, October 19, 1945, box 23, folder 7, UCLA.

11. Ned Depinet to Wyler, telegram, n.d., and Frances Harmon to Wyler, November 30, 1945, both in box 23, folder 3, UCLA.

12. Frank Capra, *The Name above the Title: An Autobiography* (New York: Macmillan, 1971), 373.

13. Quoted in Catherine Wyler's edited transcript, "William Wyler, Director" (1981), in Gabriel Miller, ed., *William Wyler: Interviews* (Jackson: University Press of Mississippi, 2010), 136.

14. David Chandler, "Willy Makes the Stars Tremble," *Collier's*, February 4, 1950, 46, file 382, WWC.

15. Talli Wyler, interview by A. Scott Berg (transcript), February 10, 1985, 36–37, for *Directed by William Wyler*, file 179, WWC.

16. Teresa Wright, interview by Jan Herman, ca. 1990s, file 10, WWC.

17. William Wyler to Samuel Goldwyn, n.d. (ca. 1945), file 8, WWP.

18. Thomas M. Pryor, "Back to Work," *New York Times*, September 16, 1945, 135.

19. Patrick Duggan to Samuel Goldwyn, memorandum, December 14, 1944, file 177, SGP.

20. John Mason Brown, *The Ordeal of a Playwright: Robert E. Sherwood and the Challenge of War* (New York: Harper and Row, 1970), 122.

21. Robert Sherwood to Samuel Goldwyn, August 27, 1945, file 177, SGP.

22. Samuel Goldwyn to Robert Sherwood, telegram, September 4, 1945, file 177, SGP.

23. Ashton Stevens, "Excursions in Stageland," *Chicago Herald-American*, January 12, 1947, box 18, folder 6, UCLA.

24. Sherwood to Goldwyn, August 27, 1945.

25. "Wyler Is Bringing Sherwood Script," *Variety*, September 12, 1945, file 218, WWC.

26. Talli Wyler to William Wyler, "Thursday" (ca. August or September 1945), file 353, WWC.

27. Talli Wyler, interview by Berg, transcript dated February 10, 1985.

28. Samuel Goldwyn to John Ford, July 14, 1945, file 177, SGP.

29. Sarah Kozloff, *"The Best Years of Our Lives"* (London: Palgrave Macmillan, 2011), 34; for another account, see Mark Harris, *Five Came Back: A Story of Hollywood and the Second World War* (New York: Penguin, 2014), 395.

30. "Summary of Budget Detail," ca. October 1945, file 154, SGP, and "Goldwyn, Inc," file 302, WWC.

31. Samuel Goldwyn to Patrick Duggan and William Wyler, memorandum, November 16, 1945, file 177, SGP.

32. Farley Granger, *Include Me Out: My Life from Goldwyn to Broadway*, with Robert Calhoun (New York: St. Martin's, 2007), 47–48.

33. Harold Russell, *Victory in My Hands*, with Victor Rosen (New York: Creative Age, 1949), 173.

34. William Wyler, "No Magic Wand," *Screen Writer*, February 1947, 6, file 180, SGP.

35. Quoted in Thomas Pryor, "William Wyler and His Screen Philosophy," *New York Times*, November 17, 1946, 77; also in Miller, *William Wyler: Interviews*, 10.

36. Jan Herman, *A Talent For Trouble: The Life of Hollywood's Most Acclaimed Director, William Wyler* (New York: Da Capo, 1997), 282.

37. Russell, *Victory in My Hands*, 169.

38. M. Howell to Patrick Duggan, memorandum, December 18, 1945, file 180, SGP.

39. Russell, *Victory in My Hands*, 174–177.

40. Berg, *Goldwyn*, 410.

41. Russell, *Victory in My Hands*, 170.

42. PJS, "Homing Flyers' Problems Delineated in Verse Novel," *Los Angeles Times*, November 25, 1945.

43. Paul Griffith, "Slick-Paper Montage," *New York Times*, November 25, 1945, and Barrett McGurn, *New York Herald Tribune*, November 25, 1945, section 7, 5, file 181, SGP; see also additional clippings in box 21, folder 5, UCLA.

44. See, for instance, *New York Times*, December 2, 1945, file 181, SGP.

45. Robert Sherwood to Samuel Goldwyn, ca. late November 1945, file 177, SGP.

46. Berg, *Goldwyn*, 246.

47. Russell, *Victory in My Hands*, 180.

48. Ibid., 181.

49. Talli Wyler, interview by Jan Herman, January 10, 1990.

50. Harold Russell, interview by Jan Herman, n.d., file 9, WWC.

51. Russell, *Victory in My Hands*, 187.

52. Ibid., 188.

53. William Wyler to Lillian Hellman, February 5, 1946, file 229, WWC.

54. Myrna Loy, interview by Mr. and Mrs. Robert C. Franklin, June 1959, 14–15, Popular Arts Project, Oral History Archives at Columbia, Columbia University.

55. Talli Wyler, interview by Jan Herman, January 31, 1990, file 348, WWC.

56. Loy interview, 25–26, 47; see also the clipping about Loy's wedding to Markey, January 3, 1946, file 180, SGP.

57. Axel Madsen, *William Wyler: The Authorized Biography* (New York: Crowell, 1973), 265.

58. Loy interview, 43. For other accounts of the Loy-Goldwyn dinner, see Herman, *Talent for Trouble*, 283, and Berg, *Goldwyn*, 410.

59. John Simon, *Esquire*, quoted in Charles Tranberg, *Fredric March: A Consummate Actor* (Duncan, OK: BearManor Media, 2013), loc. 3, Kindle.

60. See Deborah C. Peterson, *Fredric March: Craftsman First, Star Second* (Westport, CT: Greenwood, 1996), 138, 154, and Tranberg, *Fredric March*, locs. 17, 20, 207, Kindle. For March's hesitations about taking the *Best Years* role, see also Jack Wade, "Best Year of His Life," *Modern Screen*, June 1947, 62, 111–112, file 180, SGP.

61. William Wyler to Fredric March, February 15, 1946, file 8, WWC.

62. Carl Rollyson, *Hollywood Enigma: Dana Andrews* (Jackson: University Press of Mississippi, 2012), 189, 191.

63. Goldwyn letter quoted in Donald Spoto, *A Girl's Got to Breathe: The Life of Teresa Wright* (Jackson: University Press of Mississippi, 2016), 75.

64. Cast salaries in "Budget," file 154, SGP.

65. Virginia Mayo and L. C. Van Savage, *The Best Years of My Life* (New York: Beach-House, 2002), locs. 449, 521, 560, 695, Kindle; see also Virginia Mayo Oral History, November 30, 1973, DOHC.

66. Cast salaries in "Budget," file 154, SGP; see also Richard M. Sudhalter, *Stardust Melody: The Life and Music of Hoagy Carmichael* (New York: Oxford University Press, 2002), 206–207, 238, 249.

67. Joseph Wechsberg, "Dear Mr. Goldwyn," *New York Herald Tribune*, September 1, 1946, available at Reel Classics, reelclassics.com/Actresses/O%27Donnell/odonnell-article3.htm; see also an uncredited article about O'Donnell in box 18, folder 6, UCLA, and "Cathy O'Donnell" in the *Encyclopedia of Alabama*, encyclopediaofalabama.org/article/h-3947.

68. "Armless Vet Puts Wedding Ring on Bride," *Los Angeles Daily News*, January 17, 1946, file 180, SGP.

69. Russell, *Victory in My Hands*, 200–201; see also Harold Russell, "I'm a Lucky Guy," *Photoplay*, March 1947, 109, file 180, SGP.

70. Russell, *Victory in My Hands*, 193, and Russell, interview by Jan Herman, n.d., file 9, WWC.

71. Chandler, "Willy Makes the Stars Tremble"; see also Russell, interview by Jan Herman, n.d.

72. Hilton Als, "The Cameraman," *New Yorker*, June 19, 2006, 47–48, and Berg, *Goldwyn*, 184.

73. Gregg Toland, "The Motion Picture Cameraman," *Theatre Arts*, February 1947, 651, file 320, WWC.

74. William Wyler quoted in Herman, *Talent for Trouble*, 143; Talli Wyler, interview by Jan Herman, January 31, 1990.

75. Als, "The Cameraman," 51; see also Berg, *Goldwyn*, 444.

76. Als, "The Cameraman," 49, and Toland, "Motion Picture Cameraman," 652–653.

77. Preproduction details can be found in files 177 and 179, SGP.

78. Robert L. Carringer, *The Making of "Citizen Kane,"* rev. ed. (Berkeley: University of California Press, 1996), 37.

79. The underlined passage can be found in Jenkins's copy of Wyler's "No Magic Wand," file 43, George Jenkins Papers, Margaret Herrick Library, Academy of Motion Picture Arts and Sciences, Los Angeles.

80. Joshua Gleich, *Hollywood in San Francisco: Location Shooting and the Aesthetics of Urban Decline* (Austin: University of Texas Press, 2018), 21, 30.

81. Russell, *Victory in My Hands*, 203.

82. Mayo and Van Savage, *The Best Years of My Life*, loc. 914, Kindle.

83. Wyler, "No Magic Wand," 10.

84. ARI memo, December 27, 1945, and other memoranda and lists of titles, file 182, SGP.

85. William Wyler to General Eaker, March 6, 1946, file 140, WWC.

86. William Wyler, interview by A. Scott Berg (transcript), n.d., 59, for *Directed by William Wyler*, file 180, WWC.

87. Talli Wyler, interview by Jan Herman, January 25 and February 8, 1990, file 348, WWC.

Chapter 4: Underwater Again

1. Samuel Goldwyn to Robert Sherwood, April 24, 1946, file 177, SGP.

2. *The Best Years of Our Lives* screenplay, April 9, 1946, 33, box 45, folder 3, UCLA.

3. Myrna Loy, interview by Mr. and Mrs. Robert C. Franklin, June 1959, 43, Popular Arts Project, Oral History Archives at Columbia, Columbia University. The later comment by Loy appears in A. Scott Berg, *Goldwyn: A Biography* (New York: Knopf, 1989), 416.

4. Loy interview, 22, 44, 53.

5. Harold Russell, *Victory in My Hands*, with Victor Rosen (New York: Creative Age, 1949), 189.

6. William Wyler, "No Magic Wand," *Screen Writer*, February 1947, 11, file 180, SGP.

7. Mary Morris, "Stubborn Willy Wyler," *PM*, February 2, 1947, M7.

8. Harold Russell, interview by Jan Herman, n.d., file 9, WWC.

9. William Wyler to Lillian Hellman, March 25, 1946, file 229, WWC.

10. Talli Wyler, interview by A. Scott Berg, February 10, 1985, transcript, 9, for *Directed by William Wyler* (dir. Aviva Slesin), file 179, WWC.

11. Russell interview.

12. Teresa Wright, interview by Jan Herman, "Wright1," n.d., file 10, WWC.

13. Emily W. Leider, *Myrna Loy: The Only Good Girl in Hollywood* (Berkeley: University of California Press, 2011), 254.

14. Jan Herman, *A Talent For Trouble: The Life of Hollywood's Most Acclaimed Director, William Wyler* (New York: Da Capo, 1997), 287; see also Talli Wyler interview by Berg, February 10, 1985, 40.

15. Talli Wyler interview by Berg, February 10, 1985, 19.

16. Russell, *Victory in My Hands*, 203.

17. For a well-researched and compelling explanation why "the Cincinnati story" doesn't make sense, see James I. Deutsch, "*The Best Years of Our Lives* (1946) and the Cincinnati Story," *Historical Journal of Film, Radio and Television* 26 (June 2006): 215–225. My thanks to Sarah Kozloff, who cites Deutsch's article in her book *The Best Years of Our Lives* (London: Palgrave Macmillan, 2011).

18. Russell, *Victory in My Hands*, 198.

19. Ibid., 197.

20. Carl Rollyson, *Hollywood Enigma: Dana Andrews* (Jackson: University Press of Mississippi, 2012), 191.

21. Russell, *Victory in My Hands*, 194–195.

22. Samuel Goldwyn to William Wyler, memorandum, May 29, 1946, file 8, SGP.

23. See "Budget," file 154, and Sherwood's February 1946 letter to Goldwyn, file 177, SGP.

24. Gerald Gardner, *The Censorship Papers: Movie Censorship Letters from the Hays Office, 1934 to 1968* (New York: Dodd, Mead, 1987), 161.

25. Thomas Doherty, *Hollywood's Censor: Joseph I. Breen and the Production Code Administration* (New York: Columbia University Press, 2007), 5.

26. Samuel Goldwyn to Joseph Breen, July 30, 1945, and Breen to Goldwyn, August 1, 1945, MPAA.

27. Joseph Breen to Samuel Goldwyn, April 1, 1946, MPAA.

28. Ibid.

29. Gardner, *Censorship Papers*, 164.

30. Wyler quoted in Charles Tranberg, *Fredric March: A Consummate Actor* (Duncan, OK: BearManor Media, 2013), loc. 224, Kindle.

31. Leonard Leff, "The Breening of America," *PMLA* 106, no. 3 (May 1991): 443.

32. Joseph Breen to Samuel Goldwyn, April 16, 1946, MPAA.

33. Bosley Crowther, "*The Postman Always Rings Twice*, with Lana Turner in a Star Role, Makes Its Appearance at the Capitol," *New York Times*, May 3, 1946, 15.

34. "Interview with Virginia Mayo and Teresa Wright," *The Best Years of Our Lives*, dir. William Wyler (New York: Warner Home Video, 2012), DVD.

35. All quotations from Teresa Wright are from her interview with Jan Herman, "Wright2," n.d., file 10, WWC.

36. Ibid.

37. Richard M. Sudhalter, *Stardust Melody: The Life and Music of Hoagy Carmichael* (London: Oxford University Press, 2002), 249–250.

38. Ibid., 250.

39. Russell, *Victory in My Hands*, 191–192.

40. Rollyson, *Hollywood Enigma*, 199.

41. Ibid., 180.

42. Donald Spoto, *A Girl's Got to Breathe: The Life of Teresa Wright* (Jackson: University Press of Mississippi, 2016), 80.

43. Wright, interview by Herman, "Wright1."

44. Rollyson, *Hollywood Enigma*, 196.

45. Wright interview by Herman, "Wright1."

46. Spoto, *Girl's Got to Breathe*, 45.

47. Rollyson, *Hollywood Enigma*, 194.

48. André Bazin, "William Wyler, or the Jansenist of Directing," in *Bazin at Work*, trans. Alain Piette and Bert Cardullo, ed. Bert Cardullo (New York: Routledge, 1997), 11.

49. Spoto, *Girl's Got to Breathe*, 80.

50. For Andrews's account of this improvised bit, see Rollyson, *Hollywood Enigma*, 196. Harold Russell offers another version in *Victory in My Hands*, 202. Wyler credited the bit to a visitor on the set that day (Morris, "Stubborn Willy Wyler," M7).

51. Spoto, *Girl's Got to Breathe*, 82.

52. Russell interview.

53. Quoted in Spoto, *Girl's Got to Breathe*, 81.

54. Berg, *Goldwyn*, 416.

55. Robert Sherwood to Samuel Goldwyn and William Wyler, May 22, 1946, file 177, SGP.

56. Goldwyn to Wyler, memorandum, May 29, 1946.

57. William Wyler to Robert Sherwood, telegram, June 6, 1946, file 177, SGP.

Chapter 5: Fade on Kiss

1. Talli Wyler, interview by Jan Herman, January 25, 1990, file 348, WWC.

2. Army correspondence, May 1–17, 1944, file 806, WWP.

3. Talli Wyler interview by Herman, January 25, 1990.

4. Harold Russell, *Victory in My Hands*, with Victor Rosen (New York: Creative Age, 1949), 206.

5. Production reports, file 178, SGP.

6. Script clerk's notes, file 213, SGP.

7. *The Best Years of Our Lives*, shooting script, April 9, 1946, 182, file 149, SGP.

8. See clippings from *Variety* and other trade publications, ca. 1945, in file 218, WWC. The mention of Wyler's involvement with Russian War Relief appears in a document dated June 11, 1965, with other paperwork related to the Committee for the First Amendment, file 205, WWC. For membership information about the CFA, see the organization's Bill of Rights, "Statement of the Committee for the First Amendment," October 21, 1947, available from the National Archives, Docs Teach, https://www.docsteach.org/documents/document/committee-for-the-first-amendment.

9. *The Best Years of Our Lives*, shooting script; emphasis added.

10. Joseph Breen to Samuel Goldwyn, April 1, 1946, MPAA; Robert Sherwood to Goldwyn, April 22, 1946, cited in Sarah Kozloff, *"The Best Years of Our Lives"* (London: Palgrave Macmillan, 2011), 43n38; Goldwyn, press release, October 30, 1947, cited in A. Scott Berg, *Goldwyn: A Biography* (New York: Knopf, 1989), 436.

11. Script clerk's notes, file 213, SGP.

12. *The Best Years of Our Lives*, shooting script, 182–187.

13. Russell, *Victory in My Hands*, 206.

14. André Bazin, "The Evolution of Film Language," in *The French New Wave: Critical Landmarks*, ed. Peter Graham with Ginette Vincendeau (London: BFI/Palgrave Macmillan, 2009), 80–81.

15. Russell, *Victory in My Hands*, 190.

16. Jan Herman, *A Talent for Trouble: The Life of Hollywood's Most Acclaimed Director, William Wyler* (New York: Da Capo, 1997), 315.

17. Talli Wyler, interview by Jan Herman, January 31, 1990, file 348, WWC.

18. Russell, *Victory in My Hands*, 210.

19. Donald Spoto, *A Girl's Got to Breathe: The Life of Teresa Wright* (Jackson: University Press of Mississippi, 2016), 82.

20. Script clerk's notes, file 213, SGP.

21. *The Best Years of Our Lives*, shooting script, 217.

22. Ibid., 218.

23. Ibid.

24. "Armless Vet Puts Wedding Ring on Bride," *Los Angeles Daily News*, January 17, 1946, file 180, SGP; see also Kozloff, *"Best Years of Our Lives,"* 38–39.

25. Kozloff, *"Best Years of Our Lives,"* 78.

26. *The Best Years of Our Lives*, shooting script, 220.

27. Script clerk's notes, June 24 and 25, 1946, file 213, SGP.

28. *The Best Years of Our Lives*, shooting script, 206.

29. Carl Rollyson, *Hollywood Enigma: Dana Andrews* (Jackson: University Press of Mississippi, 2012), 192.

30. Ibid.

31. Berg, *Goldwyn*, 381, 382.

32. Virginia Mayo and L. C. Van Savage, *The Best Years of My Life* (New York: Beach-house Books, 2002), locs. 671, 763, Kindle.

33. Pat Duggan to Joseph Breen, April 19, 1946, MPAA.

34. *The Best Years of Our Lives*, shooting script, 200; Joseph Breen to Samuel Goldwyn, June 21, 1946, MPAA.

35. Joseph Breen to Samuel Goldwyn, April 16, 1946, and Pat Duggan to Breen, April 19, 1946, MPAA.

36. Teresa Wright, interview included on the DVD of *The Best Years of Our Lives* (New York: Warner Home Video, 2012).

37. Toland quoted in Kozloff, "*Best Years of Our Lives*," 67.

38. Mayo and L. C. Van Savage, *Best Years of My Life*, loc. 775, Kindle; Virginia Mayo, interview included on the DVD of *The Best Years of Our Lives*.

39. Kozloff, "*Best Years of Our Lives*," 68.

40. Wright interview; script clerk's notes, August 3, 1946, file 213, SGP.

41. Toland quoted in Kozloff, "*Best Years of Our Lives*," 67.

42. Production reports, July 13 and 15–17, 1946, file 179, SGP; see also Russell, *Victory in My Hands*, 197.

43. Script clerk's notes, July 15, 1946; Harold Russell, interview by Jan Herman, n.d., file 9, WWC.

44. *The Best Years of Our Lives*, shooting script, July 16, 1946 (revision to April 9 script), 193, 194.

45. Ibid.

46. Ibid., 196.

47. Joseph Breen to Samuel Goldwyn, April 1, 1946, MPAA.

48. Script clerk's notes, July 16, 1946.

49. Call sheets, file 157, SGP.

50. Charles Affron and Mirella Jones Affron, *Best Years: Going to the Movies, 1945–1946* (New Brunswick, NJ: Rutgers University Press, 2009), 226.

51. Box-office information for *Till the End of Time* can be found in Richard B. Jewell, *Slow Fade to Black: The Decline of RKO Radio Pictures* (Berkley: University of California Press, 2016), loc. 51, Kindle. For a more detailed comparison of *Best Years* and *Till the End of Time*, see Edward Gallafent, "Viewing the World in *Till the End of Time*," *Movie: A Journal of Film Criticism* 6 (2015): 86–93.

Chapter 6: Pure Emotional Dynamite

1. Lyle M. Spencer, "Veterans Make Good," *TW*, September 15, 1946, 4–5, file 181, SGP.

2. *Let There Be Light*, dir. John Huston, 1948, available on YouTube, youtube.com /watch?v=uiD6bnqpJDE.

3. John Huston, *An Open Book* (New York: De Capo, 1994), 125.

4. Mark Harris, *Five Came Back: A Story of Hollywood and the Second World War* (New York: Penguin, 2014), 413.

5. David Culbert, interviewed on the C-SPAN series *American History TV*, ca. 2012, as part of a screening of *Let There Be Light*, c-span.org/video/?309243-1/let-light.

6. Ben Shephard, *A War of Nerves: Soldiers and Psychiatrists in the Twentieth Century* (Cambridge, MA: Harvard University Press, 2001), 277.

7. Culbert interview.

8. Harris, *Five Came Back*, 413.

9. Florence S. Lowe, *Variety*, July 17, 1946, box 23, folder 8, UCLA.

10. Patricia King Hanson, "Daniel Mandell," Film Reference, filmreference.com /Writers-and-Production-Artists-Lo-Me/Mandell-Daniel.html; see also "Daniel Mandell, Won 3 Film Editing Oscars," *New York Times*, June 13, 1987, 43.

11. Daniel Mandell, interview by Jan Herman, n.d., file 269, WWC.

12. Ibid.

13. Ibid. For film footage information, see file 155, SGP.

14. Footage details in box 18, folder 2, UCLA; Mandell interview.

15. Mandell interview.

16. Ibid.

17. Catherine Wyler, telephone interview by the author, July 23, 2019.

18. Bernard Herrmann, letter to Samuel Goldwyn, July 30, 1946, file 177, SGP. Friedhofer's background is in Linda Danly, introduction to *Hugo Friedhofer: The Best Years of His Life, A Hollywood Master of Music for the Movies* (Lanham, MD: Scarecrow, 2002), 6–10.

19. Lan Adomian, "An Appreciation," *Film Music Notes*, February–March 1947, quoted in Danly, *Hugo Friedhofer*, 11.

20. American Film Institute Oral History of Hugo Friedhofer, included in Danly, *Hugo Friedhofer*, 84–85.

21. Catherine Wyler interview.

22. While Rob and his relationship with his father are fleshed out in MacKinlay Kantor's novel, the teenager's role in the Sherwood screenplay never evolved beyond a few scenes—Rob's sole function in *Best Years* seems to be as a counterpoint to the returning veterans, introducing the subject of nuclear war as a legitimate worry, particularly for the younger generation. According to Jay Levenson, the actor Michael Hall believed that he disappeared from the film because his contract ended and Samuel Goldwyn did not want to pay to rehire him; see Levenson, "In Memory of Michael Hall," *Apollo*, June 16, 2020, apollo-magazine.com/Michael-hall-collector-1926-2020. My thanks to Kyle Hall (no relation) for bringing this article to my attention.

23. Audience Research Institute, preview information, file 176, SGP.

24. Ibid.

25. Frank S. Nugent, "How Long Should a Movie Be?," *New York Times Magazine*, February 18, 1945, 18–19, 42.

26. Ken Doeckel, "William Wyler: A Great Director Has Been Reduced to Exploiting His Virtuosity," *Films in Review*, October 1971, 477.

27. "Circular on Procedure—Publicity, Advertising and Exploitation," n.d., file 187; "Samuel Goldwyn productions" in David Chandler, "Willy Makes the Stars Tremble," *Collier's*, February 4, 1950, 46; Sheila Graham, "Hollywood Chatter," *Chicago Daily News*, October 26, 1946, file 180, all in SGP.

28. A. Scott Berg, *Goldwyn: A Biography* (New York: Knopf, 1989), 418.

29. File 184, SGP.

30. Chip Boutell, "Authors Are Like People," *New York Post*, October 24, 1946, box 18, folder 6, UCLA; see also William Hawkins, "Mackinlay Kantor Likes Film Story of His Book," *New York World-Telegram*, October 24, 1946, 31, and Bill Hebert to W. Bolton, telegram, January 17, 1947, file 181, SGP.

31. The comments from Hedda Hopper are included in her letter to Samuel Goldwyn, November 12, 1946, file 184, SGP.

32. "Circular on Procedure—Publicity, Advertising and Exploitation."

33. Excerpts from letters, ca. October 1946, file 190, SGP.

34. Ibid.

35. Publicity detail can be found in files 188 and 190, SGP.

36. Promotional detail, file 185, SGP.

37. Bill Hebert to Lynn Farnol, November 7, 1946, file 186, SGP.

38. William Wyler to Samuel Goldwyn, October 28 and 29, 1946, file 8, WWC.

39. Technical specs, "Cutting Continuity," box 18, folder 2, UCLA; letter from Joseph I. Breen, October 30, 1946, accompanied by certificate #11972, Motion Picture Association of America, Production Code Administration Records, *The Best Years of Our Lives*, MPAA.

40. Talli Wyler, interview by Jan Herman, March 22, 1990, file 348, WWC.

41. "William Wyler Urges Freer Hand for Director," *Film Daily*, November 13, 1946, box 18, folder 6, UCLA.

42. Photomontage of the film's New York City premiere, *Motion Picture Herald*, December 2, 1946, 8, box 21, folder 4, UCLA.

43. Robert Sherwood to Albert Lasker, November 13, 1946, file 158, SGP; Ashton Stevens, "Excursions in Stageland," *Chicago Herald-American*, January 12, 1947, box 18, folder 6, UCLA.

44. Jack D. Grant, "'Best Years of Our Lives' Pure Emotional Dynamite," *Hollywood Reporter*, November 23, 1946, box 18, folder 6, UCLA.

45. Chuck Gay, "The Best Years of Our Lives," *Dayton Daily News*, April 30, 1947, M-1, box 21, folder 1, UCLA.

46. Kate Cameron, "'Best Years of Our Lives' Opens; It's Tops in Film Entertainment," *New York Daily News*, November 22, 1946, 62–63.

47. Bosley Crowther, "'The Best Years of Our Lives' Rings the Bell," *New York Times*, November 24, 1946, 2:1.

48. Howard A. Rusk, "New Film on Broadway Called 'Significant' Portrayal of the Emotional and Physical Problems Facing Veterans," *New York Times*, November 24, 1946, box 21, folder 1, UCLA. For background on Rusk, see Kimberly Harper, "Howard A. Rusk," Historic Missourians, State Historical Society of Missouri, https://historicmissourians.shsmo.org/historicmissourians/name/r/rusk.

49. Howard Barnes, *New York Herald Tribune*, November 25, 1946, box 21, folder 1, UCLA; Gay, "The Best Years of Our Lives."

50. Terry Ramsaye, "The Best Years of Our Lives," *Motion Picture Herald*, November 23, 1946, box 21, folder 1, UCLA.

51. John McCarten, "Goldwyn's Longest," *New Yorker*, November 23, 1946, 74.

52. James Agee, "The Best Years of Our Lives," *Nation*, ca. 1947, reprinted January 11, 2009, https://www.thenation.com/article/archive/best-years-our-lives.

53. Lillian Hellman, interview by A. Scott Berg, transcript, 28, file 166, WWC.

54. Hermine Rich Isaacs, "William Wyler: Director with a Passion and a Craft," *Theatre Arts* 31, no. 2 (February 1947): 21–24, reprinted in Gabriel Miller, ed., *William Wyler: Interviews* (Jackson: University Press of Mississippi, 2010), 16.

55. William Wyler to Gen. Carl Spaatz, December 19, 1946, file 140, WWC.

56. Interoffice memo, ca. December 1946, file 184, SGP.

57. "Goldwyn Lease on Theatres," *Daily Variety*, January 28, 1947; "Goldwyn gouge" appears in Omar Ramsey, "Stage & Screen," *Cleveland Press*, June 10, 1947, both in box 21, folder 1, UCLA.

58. Archer Winsten, *New York Post*, November 25, 1946, untitled clipping in file 181, SGP.

59. Mack Millar to Bill Hebert, ca. late November, 1946, file 180, SGP.

60. W. R. Wilkerson, "Trade Views," *Hollywood Reporter*, December 5, 1946, n.p., box 21, folder 1, UCLA.

61. Berg, *Goldwyn*, 420.

62. Samuel Goldwyn to Howard Rusk, November 24, 1946, file 158, SGP.

63. Omar Bradley to Samuel Goldwyn, December 5, 1946, file 158, SGP.

64. Premiere guest list and Bill Hebert to Lynn Farnol (source of the police chief anecdote), ca. December 26, 1946, file 184, SGP.

65. Wyler's comments appear in a letter to Harold Russell, excerpted in Russell, *Victory in My Hands*, with Victor Rosen (New York: Creative Age, 1949), 226.

66. Ibid., 222, 223; Lynn Farnol to Bill Hebert, October 7, 1946, file 180, SGP.

67. Russell, *Victory in My Hands*, 226.

68. "Critics Slap Hollywood by Picking Foreign Pix in Their 10 Best of Year," *Variety*, undated clipping in box 21, folder 1, UCLA; "Review Board Selects 'Best,'" *New York Daily News*, December 19, 1946, box 21, folder 1, UCLA.

69. Untitled article, *Box Office Digest*, ca. December 1946, file 184, SGP; "Zoom Goes the Boom in Boston," *Variety*, January 20, 1947, box 21, folder 1, UCLA; G. Hoover, Paramount Enterprises, to Samuel Goldwyn, telegram, January 17, 1947, file 185, SGP.

70. Bill Hebert to Lynn Farnol, interoffice memo (about Goldwyn's "desire to include Gregg Toland"), February 4, 1947, file 191, SGP.

71. Quoted in Mason Wiley and Damien Bona, *Inside Oscar: The Unofficial History of the Academy Awards* (New York: Ballantine, 1996), 164. For discussion of the voting changes, see, for instance, "Thomas on Hollywood," *Monrovia (CA) News-Post*, February 25, 1947, 7, and Ralph Dighton, "Hollywood's 'Oscar Derby' May Result in Photo Finish," *Greenville (SC) News*, March 11, 1947, 11.

72. Public Relations, file 203, SGP; Russell, *Victory in My Hands*, 240–241.

73. Details about the ceremony can be found in Wiley and Bona, *Inside Oscar*, 165, 166, and 1037; see also Russell, *Victory in My Hands*, 247. An unidentified New York newspaper clipping describes the crowd's response at the ceremony when Russell accepted his awards: "Russell, Handless Vet, Wins 2 Movie 'Oscars',", March 14, 1947, box 21, folder 1, UCLA. Russell's speech can be found in the Academy Awards Acceptance Speech Database on the website of the Academy of Motion Picture Arts and Sciences, http://aaspeechesdb.oscars.org.

74. Joseph McBride, *Frank Capra* (New York: Simon and Schuster, 1992), 526.

75. Transcript of the Academy Awards ceremony, file 201, SGP. Wyler's speech can be found in the Academy Awards Acceptance Speech Database on the website of the Academy of Motion Picture Arts and Sciences, http://aaspeechesdb.oscars.org. Talli Wyler, interview by Jan Herman, January 31, 1990, file 348, WWC.

76. Linda Danly, "A Portrait of Hugo Friedhofer," in *Hugo Friedhofer*, 13.

77. Deborah C. Peterson, *Fredric March: Craftsman First, Star Second* (Westport, CT: Greenwood, 1996), 156.

78. Academy Award ceremony detail, file 201, SGP. For the text of Goldwyn's acceptance speech, see the Academy Awards Acceptance Speech Database on the

website of the Academy of Motion Picture Arts and Sciences, http://aaspeechesdb
.oscars.org.

79. Goldwyn's acceptance speech.

80. Russell, *Victory in My Hands*, 249.

81. My thanks to the former Herrick archivist and author Barbara Hall for explaining
the historical details regarding the distribution of the Academy Award for sound recording. "Interview with Virginia Mayo and Teresa Wright," on the DVD of *The Best Years of
Our Lives* (New York: Warner Home Video, 2012).

82. Multiple versions of the "dynamite" story exist. In one, Russell credits Gregory
Peck with the line. I chose the version that makes the most sense given who was on or
behind the stage when Russell won his second Oscar. Russell, *Victory in My Hands*, 249;
Harold Russell, *The Best Years of My Life*, with Dan Ferullo (Middlebury, VT: Eriksson,
1981), 47.

Chapter 7: It's All the Same Fight

1. Lillian Ross, "Come In, Lassie!," *New Yorker*, February 21, 1948, newyorker.com
/magazine/1948/02/21/come-in-lassie.

2. "Kyp's Column," *Chicago Sunday Times*, December 15, 1946, box 21, folder 1,
UCLA.

3. Thyra Samter Winslow, "If You Want Him, Ask Him!," *Go*, December 1946, 39,
49, file 193, SGP.

4. For details about Hopper's radio program and interoffice memos referring to it, see
file 188, SGP.

5. *Hollywood Reporter*, April 4, 1947, file 187, SGP.

6. Ad in *Chicago Times*, May 14, 1947, box 21, folder 1, UCLA.

7. Unsigned letter, May 1, 1947, file 195, SGP.

8. W. Bolton to Bill Hebert, telegram, January 17, 1947; "Kantor Says He Wrote
Part of 'Best Movie' in New Orleans," *New Orleans Times Picayune*, March 26, 1947;
"Parks Pen to Produce," *Detroit News*, June 15, 1947; "Kantor, 'Fed Up,' to Film His Nov-
els His Own Way," *Hollywood Citizen-News*, June 23, 1947; Aline Mosby, "Mackinlay
Kantor's Changes Baffle Him," *Hollywood Citizen-News*, June 27, 1947, 14, all in
folder 181, SGP.

9. William Wyler, interview by Jan Herman for *Directed by William Wyler* (dir. Aviva
Slesin), undated transcript, 54, file 180, WWC.

10. *Variety*, March 25, 1947, box 21, folder 1, UCLA.

11. "Para. Acquires Liberty Films," *Hollywood Reporter*, April 14, 1947, file 260,
WWC.

12. Bosley Crowther, "'It's a Wonderful Life,' with James Stewart, at Globe," *New
York Times*, December 23, 1946, 19.

13. Manny Farber, "Mugging Main Street," *New Republic*, January 6, 1947, https://
newrepublic.com/article/98662/mugging-main-street-review-its-a-wonderful-life.

14. The release of *It's a Wonderful Life* is discussed in Charles Affron and Mirella
Jones Affron, *Best Years: Going to the Movies, 1945–1946* (New Brunswick, NJ: Rutgers
University Press, 2009), 219.

15. Jan Herman, *A Talent for Trouble: The Life of Hollywood's Most Acclaimed Director,
William Wyler* (New York: Da Capo, 1997), 295–296; Wyler quoted in Axel Madsen,
William Wyler: The Authorized Biography (New York: Cromwell, 1973), 288.

16. Article in the *Virginian*, March 14, 1947, box 21, folder 3, UCLA.

17. "Russell, Handless Vet, Wins 2 Movie 'Oscars,'" unidentified New York newspaper, March 14, 1947, box 21, folder 1, UCLA.

18. Harold Russell, *Victory in My Hands*, with Victor Rosen (New York: Creative Age, 1949), 227–228.

19. Ibid., 231, 233.

20. Ibid., 235.

21. Ibid., 236.

22. William Markham, "The Best Years of Our Lives," *Plain Talk* 1, no. 7 (April 1947): 35–37.

23. Richard Lloyd Jones, "An Oscar for Falsehoods," *Tulsa Tribune*, May 3, 1947, file 206, SGP.

24. Abraham Polonsky, "The Best Years of Our Lives," *Hollywood Quarterly* 2, no. 3 (April 1947): 257.

25. John Ross, "Rehabilitation a la Sam Goldwyn," *Daily Worker*, March 8, 1947, folder 42, WWP.

26. Goldwyn's response can be found in *Best Years* Publicity, file 206, SGP; see also "Over the Back Fence," *Hollywood Review*, June 6, 1947, in the same file.

27. Bohnen died of a heart attack in 1949, and while some argue that the stress of being subpoenaed killed the actor, others point out that he was being treated for a heart condition at the time of his death. Bohnen went on to make at least two films after *Best Years*, so I believe it is inaccurate to say that he was blacklisted solely because of his involvement in that film. For more information about his career, see Cynthia Baron, *Modern Acting: The Lost Chapter of American Film and Theatre* (London: Palgrave Macmillan, 2016).

28. William Wyler interviewed for the radio program *Hollywood Fights Back*, October 1947, file 596, WWP.

29. Talli Wyler, interview by Jan Herman, January 25, 1990, file 348, WWC.

30. Ibid.

31. Ibid.

32. C. A. Lejeune, "The Screen," *Observer*, March 19, 1947, and crowd detail taken from an unidentified newspaper photo, ca. March 1947, both in box 21, folder 6, UCLA.

33. Lejeune, "The Screen."

34. "Rare Hollywood Film," *Glasgow Herald*, March 7, 1947; Jean Morienval, "Le Spectacle," *L'Aube*, n.d.; notes on the film's Berlin screening, all in box 21, folder 6, UCLA.

35. Arthur Spaeth, "*Thunderbolt* Tells Operation Strangle," *Cleveland News*, August 2, 1947, box 23, folder 4, UCLA; see also "Selected Pictures," *Montclair (NJ) Times*, July 2, 1947, 20, and Mae Tinee, "Here's Another Movie Story of Horse and Boy," *Chicago Tribune*, December 13, 1947, 18.

36. Deborah C. Peterson, *Fredric March: Craftsman First, Star Second* (Westport, CT: Greenwood, 1996), 124; Charles Tranberg, *Fredric March: A Consummate Actor* (Duncan, OK: BearManor Media, 2013), loc. 240, Kindle.

37. Thomas Doherty, *Show Trial: Hollywood, HUAC, and the Birth of the Blacklist* (New York: Columbia University Press, 2019), loc. 89, Kindle.

38. William Wyler to Lillian Hellman, November 17, 1947, file 229, WWC; John A. Noakes, "Bankers and Common Men in Bedford Falls: How the FBI Determined That

It's a Wonderful Life Was a Subversive Movie," *Film History: An International Journal* 10, no. 3 (1998): 313n13. My thanks to Sarah Kozloff for including this citation in her book *"The Best Years of Our Lives,"* which led me to the article.

39. Doherty, *Show Trial,* loc. 93, Kindle.

40. Myrna Loy, interview by Mr. and Mrs. Robert C. Franklin, June 1959, 34, 39–40, Popular Arts Project, Oral History Archives at Columbia, Columbia University.

41. "Stars Fly East to Fight Film Probe," *Daily Worker,* October 27, 1947, 16.

42. Quoted in Doherty, *Show Trial,* loc. 203, Kindle.

43. Garland's full statement appears in ibid., loc. 198.

44. Ibid., loc. 60.

45. Ibid., loc. 102.

46. Details about the particulars of the hearing can be found in Doherty, *Show Trial,* and in Gordon Kahn, *Hollywood on Trial: The Story of the Ten Who Were Indicted* (New York: Boni and Gaer, 1948). J. Parnell Thomas's opening statement can be heard in the documentary *Hollywood on Trial,* dir. David Helpern (New York: Corinth Films, 2006), DVD.

47. These details can be seen in *Hollywood on Trial.*

48. Text of Johnston's statement can be found in William Bruce Wheeler and Susan D. Becker, *Discovering the American Past: A Look at the Evidence,* vol. 2: *Since 1865* (Boston: Houghton Mifflin, 1990), 280–283, available from "History Matters: The U.S. Survey Course on the Web," George Mason University, http://historymatters.gmu.edu/d/6443.

49. Excerpts from the Hollywood Ten's statements can be heard in *Hollywood on Trial.*

50. Doherty, *Show Trial,* loc. 286, Kindle.

51. "Goldwyn Says Movie Hearings Were a 'Flop,'" *New York Herald Tribune,* October 31, 1947, 7, and A. Scott Berg, *Goldwyn: A Biography* (New York: Knopf, 1989), 436.

52. Bosley Crowther, "Command Decisions," *New York Times,* November 2, 1947, D1; William Wyler to Crowther, November 6, 1947, file 694, WWP.

53. Quoted in Paul Jacobs, "Fund for the Republic," March 9, 1956, unpublished MS, file 596, WWP.

54. Wyler to Hellman, November 17, 1947; see also Lillian Hellman, interview by A. Scott Berg for *Directed By William Wyler,* transcript, file 166, WWC.

55. In press accounts and other published histories, figures for the number of attendees at the Waldorf meetings range from forty-seven to fifty. In the most recent published history of the period, Thomas Doherty claims the number was closer to fifty (*Show Trial,* loc. 300, Kindle).

56. Berg, *Goldwyn,* 437–438.

57. A segment of the newsreel, titled "HUAC Cold War," is available online from the Producers Library, https://producerslibrary.com/preview/V-0034BB_018; see also Doherty, *Show Trial,* loc. 305, Kindle.

58. Wyler quoted in Jacobs, "Fund for the Republic."

59. Wyler's FBI files reveal that by November 8, 1947, his activities had been observed and recorded for twelve days between September 16 and October 20; see FBI file #100-18990, "Communist Infiltration of the Motion Picture Industry," file 205, WWC. Dunne is quoted in Herman, *Talent for Trouble,* 338.

Chapter 8: A Training Film for All of Us

1. Harold Russell, *Victory in My Hands*, with Victor Rosen (New York: Creative Age, 1949), 266–267.
2. Ibid.
3. Ibid., 270–271.
4. Robert Cromie, "Field of Living Pays Honor to GIs Who Died," *Chicago Daily Tribune*, October 20, 1947, 1.
5. Brian T. McMahon and Linda R. Shaw, eds., *Enabling Lives: Biographies of Six Prominent Americans with Disabilities* (New York: Routledge, 1999), 19.
6. Jan Herman, *A Talent for Trouble: The Life of Hollywood's Most Acclaimed Director, William Wyler* (New York: Da Capo, 1997), 306–308.
7. A. Scott Berg, *Goldwyn: A Biography* (New York: Knopf, 1989), 439.
8. For information about the film's British release, see the *Los Angeles Examiner*, January 27, 1949, 4, file 201, SGP; for all other international details, see files 201 and 161, SGP; see also Bhupinder Singh, *World Cinema: A Film Quiz* (India: Partridge, 2019), loc. 1991, Kindle.
9. Gen. Robert McLure to Samuel Goldwyn, telegram, ca. 1948, file 201, SGP.
10. Details about *The Hollywood Story*, along with Samuel Goldwyn to William Paley, August 3, 1948, are in file 188, SGP.
11. John Hansen, untitled article, *PM*, November 14, 1948, file 201, SGP; Goldwyn to Paley, November 4, 1948, file 188, SGP.
12. Kim R. Holston, *Movie Roadshows: A History and Filmography of Reserved-Seat Limited Showings, 1911–1973* (New York: McFarland, 2012), 99.
13. Bill Hebert to Samuel Goldwyn, interoffice memorandum, ca. 1949, file 201, SGP; the excerpt from *Steve Canyon* is in box 18, folder 5, UCLA.
14. Berg, *Goldwyn*, 457–458.
15. Wood Soanes, "*Cimarron Kid, I Want You*, Routine Stuff," *Oakland Tribune*, February 7, 1952; Bosley Crowther, "Samuel Goldwyn's 'I Want You' Opens Run at Criterion—Script by Irwin Shaw," *New York Times*, December 24, 1951, 9; Art Cullison, "Goldwyn Studies Life of Today," *Akron Beacon Journal*, March 14, 1952, 42.
16. Documents related to Wyler's "Goldwyn, Inc." lawsuit, ca. 1948–1962, file 303, WWC.
17. Edwin Schallert, "Great Films Should Be Seen Over Again, Says Goldwyn," *Los Angeles Times*, February 28, 1954, sec. 4, 9; Boyd Martin, "TV Reverses a Trend and Helps Revive a Movie, *The Best Years of Our Lives*," *Louisville Courier-Journal*, January 31, 1954, 63; Loy quoted in Hortense Morton, "Play by Play," *San Francisco Examiner*, April 14, 1954, 32.
18. Goldwyn quoted in Schallert, "Great Films Should Be Seen"; Berg, *Goldwyn*, 468; attendance figures are discussed in Michelle Pautz, "The Decline in Average Weekly Cinema Attendance," *Issues in Political Economy* 11 (2002): 3; for *Best Years*' gross ca. 1946, see "Top-Grossing Movies Exhibited in 1945–1946," *Variety*, February 24, 1992, 294; *Best Years*' box-office take after its 1954 release is discussed in Leon Kaplan to William Wyler, May 11, 1962, file 303, WWC.
19. William Holden quoted in the *Hollywood Reporter*, September 9, 1954, cited in Herman, *Talent for Trouble*, 354.
20. Harold Russell quoted in the *Paterson (NJ) Messenger*, April 27, 1950, 4.

21. Herman, *Talent for Trouble*, 317; Talli Wyler, interview by Jan Herman, January 31, 1990, file 348, WWC.

22. Harold Russell, interview by Jan Herman, n.d., file 9, WWC.

23. Yvette Marrin, "Remembering Harold Russell," *Cristina Connections* 2, no. 3 (2002), 4, accessed July 4, 2018, https://www.connections.cristina.org/vol2_issues3 /printable/print4.htm (article no longer available).

24. Berg, *Goldwyn*, 505–506.

25. "William Wyler Sues Goldwyn, Asks 408G More for 'Best' Job," *Hollywood Reporter*, July 1, 1958, file 503, WWC.

26. William Wyler to Leon Kaplan, August 6, 1958, file 303, WWC.

27. Leon Kaplan to William Wyler, May 11 and October 12, 1962; Wyler to Samuel Goldwyn, October 16, 1962; legal agreement dated June 22, 1967, all in file 303, WWC.

28. John J. O'Connor, "Returning Home," *New York Times*, April 29, 1975, file 38, WWP.

29. Harold Russell quoted in McMahon and Shaw, *Enabling Lives*, 29.

30. Ken Smith, "Harold Russell, Where Are You When We Need You," *Veterans Today*, October 18, 2011, www.veteranstodayarchives.com/2011/10/18/harold-russell -where-are-you-when-we-need-you.

31. Russell interview.

32. William Wyler to Samuel Goldwyn Jr., September 21, 1976, file 9, WWC; see also Russell interview.

33. Talli Wyler, interview by A. Scott Berg, February 10, 1985, transcript, 43, for *Directed by William Wyler* (dir. Aviva Slesin), file 179, WWC.

34. Russell, *Victory in My Hands*, 189.

35. McMahon and Shaw, *Enabling Lives*, 33–34; "Actor Sells Oscar Statue for $60,500," *Fort Worth Star-Telegram*, August 7, 1992, 5.

36. Robert M. Andrews, "25 Movie Classics Named to National Film Registry," *San Francisco Examiner*, September 20, 1989, A2; American Film Institute, "AFI's 100 Years . . . 100 Movies," https://www.afi.com/afis-100-years-100-movies-10th -anniversary-edition.

37. Francis Davis, "Storming the Home Front," *Atlantic*, March 2003, theatlantic .com/magazine/archive/2003/03/storming-the-home-front/302681/?utm_source=eb. "A training film for all of us" comes from Howard A. Rusk, "New Film on Broadway Called 'Significant' Portrayal of the Emotional and Physical Problems Facing Veterans," *New York Times*, November 24, 1946, box 21, folder 1, UCLA.

38. Bruce Fetts, "'Drag Race' Makes John Mulaney Cry," *New York Times*, December 8, 2019, AR:4.

39. Mark Montgomery, "Remembering Harold Russell," *Los Angeles Times*, December 10, 2016, latimes.com/entertainment/movies/la-ca-classic-hollywood-harold-russell -20161130-story.html.

40. William Wyler, "No Magic Wand," *Screen Writer*, February 1947, 6, file 180, SGP.

41. This quotation and the one from Russell in the preceding paragraph can be found in Russell, *Victory in My Hands*, 280.

Bibliography

Select Manuscript Collections

Samuel Goldwyn Papers, Special Collections, Margaret Herrick Library, Academy of Motion Picture Arts and Sciences, Los Angeles

Harold Russell Collection, Howard Gotlieb Archival Research Center, Boston University, Boston

William Wyler Papers, 1925-1975, Arts Library Special Collections, Charles E. Young Research Library, University of California, Los Angeles

William Wyler Papers, Special Collections, Margaret Herrick Library, Academy of Motion Picture Arts and Sciences, Los Angeles

Select Primary and Secondary Sources

Affron, Charles, and Mirella Jones Affron. *Best Years: Going to the Movies, 1945–1946.* New Brunswick, NJ: Rutgers University Press, 2009.

Berg, A. Scott. *Goldwyn: A Biography.* New York: Knopf, 1989.

Bordwell, David. *Reinventing Hollywood: How 1940s Filmmakers Changed Movie Storytelling.* Chicago: University of Chicago Press, 2017.

Friedman, Matthew J. "History of PTSD in Veterans: Civil War to DSM-5." US Department of Veterans Affairs, National Center for PTSD. ptsd.va.gov/understand /what/history_ptsd.asp.

Friedrich, Otto. *City of Nets: A Portrait of Hollywood in the 1940's.* New York: Harper and Row, 1986.

Gerber, David. "Heroes and Misfits: The Troubled Social Reintegration of Disabled Veterans in *The Best Years of Our Lives.*" *American Quarterly* 46, no. 4 (December 1994): 545–574.

Harris, Mark. *Five Came Back: A Story of Hollywood and the Second World War.* New York: Penguin, 2014.

Herman, Jan. *A Talent for Trouble: The Life of Hollywood's Most Acclaimed Director, William Wyler.* New York: Da Capo, 1997.

Hoopes, Roy. *When the Stars Went to War: Hollywood and World War II.* New York: Random House, 1994.

Jones, Franklin D., Linette F. Sparacino, Victoria L. Wilcox, Joseph M. Rothberg, and

James W. Stokes, eds. *War Psychiatry*. Washington, DC: Office of the Surgeon General, 1995.

Kantor, MacKinlay. *Glory for Me*. New York: Coward-McCann, 1945.

Koppes, Clayton R., and Gregory D. Black. *Hollywood Goes to War*. Berkeley: University of California Press, 1987.

Kozloff, Sarah. *"The Best Years of Our Lives."* London: Palgrave Macmillan, 2011.

———. "Wyler's Wars." *Film History: An International Journal* 20, no. 4 (2008): 456–473.

Leider, Emily. *Myrna Loy: The Only Good Girl in Hollywood*. Berkeley: University of California Press, 2011.

Madsen, Axel. *William Wyler: The Authorized Biography*. New York: Crowell, 1973.

Miller, Gabriel, ed. *William Wyler: Interviews*. Jackson: University Press of Mississippi, 2010.

———. *William Wyler: The Life and Films of Hollywood's Most Celebrated Director*. Lexington: University Press of Kentucky, 2013.

Myers, Charles S. "A Contribution to the Study of Shell Shock." *Lancet*, February 13, 1915: 316–320.

Peterson, Deborah C. *Fredric March: Craftsman First, Star Second*. Westport, CT: Greenwood, 1996.

Rollyson, Carl. *Hollywood Enigma: Dana Andrews*. Jackson: University Press of Mississippi, 2012.

Russell, Harold. *The Best Years of My Life*. With Dan Ferullo. Middlebury, VT: Eriksson, 1981.

———. *Victory in My Hands*. With Victor Rosen. New York: Creative Age, 1949.

Schatz, Thomas. *Boom and Bust: American Cinema in the 1940s*. Berkeley: University of California Press, 1997.

Shephard, Ben. *A War of Nerves: Soldiers and Psychiatrists in the Twentieth Century*. Cambridge, MA: Harvard University Press, 2001.

Spoto, Donald. *A Girl's Got to Breathe: The Life of Teresa Wright*. Jackson: University Press of Mississippi, 2016.

Taylor, John Russell. *Strangers in Paradise: The Hollywood Émigrés, 1933–1950*. New York: Holt, Rinehart and Winston, 1983.

Time. "The Way Home." August 7, 1944, 15–16.

Tranberg, Charles. *Fredric March: A Consummate Actor*. Duncan, OK: BearManor Media, 2013.

Wyler, William. "Escape to Reality." *Liberty* 24, no. 1 (January 4, 1947). Reprinted in *Picturegoer*, March 15, 1947, 16.

———. "No Magic Wand." *Screen Writer* 2, no. 9 (February 1947): 1–14.

Index

Note: "WW" refers to William Wyler, and "SG" refers to Samuel Goldwyn.

CPSIA information can be obtained
at www.ICGtesting.com
Printed in the USA
LVHW100801170722
723473LV00006B/12/J

9 781477 318911